Ardgillan Castle

Revealed

Ardgillan Castle
Revealed

Written by Aidan J. Herron
Photography by Eamon O'Daly

Published by: Aidan J. Herron
                 aidanjherronauthor@gmail.com
                 www.aidanjherronauthor.com

© 2018, Aidan J. Herron

ISBN: 978-1-9164711-0-8

Edited by: Amy Herron

Photography: Eamon O'Daly www.outdoorstudio.ie (Picture Library)
                 www.skerriesphotography.com (Courses and Workshops)
                 Supplementary photography by Christine O'Daly and Aidan Herron

                 Photographs © Eamon O'Daly

Layout and Design: Sinéad Mallee, Graphic Designer
Printed by: KPS Colour Print Ltd., Knock, County Mayo.

The author acknowledges the financial support provided by Fingal County
Council in the production of this book.

Foreword

Following the publication of my historical novel, *To the Beat of a Savage Drum,* in December 2015, there was immediate curiosity about the militia drum used as its cover illustration. This led me to contribute a series of twenty-three articles to the *Skerries News* dealing with Ardgillan Castle and its many hidden gems, including the Donard Infantry drum. With the original content substantially rewritten and expanded, the entire series is now available in this one illustrated volume. Chapters can be read sequentially or by theme, depending on individual interest.

Although the Taylor family occupied Ardgillan for most of its existence from 1738 until 1962, very little now remains in the Castle from their time there. However, I have tried to maintain an awareness of their occupancy of the house where possible. Of those who lived and worked on the estate in distant times, only a few names have survived for us to record here. Most, unfortunately, are long forgotten. The quotations from the diaries and letters of various members of the Taylor and St Leger families give a unique insight in their lives and minds, whether they were writing about dramatic events during military campaigns or the simple trials and pleasures of daily life. Each topic is approached with the aim of 'telling a story' so that the book will appeal to the general reader as well as to those who have an interest in history.

But if I haven't fully succeeded in that, then the lavish illustrations that accompany each chapter are sure to impress all who open this book. Eamon O'Daly's superb photographs recreate the former grandeur of Ardgillan Castle, its gardens and grounds, while also revealing parts of the building that await restoration. His evocative images are poignant reminders of a bygone era lived both 'above' and 'below' stairs.

We hope that this publication will endorse Ardgillan's status as one of Fingal County Council's most popular and historically important heritage properties.

Aidan J. Herron | October 2018

The proceeds of this book will be donated to Ardgillan Castle towards the provision of suitable display facilities for its collection of historical artefacts.

" *I was as happy there as the birds that fly in the clear sky above the sea.*"

Frances (Fanny) Kemble,
writing of her recent stay in Ardgillan,
19 August 1830.

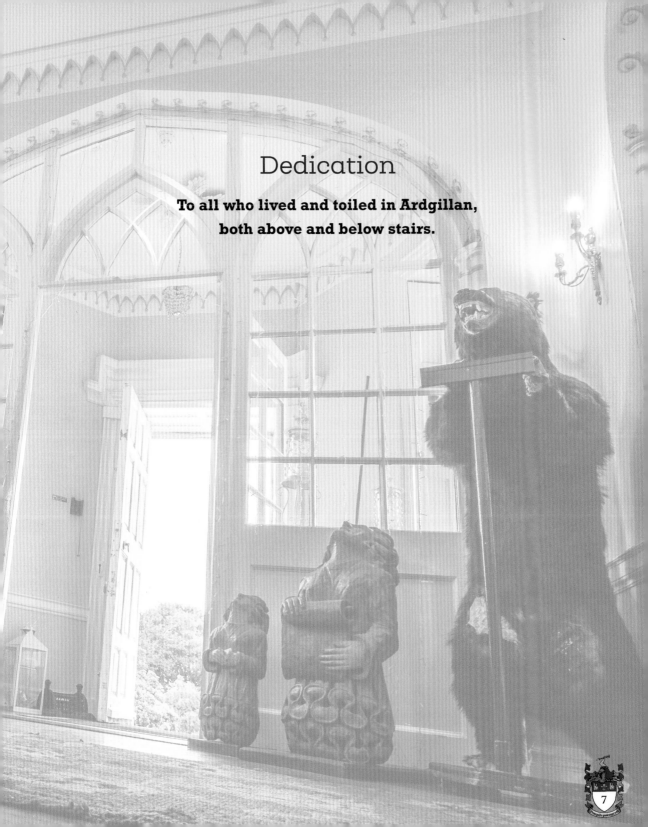

Dedication

**To all who lived and toiled in Ardgillan,
both above and below stairs.**

Contents

Part 1

THE TAYLORS
AND ARDGILLAN CASTLE

Sir Thomas Taylor and
The Down Survey

Sir William Petty
(1623 – 1687)

On the 15 August 1649, Oliver Cromwell landed at Ringsend, Dublin, at the head of his New Model Army with the objective of crushing the Confederate Catholic support for the Royalist cause in Ireland. In a short but brutal nine-month campaign, his forces swept from Drogheda in County Louth to the towns of the south and the south-east, crushing all opposition that stood in their way. The result was further massive upheaval in a society already ravaged by war.

Determined to ensure that there would be no further Papist outbreaks against Parliament, Cromwell planned on implementing drastic measures against the country's Catholic landowners including the confiscation of all their property. In a comprehensive act of land transfer, four counties, Carlow, Cork, Kildare and Dublin, were set aside for the English Government. Another ten, spread within Ulster, the Midlands and Munster, were to be divided between the officers and soldiers of his army as a means of payment. His financial backers were also repaid with land. The dispossessed Irish were to be consigned to the barren areas of Clare and Connaught to scratch out a living in any way they could. Thousands more were to be transported overseas into indentured slavery on the sugar plantations in the West Indies. There they joined the rapidly growing number of enslaved people first carried on European ships across the Atlantic from the west coast of Africa in 1619.

To ensure the orderly transfer of land, Cromwell commenced on a Survey and Valuation in 1653 that was overseen by a Government Commission. In essence, the purpose of the survey was to systematically record the area and boundaries of every townland with a view to their ultimate confiscation and redistribution. Initially, Benjamin Worsley was selected as Surveyor General by the Commission but he was soon replaced by William Petty, a brilliant, forward-thinking individual, who had been appointed Physician-General to the Army in Ireland the previous year.

Petty had proposed that, instead of just surveying the confiscated lands, the entire country should be included. In addition, he introduced more effective methods of organisation thus keeping both rates of pay and administrative costs much lower. Of crucial importance was his guarantee to Cromwell that he would complete the initial survey of the ten listed counties within two years instead of Worsley's projected thirteen. In October 1654, the Commission decided that the lands set aside as payment for the army's arrears and debts should, in their own words, 'be surveyed down as proposed by Dr Petty.' Thus, the Down Survey, a term that Petty himself used, was about to commence. Nothing on the scale of his vision of a mapped survey had ever previously been attempted.

Petty was accompanied by his friend and colleague, Thomas Taylor (1631-1687), whose father owned an estate in Ringmere (or Rigmere) in the parish of Battle, Sussex, England. Appointed Deputy Surveyor-General on the Down Survey at the age of twenty-two, and with an annual stipend of £100, Taylor would work very closely with Petty for the duration of the survey.

The process began on 1 February 1655 when Petty dispatched about one thousand well-trained men on the epic task. Although only thirty-one years of age, Petty demonstrated a genius for planning, organising and surveying. He broke the huge task down into its constituent parts and selected individuals who would be best suited to each. His teams spread out across the countryside, travelling on the primitive roads of the day and enduring every kind of hardship and exposure. Although in constant danger of ambush, Petty's astute use of ex-soldiers, trained to perform routine surveying tasks, had the added advantage of deterring potential attackers. Using a grid system for measuring area to scale as well as indicating details of the quality and typography of the land, the surveyors recorded the data in 'Books of Reference' that accompanied the maps.

The tools used by Petty's teams included the sixty-six foot (20.1m) long Surveyor's Chain and the circumferentor, a magnetic compass mounted on a tripod. The chain was made of iron links connected to each other by small, elliptical links and was used to measure distances on land. A brass handle at each end allowed the chain to be pulled taut. Each link in the chain was eight inches (403mm) long. Standardised with one hundred links, eighty chains equalled one mile (1.6km). The circumferentor, the precursor of the theodylite, was used to measure magnetic bearings from which horizontal angles could be calculated. Every detail on the maps

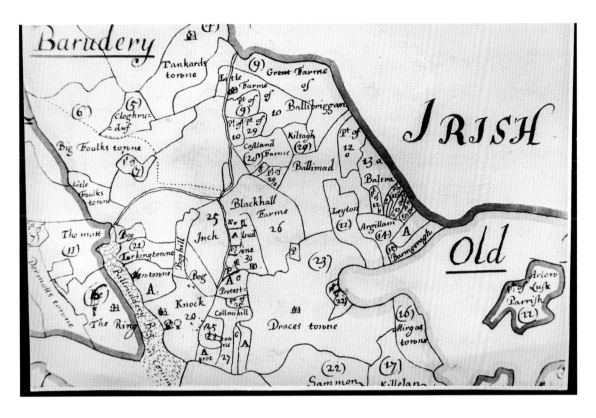

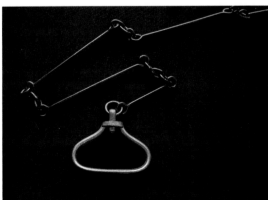

Above:
Surveyor's measuring chain

Top of page:
Down Survey Map of North County Dublin

was scrutinised by a team of examiners who checked all measurements for accuracy while keeping a wary eye out for any potential errors or fraud. All of the recorded information was sent to Dublin where skilled cartographers transferred it onto gridded paper. By the time the survey was concluded, hundreds of maps had been drawn up, millions of acres had been confiscated and the dispossessed Catholic population dispersed. Along with providing the names of townlands and parishes, the maps were rich in additional descriptive detail, indicating in certain cases, the specific ownership of land as well as commonage and bog. Properties that

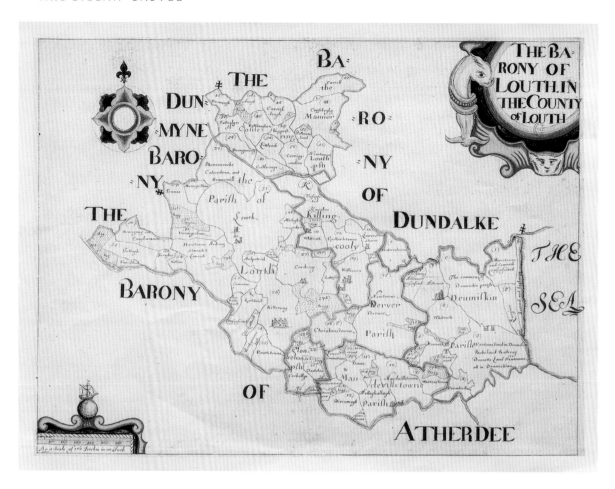

were to be left untouched were marked as 'Protestant Lands' and 'Unforfeited'. Each map had a unique cartouche, or decorative panel, reflective of certain local features, and bore the signature of its cartographer. Significantly, the signature of Thomas Taylor appeared on the cartouche of the map of the Barony of Newcastle and Upper Cross in County Dublin.

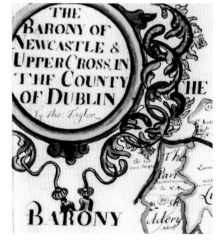

Top: The Barony of Louth in the County of Louth

Right: Cartouche with Thomas Taylor's signature

14

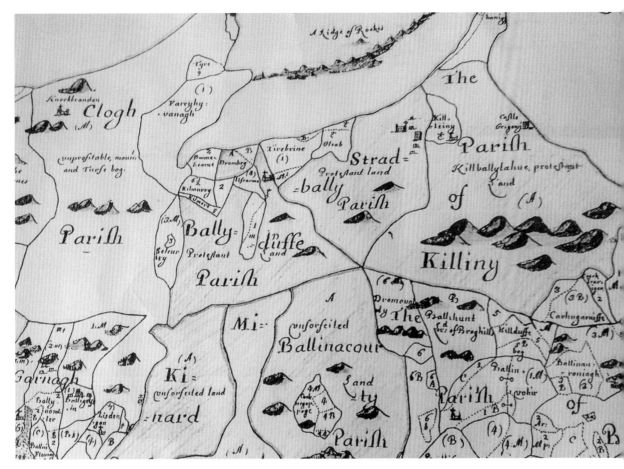

The confiscation and redistribution of land based on the Down Survey maps effectively resulted in almost the entire loss of ownership of Catholic lands. As an immediate and direct consequence of the survey, the Protestant Ascendency was established in Ireland. This was a class that would dominate the social, political, legal, military and economic life of the country for the next two and a half centuries. During the following decades, a number of prominent Catholic families managed to retrieve their property through the courts but they were relatively few.

Top: Copy of a Down Survey map showing 'Protestant land' and 'unforfeited land'

Below: Etching of scale with angelic infants wielding surveying tools

A lot of the Down Survey material was lost in an accidental fire in 1711. The maps that survived were unfortunately destroyed in the Custom House in 1922. Another set of original maps, captured by French pirates while en route to London, is in the possession of the *Bibliothèque Nationale de France*. Facimilies of these maps now, fittingly, reside in Ardgillan Castle.

When the Down Survey was completed, Thomas Taylor returned to Sussex where he married Ann Axtell in 1658. On the death of his father in 1660, Thomas sold the family estate, returned to Ireland and advantageously bought in the region of 21,000 acres in Cavan and Meath including the town of Kells where he set up residence. Although the street in which he lived was unnamed at that time, it is now called Headford Place, after Headford House, the splendid residence that he built just outside the town. Thomas was never properly accredited for his work on the Down Survey but after the Restoration of Charles II to the throne he was appointed to various official positions under the Crown. As a substantial landowner, Thomas also devoted himself to the

Coat of Arms of the Taylors of Ardgillan

development of his estates and to cattle breeding. His interest in livestock was such that he took out a lease on a site in Smithfield, Dublin, overlooking the market so that he could observe the sale of his pedigree animals. The house that was later built on the Smithfield site, designed by the renowned architect Richard Castle (Kassel), was known as Bective House after Thomas Taylor MPKP (great grandson of the first Thomas) who was created Earl of Bective in 1766.

Sir Thomas Taylor, 1st Earl of Bective

THE TAYLORS AND ARDGILLAN CASTLE

As Thomas Taylor, 2nd Baronet (1668-1757), consolidated the family residence and demesne at Headford, Kells, Co Meath, his younger brother, Robert, became interested in buying land in North County Dublin. Born in Chester in 1689, he completed his studies in Holy Orders in Trinity College Dublin and became Archdeacon in Kilmacduagh, Tuam, in 1714. Robert was appointed Precentor of Clonfert in 1722 and later became Dean of that diocese in 1726 where his sister, Salusbury, was married to Bishop William Fitzgerald.

Some years earlier, in 1721, Robert had bought parts of the townlands of Ballymad and Leytown, between Skerries and Balbriggan. When Salusbury died in Bath, Dorset, she left him 544 acres in Clontuskert, County Galway, and £800 in her will. Then in 1737, Robert bought the townlands of Ardgillan and Baltry situated beside his previously purchased properties and decided at last to build. In the Down Survey, the townland of Ardgillan was recorded as previously having belonged to a wine merchant named Robert Usher.

Down Survey Map showing townlands of Ardgillan and Baltra

Prospect House, a modest, two-storey over basement building, was completed on Mount Prospect in the townland of Ardgillan in 1738. It is not known if an architect was employed but records indicate that the house was constructed by journeyman labourers and former soldiers from County Down. The workers were paid one penny a day, provided with one daily meal and a tot of Bushmills whiskey as well as their sleeping accommodation. To commemorate the completion of his house, Robert installed an elaborate fireplace in what was then the inner drawing room.

Robert lived in Prospect House for six years until his death in 1744 aged fifty-five. As he died childless, the house was inherited by his brother, Sir Thomas, who carried out many improvements to the property and used it as a summer residence. In 1786, plans to extend Prospect were drawn up by the architect, Henry Brownrigg, but the proposed new two-storey block, complete with grand stairs, was never built. Elevated to the peerage in 1766 as 1st Earl of Bective, Sir Thomas died in 1795. Headford House and Prospect House were inherited by his son, Thomas, who became 2nd Earl.

Meanwhile, Clotworthy Taylor MP, another brother of the 2nd Earl, had married their cousin, Frances Rowley, of Summerhill, County Meath, in 1794, and changed his surname to Rowley. He leased Prospect from Thomas and as part of the process a complete inventory of contents was drawn up in 1795, combined with a description of room usage. Clotworthy did not reside there for long as on the death in 1796 of his maternal grandfather, Sir Hercules Langford Rowley, he inherited the Rowley estate at Summerhill. In 1800, Sir Thomas was created Marquess of Headford and Clotworthy Rowley became Baron Langford, both having voted in favour of the Act of Union.

The Rev Edward
(Henry Edward) Taylor
(1768-1852)

In 1807, the Rev Edward Taylor (Henry Edward), youngest brother of the Marquess, married Marianne St Leger, daughter of the Hon Richard St Leger, from Doneraile, County Cork, and Anne Blakeney. The couple took up permanent residence in Prospect House in August of that year and raised their family there: Marianne Jane (b.1809); Thomas Edward (b.1811); Elizabeth (Eliza) Agusta (b.1812); Louisa Catherine (b.1815); Henrietta Frances (b.1817); Richard Chambre Hayes (b.1819); and Hercules Langford Barry (b.1824), who died young. Around this period Prospect House became known as Ardgillan, the name being a derivation from the Irish, *ard choill,* meaning 'high wood'.

The Headford Taylors changed their surname to Taylour in 1815 and continued to develop the estate at Kells. In 1831, Sir Thomas, 2nd Marquess of Headford, was created Baron Kenlis in County Meath, a position which granted him and his successors an automatic seat in the House of Lords. He served as a Government Whip in the Whig administration of Lord Melbourne.

At Ardgillan, Edward and Marianne also engaged in developing the grounds of the demesne during the early to middle decades of the nineteenth century and carried out further extensions to the building. A map of Ardgillan Estate by George Conroy, dated 1844, contains an inset of the north view of the building showing how it looked in that year (see page 20). The original house, with its added turreted entrance and wing extensions, had been castellated with the battlements extending along the front. A copy of this map is on view in the Castle.

Between 1842 and 1844, the Dublin to Drogheda railway line was constructed. Rather than run along the cliffs beyond Skerries, the Rev Edward permitted the track to cross his estate. In recognition of this, the Dublin and Drogheda Railway Company built a pedestrian bridge, now known as The Lady's Stairs, to facilitate access to bathing facilities at Barnageeragh, and agreed to the placing of a private halt on the estate for the exclusive use of the Taylors and their heirs in perpetuity. The line opened in May 1844.

Above:
This 1808 portrait of Marianne St Leger Taylor (1780-1859) now hangs in the Morning Room of Ardgillan Castle.

Below:
Marriage Certificate of Edward Taylor and Marianne St Leger dated 10 February 1807. Lord Guilford, a friend of Marianne's, signed as witness.

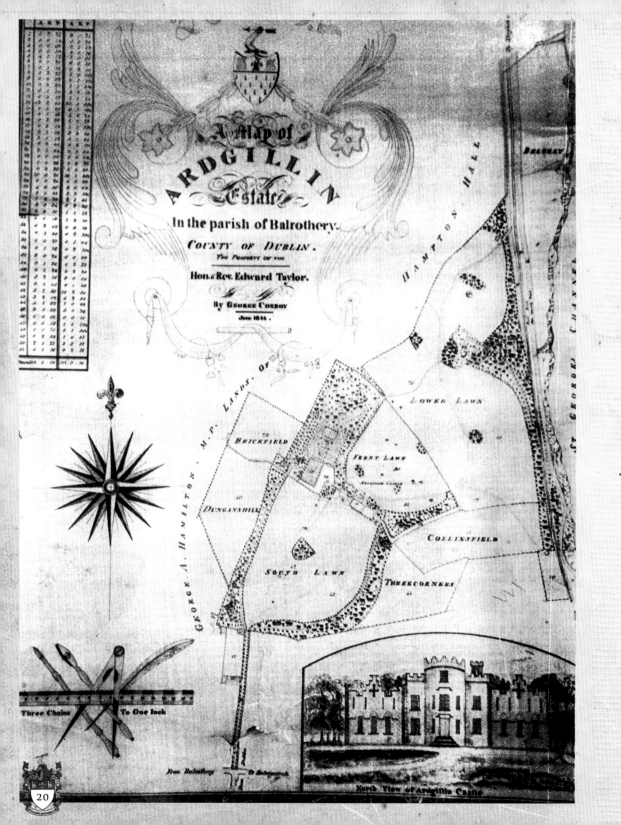

A Map of
ARDGILLIN
Estate
In the parish of Balrothery.
COUNTY OF DUBLIN.
The Property of the
Hon.᷂ Rev. Edward Taylor.
By GEORGE CONROY
June 1844.

Three Chains   To One Inch

North View of Ardgillin Castle

The failure of the potato crop during the Great Famine brought extreme hardship to North County Dublin, as with the rest of the country. A letter written by Louisa Taylor on 18 January 1847 to her brother, Richard, stationed at Gibraltar with his regiment at that time, describes being 'overwhelmed' at 'the perpetual crowd of hungry naked creatures' that arrived daily at Ardgillan seeking food but that everybody seemed to be 'doing their best to assist them'. Personal tragedy visited Ardgillan on 5th November, 1853 when Louisa Augusta Rowley (neé Conolly), Baroness Langford, who was staying there at the time, decided to go swimming at Barnageeragh. Louisa was married to the Rev Edward's nephew, Clotworthy Wellington Robert Rowley, and lived at Summerhill, County Meath. Her husband was away grouse shooting with Edward Taylor in Scotland at that time. Ignoring advice from her servant about the sea conditions, Louisa entered the water but soon got into difficulties. When she was retrieved from the sea an hour later, her lifeless body was carried back over the bridge to the Castle. Just thirty-one years of age, Louisa was

Facing page:
A map of Ardgillan Estate by George Conroy, 1844

Above:
A view of Ardgillan before the wing towers and conservatory were added on

the mother of four small children. Heart-broken, her husband, Clotworthy, died the following year after a short illness, leaving the children orphaned.

Along with maintaining close connections with their relatives in England and Ireland, the Taylors were part of a wide social circle that included many prominent and wealthy families in North County Dublin and Meath. The highlight of the year in Ardgillan, as in other Big Houses, was the annual ball when they entertained lavishly. The Taylors also loved the theatre and regularly attended plays and concerts at the popular venues in Dublin. They enjoyed the outdoors also with horse racing, cricket and archery among their favourite sports while swimming was a regular activity almost all year round according to Marianne's diaries. As with many Ascendency families, they undertook the 'Grand Tour' of Europe on a number of occasions, keeping extensive journals and sketchbooks as records of their travels.

Drawing by one of the Taylor family while on the European Tour

It was on their last European tour in 1852 that the Rev Edward, aged 82, died near Lake Como, Italy, after a short illness. His remains were returned to Ireland for burial in the family vault in St George's Church, Balbriggan. After a period of mourning, Marianne resumed her active social life with family and friends until her death seven years later. She was buried in the family vault alongside her husband.

Their eldest son Thomas, a captain in the 6th Dragoon Guards, was elected as a Conservative MP in Westminster in 1841. He subsequently retired from the army in 1846 and devoted himself fully to a career in politics. He was a party whip for the Conservative Party for seventeen years before being appointed Chief Government Whip in 1866. He held the cabinet post of Chancellor of the Duchy of Lancaster in the Disraeli Government. As Thomas had inherited Dowdstown House, Navan, from their uncle, General Robert Taylor, Marianne left Ardgillan Castle and Demesne to his younger brother, Richard, who was by then a brigadier general in the British Army. However, the two brothers agreed to exchange properties so that Richard became owner of Dowdstown while Thomas took up residence once again in Ardgillan.

In 1862, Thomas married Louisa Tollemarche. Together, they had five children: Edward Richard (b.1863); Basil Richard (b.1865); twins Cornelia Marianne and Beatrix Louisa (b.1866); and Wilfred (b.1868). Thomas continued the work of developing the castle and the grounds of the demesne. By then, the towers had been added to the two wings, thereby completing the front aspect of the castle as it is today. The gardens were extended and new trees planted in the woodlands. The Yew Walk with twenty-one yew trees, twenty green and one golden, was planted to celebrate a twenty-first birthday in the family. It became a favourite place for evening strolls.

Above:
Col Thomas Edward Taylor MP

Below: Caricature of Col Thomas Taylor MP for Vanity Fair magazine, July 1881

Colonel Thomas Edward Taylor M.P.
(1811–1883)

(Illustration for Vanity Fair, July 1874)
Artist: Carlo ('APE') Pellegrini
Pencil and Watercolour with white highlights on blue paper
Photograph courtesy of the National Gallery of Ireland Cat. no. 2653

Ardgillan Castle
front aspect, 2018

Above: Millicent, Constance, Evelyn and Gertrude, daughters of Gen Richard CH Taylor and his wife, Lady Jane Hay

Right: Captain Edward Richard Taylor's entry in *Kelly's Handbook* to the Titled, Landed and Official Classes, 1916

1428   KELLY'S HANDBOOK—1916.

Taylor, capt. Edwd. Richd., eld. s. of rt. hon. T. E. Taylor, P.C., M.P. of Ardgillan Castle, co. Dublin (*d*. 1883); *b*. 1863; J.P. co. Dublin, served in Soudan campaign 1885, capt. gren. gds. 1894-8; Carlton and Guards' clubs; Ardgillan Castle, Balbriggan, co. Dublin.
Taylor, Edwd. Russell, J.P. (1910) Cheshire: King-court, Liscard, Cheshire.
Taylor, Edwd. Sydney, J.P. (1912) Flints: Sandycroft, Chester.
Taylor, lt.-col. Ernest Fitzwilliam, C.B. (1915); *b*. 1867; served in S. African war 1899-1901, A.A.Q.M.G. from 1915, lt.-col. A.S.C. from 1911.
Taylor, lt.-col. Fras. Pitt Stewart, C.M.G. (1915); *b*. 1869; served with Nile expdn. 1893,

When Thomas Taylor MP died in 1883, Ardgillan was inherited by his eldest son, Edward Richard, then a captain in the Grenadier Guards. It was during his life that Ireland experienced radical change and the age of the big estates was brought to a gradual end with the shift of ownership of the land back to the people. However, between 1886 and 1889, Edward Richard managed to put his mark on the house by commissioning the Guardorici brothers from Italy to design and carve the marvellous oak panelling and double doors in the Dining Parlour. Edward Richard married Ada Bodley in 1935 and died childless in 1938. He was the last resident Taylor to be born in Ardgillan.

Meanwhile, Edward's brother, Basil, had joined the Royal Navy (RN) and spent most of his life posted overseas. While Basil was in Hong Kong, he adopted the Headford version of the family surname, Taylour, to avoid confusion with other RN officers. He married Harriet Mary Clendenin in 1903 and their first child, Richard, the eldest of four, was born in Hong Kong in 1904. As Basil had died in 1936, it was Richard, by then a qualified barrister in England and the Colonies, who inherited Ardgillan in 1938 from his

Uncle Ned with rain gages Ardgillan opposite Greenhouses—

Captain Edward Richard Taylor in the gardens at Ardgillan

uncle Edward. Three photographs of the interior of Ardgillan were sent to him to encourage him to come and view the property. Richard arrived from Singapore with his wife, Gwen, and their two small children, Jeremy and Terence, accompanied by a Chinese *amah*, or nurse. Although Richard intended selling the estate and returning to Singapore with the proceeds, war broke out in 1939, making this impossible.

From that year on, the demesne continued to be run as a mixed farm with a pedigree dairy herd also being maintained. During the Second World War, Ardgillan's power needs were met by its own gasworks and electricity generator as well as by a wind charger on the east tower. When war ended, the burden of running the estate became progressively more difficult. In 1958, one of the original features of the house, the black Kilkenny limestone fireplace was sold, finding a new home in Leixlip Castle. However, the Rev Robert's plaque remained untouched.

But Richard and Gwen Taylour's time in Ardgillan was nearing a conclusion. Inevitably, the end came in 1962 when the Castle and what was left of the demesne were sold to Heinrich Pott, a German industrialist, who intended using it as a second home. But Herr Pott died in 1966 and, although his family continued to visit on holidays occasionally, Ardgillan was again placed on the market in 1981. The following year, seeing its potential to complement Malahide Castle and Newbridge House as amenities in North County Dublin, Fingal County Council purchased Ardgillan and, by 1986, the grounds had been sufficiently redeveloped to allow the demesne to be opened to the public.

Captain Edward Richard Taylor, Grenadier Guards (1863-1938)

Captain Basil Richard Taylor, RN (1865-1936)

Tea
Rooms
&
Castle Tours

30 | 14 D 120001

Vintage cars in front of Ardgillan Castle in 2017

In spite of the maintenance work carried out by Richard during his occupancy, the house was found to be in need of immediate conservation work. Between 1989 and 1992, restoration work on the Castle itself was carried out with a view to retaining or repairing the original features that graced the building. Unfortunately, practically none of the original family furniture remained, having been sold off at auction. However the Castle is now home to a range of period furniture and antiques from the eighteenth and nineteenth centuries either purchased by the Council or offered privately on loan.

In May 1992, Ardgillan Castle was officially opened to the public by the then President of Ireland, Mary Robinson, who planted a tree in the demesne to mark the occasion.

In May 2017, on the twenty-fifth anniversary of the Castle's opening, President Michael D. Higgins visited Ardgillan and also planted a tree on the grounds.

Ardgillan Castle and Demesne, one of eight properties in Fingal County Council's heritage portfolio, continues to be one of the most popular attractions in North County Dublin.

L-R: Paul Reid, CEO, FCC, President Michael D Higgins, Cllr Darragh Butler and Kevin Halpenny, FCC, at Ardgillan, 2017.

ARDGILLAN'S GARDENS AND LANDSCAPE

The Rev Robert Taylor, proud owner of the townlands of Ballymad, Leytown, Ardgillan and Baltry, must have watched with delight as his new home took shape on Mount Prospect in 1738. Taking advantage of the spectacular vista of the Mourne Mountains and the grey-green of the Irish Sea, the house has a unique north-south aspect in contrast to other contemporary houses that were positioned east-west to take advantage of the rising and setting of the sun. Although now reduced to an area of about two hundred acres, Ardgillan Demesne, lovingly maintained by Fingal County Council staff, has become one of the most-visited family amenities in Dublin.

On arriving at the middle gates, many keen walkers prefer to turn either left or right as these paths lead to the looped trail around the perimeter of the demesne, some five kms in length, where the rolling parkland and mature woods can be appreciated at their best. A long avenue sweeps down from the middle gates towards the castle, cutting through what is known as the South Lawn. It was here that a cricket match was played by opposing teams from Balbriggan and Skerries on 12 August 2016 to commemorate

A panoramic view of Ardgillan Castle

an earlier cricket match held at Ardgillan during the summer of 1829. Marianne Taylor documented the occasion in her diary of that year, making it one of the earliest references to the game being played in Ireland.

Approaching the Castle by the main avenue, the visitor soon comes across one of Ardgillan's most charming and unusual landscape features, the 'haha' wall, so-called because one comes upon it unexpectedly and exclaims in surprise, "Haha, it's a wall." Not many such recessed boundaries survive now. Originally utilised by the French military as part of a defensive system, it was adapted by landscape gardeners as a means of separating the

The Haha Wall and Yew Tree Walk

pasture areas of an estate from its garden amenities while preserving an open, uninterrupted view over parkland. This was not the garden's only line of defense against straying livestock. The row of yew trees beyond the sunken wall provide another disincentive to animal incursions as yew leaves are toxic.

Standing like an exotic, green custodian at the turreted, side

entrance to the Castle is a monkey puzzle tree (*Araucaria araucana*). First discovered by Europeans in Argentina and Chile in the 1780s, this species was cultivated in England in the 1850s. By then, huge tracts of land where the tree flourished had been destroyed by fire to create open space for agriculture. Known as a living fossil due to its long life span, the monkey puzzle is now an endangered species.

On approaching the main building, the high stone wall shelters the two cobbled courtyards and the various work sheds that were once hives of activity. Passing in front the Castle, the gravel path leads to the ornamental walled gardens. The original and much smaller enclosed garden would

Apple – Blood of
the Boyne, 1676

Link from upper
yard to lower yard

have provided fruit and vegetables for the kitchen of Prospect House. But as the main building was extended in the late 1700s, the Walled Garden also grew substantially so that, by Victorian times, it was one hectare (2.27 acres) in area, subdivided into five separate sections. As well as providing shelter from the wind, the high brick and stone walls absorb heat during the day and release it by night, thereby creating a microclimate in which plants can thrive. Framed by neatly trimmed box hedges, an extensive range of plants flourish while, in a separate area, rows of low fruit-producing trees are espalier-trained on wires. Among the old varieties of apple in the garden is the 'Blood of the Boyne' dating from 1676. A fruit wall with twenty alcoves, commissioned it is believed as a Famine Relief measure, still provides enhanced shelter for more tender fruits including nectarines and peaches.

Above: The Alcove Wall

Below: The Alcove Wall
– detail

There is evidence that the Taylors stayed abreast of the latest developments in fashionable garden design as, in a letter home while on military service in India in 1857, Brigadier General Richard CH Taylor enquired how the 'pleasaunce' was coming on. He was referring to a trend popular in the 1800s of having a garden for the sole purpose of giving pleasure to the senses, an idea that had also been adopted by their neighbours, the Hamiltons, who had one at Hampton Hall. The gate the families used when visiting each other, on the path leading down to the railway track, is now rusted with age and embedded in a tree.

The idea of utilising a controlled environment for growing plants derives from Ancient Rome where the process of heat regulation was well understood. Fast-forwarding through time, by the thirteenth century, the glass greenhouse as we know it today existed in parts of Italy and elsewhere. These were erected to house the many exotic plants that explorers were bringing back from their travels. When the New World opened up, ships laden with every kind of tropical plant returned to a Europe where garden design had moved far beyond monastic utilitarianism. By the seventeenth century, the Netherlands and England were to the fore in greenhouse development as it was only within such shelters that these plants could survive the harsher weather of northern climes. But, as these early structures were very labour intensive, only the wealthiest could afford them.

By the mid-nineteenth century though, greenhouses had become much more widespread for a number of reasons. The abolition of the glass tax by Sir Robert Peel's government in 1845 coincided with the introduction of improved methods of glass production, especially cast plate glass, which was developed by James Hartley in 1848. A separate window tax, based on the number of windows in a house, had also existed in the seventeenth and eighteenth centuries. In order to reduce the amount due, many buildings were completed with bricked up windows, pending the day that this unpopular tax would be abolished. It was finally discontinued in 1851, the same year that Joseph Paxton's Crystal Palace opened to an incredulous public. With these contemporaneous developments, the golden age of the glass greenhouse had arrived on a grand scale. But if London had the Crystal Palace, Dublin was not to be outdone. Richard Turner, planner of Kew Gardens, designed the Curvilinear Range of glasshouses for the Botanical Gardens, Glasnevin, from 1843, with extensions added on later. By 1860, the stately Palm House in the Botanical Gardens was also completed.

And Ardgillan was not left behind. Along with the lean-to, corner greenhouses in the Walled Garden, the Castle also possessed an imposing glass conservatory in the Rose Garden manufactured in 1880. Similar to the conservatory in Balmoral Castle, this wonderful structure awaits restoration to its former glory. The Rose Garden, now faithfully reproduced as recorded in the Ordnance Survey Map of 1865, is laid out with formal

The rusted gate into Hampton Hall embedded in a tree

The old glass conservatory in the Rose Garden

Above:
Old ridge tiles
from the middle
gates lodge

beds providing bursts of vivid colour during the summer months.

But if Ardgillan's gardens have been restored, the four gate lodges that marked the various entrances to the demesne are gone forever. Named after the families that once occupied them, three were to be found along the railway tracks. Fottrell's Gate Lodge, last occupied by the Harmon family, stood at the Balbriggan end of the demesne; a lost lodge (occupants unknown) that stood adjacent to where the Lady's Stairs are now to be found was dismantled pre 1844 to make way for the railway; Casey's Lodge was located at the Skerries end of the demesne; and Fedigan's Lodge stood just inside the middle gates. All that is left of the middle gate lodge are two ridge tiles from the roof leaning poignantly against the wall and a few stones from the garden. Of the three railway lodges, only the ruins of a small outhouse to the rear of Fottrell's remains.

Since taking ownership of Ardgillan Demesne, Fingal County Council has painstakingly returned the gardens to their original design and layout but with one significant extra feature. The Castle is now home to the National Plant Collection of Shrubby Potentillas. With more than two hundred cultivars and varieties on display, this unique addition to the formal gardens is one of which the Parks Department can be truly proud.

Below:
Lilies in bloom
at Ardgillan

THE ICEHOUSE

In 1985, Fingal County Council staff who were engaged in some site clearance beyond the Walled Garden discovered the entrance to what they thought was a tunnel. To their amazement, they had in fact found an icehouse.

From the seventeenth century on, icehouses were constructed at stately homes in response to the demand for ice cold drinks, ice-cream and exotic, sorbet desserts, as well as for the preservation of perishable foods. They were constructed with a north-facing tunnel giving entrance to a vaulted, underground chamber in which ice could be packed. Earth was then

35

banked over the roof to provide additional insulation. The tunnel kept out the warmer, exterior air, while two or more doors gave further buffering.

The icehouse at Ardgillan, tucked away in a tree-covered bank, can be found below the walled garden. Although the outer doors have been modified, the hooks of the original doors are still there on the side walls of the entrance tunnel. The interior remains intact with the beautiful, red-bricked arched roof in a remarkable state of preservation. The base is concave in shape, with a sump hole into the ground to allow for drainage. It was designed specifically to ensure that the temperature within remained at almost freezing point so that the packed ice would last well into the summer months and beyond.

Sourcing ice two centuries ago was not as problematic as one might think as winters were generally more severe then and sufficient ice from nearby frozen rivers and lakes could be harvested to satisfy demand. However, by the early decades of the nineteenth century, with a rise in the average winter temperature, ice had to be found elsewhere, namely, in the mountain lakes of the east coast of the newly independent United States.

From the early 1800s, the well-to-do people of Boston, Massachusetts, already enjoyed the cooling benefits of ice during the summer months. Although the local trade was well established, the work of harvesting ice was harsh and difficult. Horse-drawn scrapers removed the surface layer of slush revealing the solid ice beneath. This ice was grooved into blocks by a knifelike plough before being cut with handsaws and separated with crowbars. The blocks were then stored until shipment. When Ardgillan's icehouse was constructed, the procurement and transport of ice had progressed considerably, mostly through the foresight and perseverance of a man from Boston, Frederic Tudor, the Ice King.

It is said that while attending a garden party in Boston in 1805, someone suggested to Tudor that he should ship ice overseas. Whether or not this was said in jest is unknown but Tudor took it seriously and set up the Tudor Ice Company in 1806. Skeptics who had doubted the wisdom of ships carrying frozen water over large stretches of ocean were proved utterly wrong as within a few years Tudor's refrigerated vessels not only sailed to the Caribbean but also successfully crossed the Atlantic. When loading,

Tudor used sawdust and wood shavings, previously a waste by-product from the mills, to insulate the ice blocks and thus was able to carry the purest of glacial water to Liverpool and London. Labelled 'Crystal Blocks of Yankee Coldness', no ice could compare with that from Wenham Lake near Concord, MA. It became world famous for its quality and purity, and could be found on the most distinguished royal tables all over Europe, including that of Queen Victoria who insisted upon having it.

In time, however, the convenience of more easily sourced ice from Norway took precedence over the quality product from New England and, by 1860, the transatlantic trade had fallen off. Gradually, with the introduction of refrigeration, icehouses became redundant and, eventually, the industry disappeared altogether during the early 1900s, as did the Castle's icehouse when the entrance was covered in and forgotten.

Today, Ardgillan's rediscovered icehouse is a reminder of the extraordinary innovation that allowed the Taylors to enjoy what is now taken for granted – the joy of a chilled drink or an ice-cream on a warm day.

Close-up of the entrance tunnel to the Icehouse

THE COMING OF THE RAILWAY

Following the success in 1829 of Stephenson's Rocket, the first steam locomotive, there was huge interest in the development of new railway routes all across Great Britain. In Ireland too, potential investors met to plan railway lines that would link towns and communities which, until then, were remote from the major centres of Dublin and Belfast.

When a wealthy property-owner named Thomas Brodigan of Piltown House, Drogheda, proposed the construction of a railway line between his native town and Dublin, the idea won approval from many who wished to invest in the enterprise. The grand vision was for the eventual linking of Dublin and Belfast. Initial meetings were held in Dublin and a Board of Directors was elected with Mr George A Hamilton, neighbour to the Taylors, appointed Chairman. However, the proposal soon met with serious opposition from a group that favoured the interior route to Armagh passing through Trim and Navan but with a spur along the River Boyne to Drogheda. As there was no possibility of reconciling the two sides, a provisional committee commissioned an independent survey of both routes to be carried out by Sir William Cubitt, a highly-esteemed engineer, and then to recommend the better one. Cubitt decided in favour of the coastal route. This failed to resolve matters and, after further argument, a Parliamentary Committee chaired by the Great Liberator, Daniel O'Connell, was formed.

Those in favour of the coastal route highlighted the greatly reduced travelling time between Drogheda and Dublin, the potential benefits to the citizens of Dublin of having fish brought from the north county ports to the markets more quickly than by road or sea, and the reduced costs of transporting cotton and linen merchandise from the local mills to the main centres of population. Supporters of the inland route proposed the advantages of opening up the Meath hinterland and the easier transportation of agricultural produce and livestock. Once again the coastal route won out and it was brought to the House of Commons. But even when it had been passed by the House, with tenders to build accepted and contracts issued, the opposition still continued. The matter was then raised

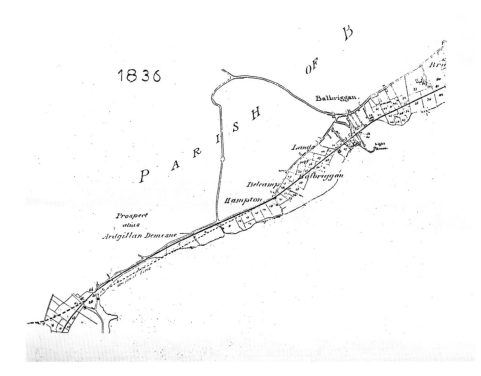

The proposed railway route from Skerries to Balbriggan, 1836

in the House of Lords where at last, following final heated debates, an accommodation was reached. The Act of Parliament approving the coastal route was passed and, by August 1839, work had commenced in earnest.

Objections to other proposed railway routes continued, especially to those that would compete with both the Royal Canal and the Grand Canal whose shareholders saw the devastating impact that the new transport system would have on their businesses. Coach operators, hauliers and carters agreed, seeing the whole venture as a threat to their livelihoods. However, while the Dublin and Drogheda Railway did not compete directly with the canals, it would certainly have a more immediate effect on road traffic, in particular, that on the Dublin to Dunleer Turnpike.

Turnpike roads, introduced with the first Turnpike Act in 1729, had gate-like barriers, or toll booths, at roughly eight-mile intervals from each other. The accumulated tolls were intended for the maintenance and upgrading of each stretch of road – a major initiative at the time. Prior to

Milestone from the Dublin to Dunleer Turnpike preserved at Ardgillan

this, long-distance travel by coach was a demanding and arduous affair, especially during the winter months when road conditions were grim, causing great discomfort to passengers. Gradually, as the roads were upgraded and the design of vehicles improved, there was a corresponding growth in coach travel. To assist road users, milestones were erected at regular intervals along the route to indicate the distances to and from the nearest towns. A surviving milestone from the Dublin to Dunleer Turnpike stands in the grounds of Ardgillan beside the lower car park.

To service this increase in traffic, roadside inns offering food, accommodation and overnight stables sprang up along the turnpike routes. The Man O'War Inn, located on the Dublin to Dunleer Turnpike, became a popular halting place but its location on the brow of a hill presented a real problem for hard-pressed mail coach drivers and their operators. The long, uphill haul from either side exhausted the horses and slowed journey times down so considerably that eventually an alternative route bypassing the Man O'War had to be constructed. The new stretch of road that opened in 1834 resulted in a significantly reduced traffic flow past the inn. The coming of the new railway would bring further decline to the turnpike until it finally closed in 1855.

Initially, according to the transcripts of the Select Parliamentary Committee (1836), the Dublin train terminus was to be near the General Post Office in Sackville Street, now O'Connell Street. However, as a substantial number of dwellings were in the way, it was moved to the current site on Amiens Street, advantageously close to the Port of Dublin, the Customs House and the River Liffey. The central campanile of the station was strategically located in order to be easily seen from Sackville Street.

But the railway continued to meet strong local resistance. Prominent objectors included Sir John Vernon of Clontarf and Lord Howth of Howth Castle who feared for the value of their property. Even the residents of Dollymount argued that the railway would have a detrimental effect on bathing facilities there. To appease the locals, the line beyond the North Strand was subsequently adjusted to its present location although it required the construction of a high embankment and a bridge at Clontarf. As work progressed along the line, the material from each cutting was used to create embankments, including those that crossed the estuaries at Malahide and Rogerstown.

But closer to Skerries more problems arose concerning the planned route through Milverton, the estate of George Woods, Esq., where not only a long, deep cutting would be required but also a stretch of tunnel, both costly and troublesome processes. The issues were solved by moving the line closer to the coast along a high embankment that crossed what was deemed at the time to be 'a handsome bridge over the high road from Dublin to Skerries.' George Woods benefitted substantially from this alteration as on his estate were 'excellent quarries affording the finest building-stone, a good deal of which was used in the construction of some of the works on this line.' *The Hand-Book to the Dublin & Drogheda Railway (1844)*. At Skerries, the proposed purchase of a piece of land for use as a ballast pit was a matter of contention between the owner, Mr Ion Trant Hamilton MP, later 1st Baron Holmpatrick, and the railway company. Due to the higher cost to passengers travelling beyond Malahide, Mr Hamilton deemed it an injustice to the residents of Skerries and Balbriggan and therefore used the sale of the land as a means of achieving a reduction in the fare. After a long deliberation, the company conceded that they would reduce the fare accordingly but that this was to be understood as separate from Mr Hamilton's decision on whether or not to sell the land for the ballast pit.

Further challenges faced the engineers when the line progressed north of Skerries due to the difficulty of traversing a stretch of high shoreline cliff. The solution was to approach the Rev Edward, already a shareholder in the company with ten shares valued at £1,000, for permission to lay track across Ardgillan Demesne, which he duly granted. In acknowledgement of his generous gesture a pedestrian bridge, The Lady's Stairs, was erected across the line near Barnageeragh and bathing facilities that included a screening wall to block the roving eyes of future passengers were constructed. The Rev Edward also requested that his family would be

"I think Papa will soon grow as impatient as we all are to have our platform erected and our station finally established here, for he is getting rather weary of the continuing demand for the carriage or the car to take our friends to Balbriggan station. They are at last beginning preparations for our pass down to the sea though the bridge cannot be commenced until Sir John McNeill returns from England."

Marianne Jane to Richard CH Taylor (Dick), April 22nd, 1847.

41

provided with their own personal halt on the demesne, complete with wooden platform for their private use, for as long as the family was resident in Ardgillan. The granting of a stop on private property, a unique concession at the time, meant that the original Act of 1836 had to be amended as follows:

> *'Be it therefore enacted, That the said Company shall at all Times cause all the Trains running on the said Line between Dublin and Drogheda...to stop at the North Gatehouse of Ardgillan, for the Convenience and Accommodation of the said Edward Taylor, his present Issue, and the Heirs of the said Edward Taylor, being owners of Ardgillan Castle as aforesaid, when travelling or intending to travel by the said Railway.'*

The special rail halt shelter built for the Taylors. Photo courtesy of Joe Curtis

Work on constructing the line was arduous and backbreaking for the labourers who were known as 'navies', from the 'navigators' who built the canals of the Empire. Thousands of men were employed over the years, working in double shifts in all weathers. Although pay and conditions were good for the time, they and their families lived like nomads in temporary dwellings that could be taken down and re-erected as work progressed. However, local residents often objected to the shanty type of encampments that sprouted up near their houses. Accidents among the workers were

common and deaths also occurred. In one month alone in 1841, eight men are said to have died and 103 were injured. Notwithstanding the risks, working mostly with pick and shovel, the navies shifted tons of earth and rock as the line slowly took shape.

Eventually, on 18 March 1844, an experimental run with 565 people on board was made from Dublin to Drogheda and back. The Rev Edward was among the invited dignitaries and guests. Pulled by the engine, *Norah Creina,* it was a resounding success, reaching Drogheda in a reported one hour and eighteen minutes including stoppages and returning to Dublin in an hour and fifteen minutes. After further successful trial runs in April, the line opened to the public on 24 May 1844. Wildly enthusiastic crowds and detachments of the coastguard cheered the first train as a marvel of technological invention and achievement as it arrived at each station along the line.

The Taylors immediately became regular users of the railway, often

Fottrell's lodge at the Balbriggan gate, now sadly demolished. Photo courtesy of Joe Curtis

The Boyne River would not be crossed until Sir John Benjamin McNeill's magnificent bridge was completed in 1855, coincidently the same year that the Dublin to Dunleer Turnpike closed.

stopping off to visit the Talbots of Malahide Castle and the Cobbes of Newbridge House, or making frequent trips into Dublin where they attended the theatre. While they undoubtedly travelled in the comfort of first class, the third class passengers endured the entire trip while standing in open carriages breathing in air fouled by billowing smoke.

But it wasn't just the convenience of easy travel from the halting station at Ardgillan that the Rev Edward enjoyed. This new venture also presented him with a novel business opportunity. As the railway opened up Skerries with its broad, sweeping strand to a whole new tourist market, a group of astute businessmen decided to build a row of quality houses for the rental market. In 1845, the Skerries Building Society was founded with a provisional board of directors onto which the Rev Edward was elected, as was George Woods of Milverton. Building proceeded swiftly and their first project, Holmpatrick Terrace, was ready for rental the following year. The enterprise lasted a number of decades before going into liquidation in 1881 but by then Col Thomas Taylor MP, son of the Rev Edward, had replaced his father among the named directors.

The gate lodge and rail crossing at Ardgillan
Photo courtesy of Joe Curtis

Just as no trace remains of the lodges that once existed on the estate, nothing is left either of the private platform or the brick shelter that was built for the Taylors whose privileged use of the railway ended only when the last of the family left in 1962. Gone too is the screening wall and the private bathing facilities they enjoyed at Barnageeragh. The sole, remaining link left between the Rev Edward and the coming of the railway to Ardgillan in 1844 is The Lady's Stairs, now renovated but still in its original position, providing easy pedestrian access to the Castle and Demesne from the scenic coast road above the shore.

On display in the Drawing Room is an early copy of John D'Alton's (1844) celebrated drawing immortalising the coming of the railway to Ardgillan.

'It may be here stated that, subsequently, owing to the considerable kindness and liberality of the Hon and Rev Mr Taylor of Ardgillan Castle, in permitting the Company to run the line through his demesne, a considerable additional saving was effected, so that the capital of the Company was thus reduced from £600,000, in 6,000 shares of £100 each, to £450,000 in 6,000 shares of £75 each.'

'It was originally intended that the line should run along the steep cliffs to the right, which would have involved the Company in considerable expense for the necessary embankments and parapet walls; but with a liberality that cannot be too highly appreciated, Mr Taylor, without any pecuniary compensation, permitted a more inland course through his demesne to be taken.'

The Hand-Book to the Dublin & Drogheda Railway (1844)

D'Alton's (1844) depiction of the train heading towards Skerries with Ardgillan on the hilltop

45

Fottrell's Lodge circa 1870s. It was then occupied by the Mason family, five of whom are visible in the photograph. From left to right are Rebecca, Elanor, then Emily and Richard standing together, with Louisa in the doorway. Their names have been kindly confirmed by Diana Cornell who is related to them.

Part 2

UPSTAIRS
AT ARDGILLAN

The Main Hall

On entering Ardgillan, having remembered to use the boot scraper outside, the visitor steps into the Main Hall. To the left, the Drawing Room lies behind the prominent white door at the end and to the right is the corresponding entrance to the Dining Parlour. Immediately in front, another wide door in the closed-up archway hides the stairway to the upper floors and to the basement area. The span from left to right marks the width of the original Prospect House. When the wing extensions were added on, it necessitated the removal of two internal walls, the creation of entrance doors to the new rooms and the closing up of the stairwell area. The decorative arches show where the internal walls once stood and indicate the size of the original rooms.

The result of all this was that Prospect House lost its entrance hall as the enlarged area became a reception room with two fireplaces. However, the addition of a semi-turret with a small doorway to the front of the house not only created a small step-in hallway but also helped to retain inner warmth. The fireplaces that once heated the smaller rooms are now closed up but the photograph dated 1938 on the wall beside the Dining Parlour door clearly shows where they were. Two hidden, or jib, doors give access to other parts of the house. These were generally intended for use by servants. By contrast, the wider dimensions of the doors leading into the Drawing

Main entrance
and hall

48

DECLINE OF THE BIG HOUSE

The eighteenth and early nineteenth century was a time of great prosperity for Big Houses in Ireland. Landed estates were prevalent all over the country with lavish and highly decorated houses in every county in Ireland. In the mid-nineteenth century things began to change and their decline became imminent.

These grandiose estates with their sprawling grounds, meticulous gardens and exquisite interiors came at a cost and in many houses the money needed to fund the estate was borrowed. The families in these houses would borrow to extend and decorate the house; it was important to keep up with the fashion of the day. This meant that when the downturn came, landlords were set in a position to repay their loans or manage the upkeep of their properties. The Wall Street Crash of 1930 had a huge impact on these wealthy families. Many houses were rented out to generate money for their upkeep, the family moving to a smaller and more manageable estate or often to England. Some houses were abandoned completely.

In the 1930s the Taylors of Headfort House were spending £2000 annually on maintaining their estate, this dropped to £500 in the 1950s. Managing an estate of such magnitude meant having a healthy income and many of these families began to struggle. Headfort was eventually leased to a preparatory school and the family never returned to their great estate. At Ardgillan, the Taylors managed to maintain the estate until the 1960s, however, it was at a cost with the house in need of major repairs when it was sold.

BASIL RICHARD TAYLOUR (1935-1996)
THE LAST TAYLOUR TO OWN ARDGILLAN CASTLE.

49

Photograph of Main Hall taken in 1938 *(above)* and in 2018 *(facing page).*

Room and the Dining Parlour were to accommodate the style of ladies' attire in those days. Entry to both rooms is made by passing through two doors with the buffer in between showing the thickness of the original external walls before the wings were added on.

The Main Hall has been restored with antique furniture and fittings reminiscent of those which would have been there when the Taylors were in residence. The model of the pond yacht on display in the glass cabinet is one of the few reminders of their time in Ardgillan with the original sails in a frame on the wall beside it. It is now rigged as a Brig, a type of ship that was once common on the Irish Sea. This was a perfect toy for both floating or sailing.

Hall Clock

Pond Yacht

The Carabinier Breastplate

On the wall of the Main Hall hangs a splendid example of a breastplate, or cuirass, that once belonged to a French cavalryman, an officer in the Regiment of Carabiniers, the elite among Napoleon's feared heavy cavalry. Their name derives from the carbine or shortened musket they carried in addition to their long, straight, heavy sword and a pair of pistols. The Carabiniers, with their black bearskin headdress, blue jackets, buff trousers and white gloves, were usually deployed at crucial moments on the battlefield throughout Napoleon's many, bloody campaigns. However, in 1809, they suffered such horrendous casualties that he ordered them to wear the cuirass, the iron breastplate worn by the other regiments of heavy cavalry in the French Army. Initially, they took this instruction as an insult to their courage under fire and also argued that this would make them look the same as other cuirassier regiments. As a result, Napoleon permitted them to have a polished brass overlay on their breastplates adorned with the Imperial Eagle.

The Carabinier's breastplate with crossed halberds

Centre right: Close-up of the Napoleonic Eagle crest

The earlier bearskin was replaced with a new helmet made from yellow copper with the letter 'N' in front and a metal chinstrap. It was topped with a splendid, raised red comb instead of the trailing, black, horsehair plume of the cuirassier. Incidentally, that long plume wasn't just for ornamentation. Being a very stiff fabric, horsehair also provided very effective protection to the back of the neck from a sword slash as did the rolled blanket over the shoulder for other regiments. These changes made the Carabinier trooper one of the most visually astounding sights on the battlefield, especially when the sun shone on their massed ranks.

Prior to the Battle of Waterloo on 18 June 1815, Wellington's men had never faced Napoleon's heavy cavalry. In the afternoon of that fateful day, the Emperor's cavalry swirled around the packed squares of the Allied Army and came under such intense musket fire that one officer later compared the sound of the balls hitting the French armour with that of hailstones on a tin roof. After the battle, some of Wellington's exhausted soldiers collected the discarded breastplates and used them as vessels in which to cook their food. Of the few samples of the cuirass that have survived to this day perhaps the most internationally recognised is that which belonged to twenty-three year old Francois-Antoine Fauveau. According to family legend, Francois-Antoine was about to get married on the day he was called up so his brother took his place and enlisted. And it was this brother who died on the battlefield when struck by a cannonball. His shattered front armour still presents as one of the most shocking images of the horrors of Waterloo.

Cromwell's New Model Army breastplate

In addition to the Carabinier officer's body armour in the Main Hall, two breastplates worn by soldiers of Cromwell's New Model Army are also on view there. They are considerably smaller and lighter than the Carabinier's cuirass, their size offering a clear indication of the typical physique of a Cromwellian-era soldier. Although Cromwell's cavalry were known as Ironsides for their ability to cut through opposing ranks, the troopers' armour only covered the chest and the back, with a 'lobster tail' helmet offering protection to the head. They were so well trained tactically that they retained their discipline when in action against the Royalists, and usually emerged victorious. However, when they came to Ireland in August 1649, even this armour wasn't enough to prevent the New Model Army from suffering its greatest defeats some months later at both Waterford and Clonmel, shattering its aura of invincibility.

While Ardgillan's rare breastplates can be viewed in the Main Hall of the Castle, Fauveau's holed breastplate can be accessed online as part of 'Waterloo – 200 Objects', the 2015 Exhibition that commemorated the 200th anniversary of the Battle of Waterloo.

The Polearms Collection

On display in the Main Hall in conjunction with the Carabinier's cuirass are pairs of crossed halberds, those crude, fearsome weapons from the Middle Ages that are seldom seen in public now except perhaps when carried ceremoniously by the Swiss Guard in the Vatican. Once wielded by the bulk of the common soldiery, they dominated the battlefield for centuries. Even when firearms started to replace them, it was a long time before they disappeared completely.

The word 'halberd' comes from two Middle High German words, *halm* meaning 'handle' and *barte* meaning 'axe'. Cheap and easy to manufacture, polearms are exactly that, weapons with long handles to keep one's enemy at a distance and, in the hands of trained and experienced soldiers, they were deadly. The halberd, with its combination of spear and battleaxe, was the product of years of chilling development and refinement and could inflict injury in different ways by chopping, skewering, stabbing or crushing, depending on which blade was used.

Usually, only the front row of a phalanx of soldiers wore breastplates to protect them from the polearms of the opposing army, with the following ranks being unarmoured. Companies of soldiers moved in large columns with their long pikes carried in the vertical position. When two such bodies of men came into contact, the front ranks advanced with lowered weapons to attack, while the men in the outer ranks slashed to the side of the opposing column. The pressure from within a large body of men to keep moving forward built up until the column's advance became

Wall-mounted crossed halberds displayed in the Main Hall

unstoppable, crushing the foremost ranks against each other, hence the need for armour. This was the tactic known as 'push pike' and it led to carnage.

The long weapon was particularly useful when infantry faced cavalry. The soldiers dug the handles of their halberds into the ground presenting a hedgehog of spear tips onto which horses, sensibly, would not charge. Cavalry usually resorted to swirling around the outside of the formation looking for a gap. If the wall of halberds held firm, cavalry were forced to withdraw. Of course, the obvious disadvantage of the polearm was that it was too long to be used in close combat. Once an opponent got beyond the blade, the ungainly weapon was useless and soldiers then had to resort to the sword, dagger or mace for personal defence.

The polearm collection in Ardgillan contains some splendid examples, including a number of halberds with faded red tassels, a sergeant's spontoon and a unique, crude homemade pike. The business end of the halberd consists of three standard elements: blade, point and beak; the blade for chopping, the point for thrusting and the beak for unhorsing cavalry. The tassels were for dispersing blood and gore when held upright during use to prevent the handle from becoming slippery. However, it seems unlikely that the Ardgillan halberds were intended to be used in battle since they do not have the studded leather covering which would provide grip to the handle nor are they pointed at the base. The crest detail and motto, *Alta Peto*,

Three types of polearms showing a variety of blades.
Lower right:
Close-up of tassel

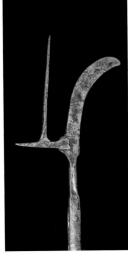

meaning 'Aim High', on each halberd belongs to the Smethurst family, whose origins can be traced to pre-Norman Lancashire, England.

Also in the collection is a spontoon, a nine-foot long shaft topped by a simple blade with cross bars. This was carried by sergeants to keep troops in line as they marched and manoeuvered, and as a rallying-point for dispersed soldiers on the battlefield. Spontoons were in use in many European armies as late as the middle of the nineteenth century.

But perhaps the most extraordinary polearm preserved in Ardgillan is the homemade pike from the late 1700s. It looks innocuous enough now, consisting of a farm labourer's bill (a kind of sickle) attached to the end of a long, wooden shaft, similar to a traditional English infantry weapon. This unique example also has a craftsman's hammer, stripped of its wooden handle and with its metal shaft sharpened to a point, crudely forged to the curve of the bill, thus creating a primitive and deadly weapon.

A monument erected outside Ballyboughal on the Oldtown Road commemorates the activities of the men of North County Dublin, reinforced by insurgents from Wexford in 1798. It was mainly homemade pikes of this type that they used in the uneven fight against the muskets and artillery of the outnumbering militias.

Above:
Sergeant's spontoon with metal cross bar

Top right:
A homemade pike

Below:
Beautifully landscaped grounds at Ardgillan

The Ships' Figureheads

As though celebrating the Castle's panoramic view of the Irish Sea, four wooden ships' figureheads stand in the Main Hall just inside the front door. Judging by their weather-beaten appearance, they have survived many long voyages. Figureheads like these were once a common sight on the schooners that plied their trade from Skerries and Balbriggan harbours and indeed have adorned ships worldwide since antiquity.

From as early as 500 BC, mariners in the Mediterranean Sea decorated their ships with symbols as a means of identifying them. In predominantly illiterate, yet otherwise sophisticated societies, these images were significant as they also embodied specific meanings. Greek and Phoenician boats carried the Eye of Horus to ensure safe passage at sea, a custom that endures to this day. Romans decorated the ram bows of their war galleys to further intimidate enemy vessels using the centurion to denote valour. Greeks adopted a boar's head to symbolise vision and ferocity. In Northern Europe, bulls, serpents, dragons and dolphins were popular among seafarers and the Vikings added menace to their longships with the high curved bow depicting a gaping-mouthed sea creature. Later, during the thirteenth century, the swan made an appearance, signifying mobility and grace.

As ship design and construction improved, the stem, an extension of the keel, was strengthened and it became possible to attach bulkier figureheads under the bow spit. The Renaissance saw a move towards religious imagery and it was not long before this was reflected in ships' figureheads as sailors sought Divine Protection on their voyages. So it is little wonder that when the Spanish Armada set sail in 1588 many galleons were named after popular saints and carried ornate figures of Christ or the Virgin Mary.

Ship's figurehead – detail

But it was during the Baroque period (1600-1750) that both commercial and naval ship ornamentation was carried to an extreme, arguably reaching a zenith in the 1700s. An army of carvers was employed in Europe's shipyards with many sculptors becoming

just as renowned as the great painters of the period. Figureheads, often comprising separate parts carved from massive pieces of hard wood were assembled and attached to the stem while the stern was decorated with repeating patterns and motifs of extraordinary grandeur. By contrast, British ships became more understated in their decorative work tending to incorporate smaller figureheads and, on occasion, just a scroll or fiddlehead at the bow. It was said that English crews admired French figureheads while the French sneered at their restrained English counterparts. Regardless of nationality, the visual impact of these carvings, the product of flamboyantly creative minds, reflected the wealth and prestige of the state or the merchant shipping companies that owned them. But heavy sculptures had severe disadvantages in that they affected the handling of the ship and they were costly.

Around the time of Napoleon there was a move away from the full, complex, ostentatious figure to more simple, waist-up depictions of the human form, male and female, but which still reflected the identity of the ship. The images of the female body, both covered and partly-covered, included mermaids in various, flowing poses. While sailors always believed that the symbols brought good fortune to their ship, there was the additional superstition that the bare-breasted female spirit could calm a stormy sea, hence its popularity. In times of war, it was customary to rename a captured vessel after renovation but the figurehead was always left untouched.

These dramatic carvings were the eyes of the ship, always looking ahead across the sea. Sailors trusted in them and went to extraordinary lengths to care for them. For instance, a figure with outstretched arms had the arms removed as soon as they were clear of a port. They were then stored safely in the hold until their next port of call was neared when they were reattached. The exhilarating image of an outstretched female figure is imitated in the famous bow scene from the film *Titanic*.

As the 1800s progressed, the popularity of figureheads increased and a Turk's Head or a Native American Chief's head became a common sight on sailing ships. By the time the tea clippers were masters of the sea, they had become much smaller and lighter but no less symbolic. Perhaps the most famous of the clippers was the *Cutty Sark* which carried a bare-

Above and facing page:
Ships' figureheads

breasted female, the witch Nannie wearing a 'cutty sark', a short chemise or undergarment. It is no surprise then that some captains paid for a carving, respecting the crew's preference to sail in a ship that carried one. But whether it was that of a beast, a person or a mythological character, sailors wanted the carving to be ornate and imposing and they lovingly restored them when in port. When the age of sail ended, demand for figureheads largely disappeared. As a consequence of this, some carvers adapted their skills to a growing market for full-size, Native American figures that were then used as advertising both inside and outside tobacco shops. However, much simpler symbols have continued in use on vessels, in the shape of a crest affixed to the bow or the bridge of a ship, or as artwork on the conning tower of a submarine.

As for the four figureheads in the Castle, two are from larger vessels and two from smaller ones, probably the size of the Skerries and Balbriggan schooners of old. Each represents a female with windswept hair, peering eyes and with their garments gathered at the waist. Traces of their once-bright paintwork can still be seen. At the back of each figure, the chisel work is crude and the nails and screws that attached them are rusted and bent. Unfortunately, there is no identifying artisan's trademark on any of them.

Apart from Ardgillan's figureheads, this part of coastal North Dublin is familiar with two other such examples. One, the Turk's Head, was once atop a plinth outside the Man O'War Inn a few miles away but was removed in the 1880s and is now in private ownership. The other, a female figure from the waist up with flowing hair, a torc, and a Tara Brooch affixed to her cloak, can still be seen on the gable wall of the public house previously known as Fingal's Cave, on Church Street, Skerries.

Ship's figurehead
- detail

Traditionally, when a wooden ship was being broken up, the figurehead was given to its last captain. At this remove, and in the absence of captains' logs, there is no way of finding out the names of the ships that Ardgillan's wonderful sculptures once watched over. However, with the long, sea-faring tradition that exists along the North Dublin coast, the presence of these rare pieces of maritime history serves as a reminder of all who sailed in these waters.

THE BILLIARD ROOM

On entering the Billiard Room with its large, feature window and decorative, plaster ceiling rose, the eye is drawn immediately to the plaque on the wall over the Carrara marble fireplace. Placed there in 1738 by the

Rev Robert on completion of Prospect House, it looks very impressive with its Latin inscription in keeping with its owner's classical education. The obvious mismatch between the curved corners of the marble fireplace base and the rectangular limestone foundation on the floor has a simple explanation. The Carrara marble fireplace, with its detailed sculpting of feeding birds on either side of the coat of arms, is not the original that graced the Billiard Room. The earlier limestone fireplace, now in Leixlip Castle, was a truly beautiful piece of craftsmanship into which Robert's plaque was embedded. At a certain stage, the family decided to sell the black one and replace it with that which is currently in situ. However, this new fireplace of white marble with buff columns is also of considerable significance as it was made originally for the Nugents, the Earls of Westmeath, whose coat of arms and motto, *Decrevi*, 'I have decided', adorns it. It once stood in Clonyn Castle, a Victorian baronial residence, built near the site of an earlier Nugent castle at Delvin in County Westmeath.

What is often referred to as Kilkenny marble is actually a high-quality limestone found on the banks of the River Nore. Today, a signed footpath along its shady banks in the direction of Bennettsbridge passes through Maddoxstown where William Colles of nearby Blackrath opened his limestone quarry, the high cliffs of which are now partially obscured by tall aspen trees. This peaceful area was once a hive of activity as the black fossil stone was removed, cut into blocks at the nearby watermills and then carried by boat to Kilkenny where flagstones and tiles for paving and

Above:
The coat of arms of the Earls of Westmeath, the Nugents

Facing page:
The ornate fireplace in the Billiard Room with the Rev. Robert Taylor's commemorative plaque

D O M
favente
Has Ædes extruxit
ROBERTUS TAYLOR
Decanus Clonfertensis
Anno Salutis 1738.
Procul hinc
Mendacium. Rixa, Clamor, Luctus, Ira.
Adsint
Amicitia, blanda Quies, alma Faustitas,
nuda Veritas, jocorumq. Chorus.
————Dicimus integro
Sicci mane die: dicimus Uvidi,
cum Sol Occano Subest.
Hor: L4 Od:5

flooring were produced. The highest-grade stone glistened with a white fleck when polished and was used in the carving of ornate fireplaces, memorial tablets, sculptures, columns, ornamental monuments and countertops. It was this precious stone that Robert chose for the astonishing fireplace that he installed in his home, its speckled black surface a stark contrast to the white marble plaque encased within it.

Inscriptions over portals and fireplaces were common from the Middle Ages but in Robert's time it was fashionable to display a worthy verse from a Roman or Greek poet to demonstrate one's regard for, and knowledge of, the classics. In selecting Quintus Flaccus Horace, better known to us today as Horace, Robert could have chosen one of his most popular quotes, for example, *Carpe Diem,* 'Seize the Day' or *Nil Desperandum,* 'Never Despair'. Instead, he opted for lines that were much more obscure but obviously had some personal appeal:

Dicimus integro,
Sicci mane die dicimus Vivandi,
cum Sol Occano Subest

(Thus, dry lipped we pray when day begins,
so we pray flushed with wine
when the sun sinks beneath the oceans.)

Horace, Book 4, Ode 5, Lines 38-40

Ceiling plasterwork
and chandelier

Feature window in
the Billiard Room

THE DRAWING ROOM

The Drawing Room was the centre of social activity in Ardgillan, its wide door giving entry to the large, bright space complete with wooden floor, tall windows and high ceiling.

Above the marble fireplace, the large mirror, framed with sculpted, Gesso-style moulding covered in gold paint, reflects the magnificent view from the north-facing windows down the sloping parkland to the tree line (Wilfred's Wood) and the sea beyond. Hidden behind the trees are the Dublin to Belfast railway line and the scenic coastal road between Skerries and Balbriggan. Double doors lead through from the Drawing Room into the airy conservatory. A black-and-white photograph on the wall shows the room as it was in 1938, the same year in which Edward Richard, the last Taylor to be born in Ardgillan, passed away.

The Drawing Room looking towards the conservatory

It was here that the Taylors formally received their relatives, guests and many visitors. Indeed, the long list of signatures in the guest books show how strongly connected the family was to prominent and wealthy members of society in North Dublin and the surrounding counties. Their regular invitees included their neighbours, the Hamiltons from Hampton Hall; from Skerries, the Woods of Milverton Hall and the Hamiltons of Hacketstown House; from Balbriggan, the Macartneys of Lother Lodge; the Palmers from Kenure House, Rush; and from further afield, the Cobbes of Newbridge House, Donabate, the Talbots of Malahide Castle, the Prestons of Gormanston Castle and the Hamiltons of Sheephill Park and Holmpatrick.

Apart from the names of family and friends, the guest books show that the Taylors entertained the most distinguished and influential members of society year after year at Ardgillan. On 10 February 1879, John Winston Spencer-Churchill, 7th Duke of Marlborough, accompanied by his wife,

The fireplace with mirror and Gesso-style surround

Frances Anne, visited the Castle. Marlborough was Lord Lieutenant of Ireland at the time, a post he held under Disraeli from 1876 to 1880. Their grandson, Winston Churchill, the future Prime Minister of Great Britain, was already five years old when the Marlboroughs signed their names in the guest book. Another significant date was 3 January 1882 when the Earl of Bective visited, along with Lords Longford and Inchiquin, a Hamilton (most likely Ion Trant Hamilton, later to become Baron Holmpatrick), Adelaide Lisgar and her second husband, Francis Tourville of Bosworth Hall, Leicestershire. (Her first husband was John Lisgar, Governor General of Canada.) The conversation must have been sparkling on that occasion as Hamilton wrote 'Great Meeting Day' beside his signature. While many who visited the Castle are unknown today, one signature from 1869 still instantly recognisable is that of Arthur E Guinness, first used as a trademark label by the Guinness brewery in 1862.

As they moved within the highest levels of social and political life, the Taylors engaged

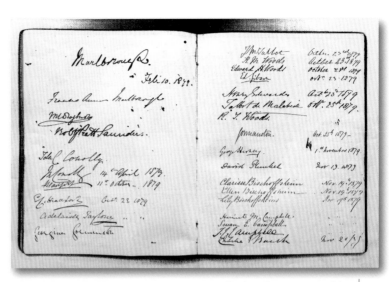

Guest book with signatures of the Lord Lieutenant, Lord Marlborough, and his wife, Frances Anne

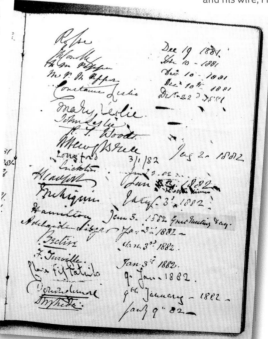

Names of distinguished guests present at the 'Great Meeting Day' on 3 January, 1882

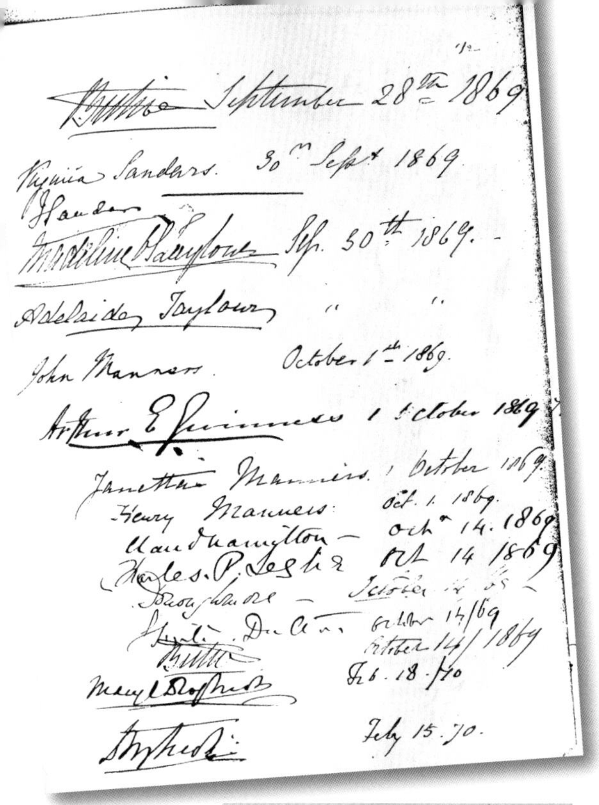

Guest list featuring the famous signature of Arthur E Guinness

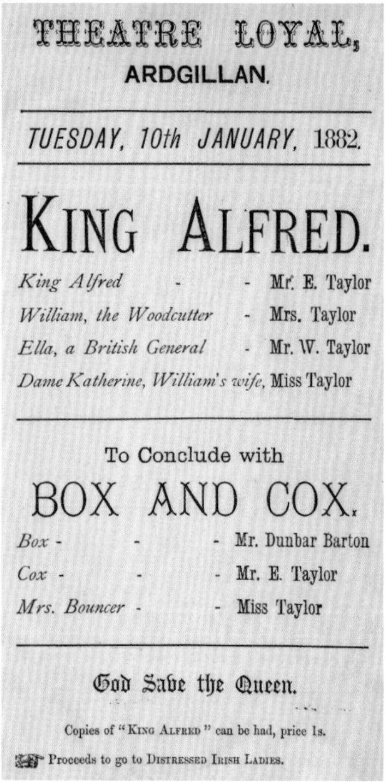

[handwritten guest list entries:]

Kythe — September 28th 1869
Virginia Sandars. 30 Sept 1869
Flander
Madeline Barrymore Sep 30th 1869.
Adelaide Taylour " "
John Manners October 1st 1869.
Arthur E Guinness 1 October 1869
Janetta Manners 1 October 1869.
Henry Manners Oct. 1. 1869.
Maud Hamilton Oct 14. 1869
Charles P. Leslie Oct 14 1869
Rosy Moore Octbr 14 69
Egidia DuCane Octbr 14/69
Kythe Octbr 14/ 1869
Mary E Bofhes Feb. 18 70.
S Kythes Feby 15. 70.

Home-printed programme for the Theatre Loyal

THEATRE LOYAL,
ARDGILLAN.

TUESDAY, 10th JANUARY, 1882.

KING ALFRED.

King Alfred	-	-	Mr. E. Taylor
William, the Woodcutter	-		Mrs. Taylor
Ella, a British General	-		Mr. W. Taylor
Dame Katherine, William's wife,			Miss Taylor

To Conclude with

BOX AND COX.

Box	-	-	Mr. Dunbar Barton
Cox	-	-	Mr. E. Taylor
Mrs. Bouncer	-		Miss Taylor

God Save the Queen.

Copies of "KING ALFRED" can be had, price 1s.
Proceeds to go to DISTRESSED IRISH LADIES.

---

in frequent and lavish entertainment. With relatives and guests staying at Ardgillan for prolonged periods, the demands on the household were considerable, especially upon the servants who bore the brunt of the work. But, undoubtedly, the highlight of the social year in a Big House was the annual ball when the Drawing Room was the centre of activities. Generally the season for debutante balls lasted for around six weeks, culminating with the Levée at Dublin Castle. It was on occasions such as these that a young girl in a family emerged as an adult and the search for an agreeable match with an eligible gentleman began. Indeed, mixing and conversing in the Drawing Room was seen as part of formative social training for girls when they could display their skill with a musical instrument, entertain guests with their singing or demonstrate their poise when pouring tea.

When the Taylors indulged their passion for amateur dramatics by performing plays in front of invited guests, all of the family members were allocated parts in the production. The Drawing Room was amusingly renamed 'Theatre Loyal' on these occasions. An inlaid piano once provided the accompanying music to the performances but, as with the rest of the original Taylor furniture visible in the 1938 photographs, it is now gone. The actress Frances (Fanny) Kemble was a close friend of both Harriet and Marianne St Leger prior to the latter's marriage to the Rev Edward. Fanny visited Ardgillan on a number of occasions and retained such fond memories of the place that she refers to the castle on several occasions in her writings, describing herself as being 'as happy there as the birds that fly in the clear sky above the sea' (*Records of a Girlhood*, Fanny Kemble, 1878).

Unlike other grand residences of the period, the soft furnishings, curtains and bed fabrics were made from cotton and linen, materials readily available in the area due to the two mills that were in operation in Balbriggan. Developed from a cottage industry, George Hamilton (d.1793) of Hampton Hall was instrumental in the development of the mills since 1780 and from the 1800s on the quality of cotton and linen from Balbriggan achieved world recognition for excellence. Today, the curtains that hang in Ardgillan reflect the modest style of fabric that would have been seen in the time of the Rev Edward and Marianne when they entertained distinguished guests in the Drawing Room.

The Wedgwood Clock in the Drawing Room

Above:
The Marble Fireplace

Left:
Corner embellishment
in the Drawing Room

Below:
Detail of
Gesso-style mirror
surround

THE BELL SYSTEMS

Like all Big Houses of the period, Ardgillan was equipped with an internal bell system for summoning servants within the house and an external bell for the estate workers.

Early internal bell systems were of the pulley and copper wire type. In formal rooms, such as the Drawing Room or Dining Parlour, the pulley would have been disguised with a length of tapestry ribbon with a metal ring on the end. Later on, the wiring system was hidden within the wall and operated by use of a knob. When pulled, the vibration passed along the wire and sounded a single bell from among a row hanging on the wall near the kitchen. Each bell was of a different size and therefore each possessed an individual sound. Servants learned to associate each tinkle with a specific room in order to respond speedily. When electrical systems were introduced, the wire pulleys were replaced with push button fittings. Those in the Dining Parlour are cleverly disguised into the oak panelling while the Library still retains both wire pulley and push button models.

Above: Pull and press bells in the Library
Below left: The disguised Dining Parlour bells
Below right: Drawing Room bell

Although the row of internal bells that once hung near the kitchen has unfortunately disappeared, a large external bell still hangs high up on the gable wall of the castle overlooking the Rose Garden. The ringing of this bell, once heard all over the Demesne, controlled the working day of the gardeners and the field labourers.

The gardener's bell – close-up

The bell tower on the gable
of the Castle building

Afternoon Tea

By the time that the Rev Edward and Marianne took up residence in Ardgillan in 1807, tea had largely displaced coffee as the drink of choice of the upper classes. As the quantity of tea being imported and smuggled throughout the early 1800s increased dramatically in Ireland and Great Britain, its popularity and consumption also rose rapidly. Of course, this trend was soon followed by the rest of society as the price gradually fell and the Irish love affair with tea began.

Among the wealthy, a whole etiquette surrounding the drinking of tea developed. Before cups were introduced, the beverage was served in a small dish called a tea bowl and, as time passed, afternoon tea and tea gardens became fashionable. In poorer households tea became a daily necessity and, eventually, a symbol of warm hospitality. Initially, it was so expensive that it was common for tea leaves to be dried and then reused, or stewed all day with more and more water being added. While medical journals of the period reflect widespread concern about the over-consumption of tea among the poorer population, the fact that tea contains natural antibacterial qualities and that water had to be first boiled, meant that it was a far safer drink than the water available in the towns and cities at that time. In factories, the introduction of a tea break gave workers an added injection of energy so that they could sustain longer shift hours, while in Big Houses it replaced 'small beer', or watered down beer, as the regular drink among servants. In Leinster House, for instance, such was the contaminated state of the water in Dublin, that the servants of the Earl of Kildare enjoyed small beer on tap.

"There was cricket and dinner of beef and pudding for the labourers; and a Servants' Ball in the evening at which Edd (Thomas Edward) led off with Miss Thorp." Marianne Taylor to her son, Dick, in Gibralter, 14 Sept. 1847.

Lockable containers for tea and sugar. Tea was locked away in a caddy. The word 'caddy' derives from the word 'catty', a standardised weight measurement used in the Far East.

M.SUGAR

73

Due to the bitterness of black tea in contrast to green tea, sugar and milk were often added. Vast quantities of sugar came from plantations on the islands of the Caribbean to which many Irish had been transported following Cromwell's land confiscation. When the 1733 Molasses Act was passed in Westminster, it protected the British sugar islands while heavily taxing sugar and molasses from elsewhere. Sugar arrived in the form of a sugarloaf from which pieces were broken for ease of use. Along with tea, sugar soon became another essential ingredient and was used mostly in the preparation of exotic and eye-catching desserts to impress dinner guests. As demand grew, profits from the importation of sugar made merchants so wealthy that it was called 'the White Gold'.

From their obsession with all things sugary, the aristocratic sweet tooth contributed largely to the widespread dental decay that afflicted the wealthy from the seventeenth century on, leading to a demand for false teeth made from porcelain – or for real teeth. With dentistry in its infancy, advertisements even appeared in newspapers in the late 1700s seeking human teeth from the continent to replace the rotten teeth of the aristocracy. The demand was partly met during the Napoleonic Era as unscrupulous individuals harvested the teeth of the huge numbers of young men killed in battle. For example, dentures made from the teeth of soldiers killed at Waterloo, known as Waterloo teeth, were widely available after 18 June 1815. More frivolous

Far left: Samovar for hot water on display in the Drawing Room

Left: Sugar came in the form of a sugar loaf which was then broken into lumps

generalisations made by commentators were that chambermaids lost their bloom through their habit of sipping tea and that it encouraged gossip.

Concern with people's health due to the increased consumption of sugar led to protests across Europe in the form of the Anti-Saccharite Society. Because West Indies sugar was linked inextricably with slavery, an effective boycott was organised in 1791, which led to a dramatic fall in demand as people heeded the call to say 'no' to Caribbean 'slave sugar'. In an effort to improve their public image, and to counter diminishing sales, the Honourable East India Company printed an ad stating: 'East India sugar not made by slaves'.

The question of slavery continued to be debated in the British Parliament until it was eventually abolished in 1833, four years after Catholic Emancipation in Ireland. Meanwhile, the territories in the possession of the East India Company would have to wait another ten years before slavery was ended in 1843, the year before the first train ran across Ardgillan Demesne. As for commodities such as tea and sugar, the steady increase in their supply meant that the price of each dropped and in time it was no longer necessary to keep them under lock and key at night.

Enjoying tea and perhaps a cigar or a pipeful of tobacco purchased at G Mitchell's of 20 Sackville Street, Dublin, was a regular occurrence in houses such as Ardgillan. While the guest lists record the names of those who were

Above right: Silver tea pot on display in the Drawing Room

Right: A cigar box from G Mitchell's, Importer of Havana cigars, tobacco, etc., and Wine Merchant, of 20 Sackville St, Dublin, by appointment to his Royal Highness, The Prince of Wales and His Excellency, the Lord Lieutenant

formal invitees to the Castle, family diaries reveal details of their more casual visitors in wonderfully familiar ways such as '3 Cobbes 6 Woods to tea'. Among the Cobbes would have been Frances Conway Cobbe of Newbridge House, a lifelong friend of Marianne's. Frances' son, Charles, who seconded the nomination of Thomas Edward Taylor when he first went for election in 1841, while her daughter, Frances Power Cobbe, was a particular friend of Harriet St Leger. These connections illustrate the closeness of the friendship between the families. Perhaps the conversations they had around the fire in the Drawing Room over a cup of tea included such weighty matters as their political ambitions and achievements as well as more trivial, everyday topics.

CANDLES AND CHIMNEYS

Today candles are decorative accessories associated with celebration, the warm glow of the naked flames creating a soothing and relaxed atmosphere. Until the advent of gas and electricity, dipped candles and oil lamps were the principal source of domestic lighting, undergoing many refinements along the way. In Europe, tallow, or animal fat, was the primary material used in candle making but these gave off an offensive odour when lit, a real disadvantage within a room. They also tended to bend over while burning, making them a serious fire hazard. This was not the case with sweet-perfumed beeswax candles that are highly flammable, burn brighter, last longer and most importantly do not bend over while burning. Like others of their class, the Taylors would have used beeswax candles extensively throughout the Castle even though they were much more expensive to purchase.

The more humble dwellings of the poor were illuminated by rushlight, a means that was at once both inexpensive and easy to produce. In late summer or autumn, rushes were gathered, peeled and the inner pith was dried. After this, the pith was steeped in grease or fat and sometimes a

Oil lamp on
the wall in the
basement

little beeswax was added to make it burn longer. A metal clip held the burning rush at an angle as this gave off more light than if held in a vertical position. In turn, the holder was based on a tripod, a metal base or on a block of wood. A large collection of antique rushlight holders is preserved in the Castle, some of which are on display as exhibits in the rooms.

A variety of rush lights from the collection in Ardgillan

In Big Houses such as Ardgillan, elaborate chandeliers supplemented by wall-mounted candles with backing mirrors were the main sources of light in the formal rooms before the introduction of the incandescent bulb. The chandeliers now hanging from the centre of the decorative plaster roses in

the Drawing Room and the Dining Parlour are replacements for the originals that were candle-lit. The glow from so many candles added cheer to the surroundings and supplemented the warmth from the crackling, log fire. However, with so many naked flames to monitor, the risk of fire was a constant reality in the Castle and with no running water available the consequences were potentially catastrophic. Hence, the necessity for the Master or the butler to check the house last thing at night to make sure that all candles were properly extinguished, the fires stoked down and that all had withdrawn to bed.

The task of keeping Ardgillan's fires going fell to the housemaids starting first with the range in the kitchen. This was followed by the opening of the shutters in the Main Hall, the Drawing Room and the Dining Parlour, and then the cleaning out of the fireplaces. Ashes were sifted before being disposed of and any cinders kept for reuse in the kitchen. Having blackened the grates and accompanying firedogs or andirons, the fires were then set. The same process then continued in each of the upstairs rooms that were occupied. The housemaid's box held different kinds of dusters for cleaning the various surfaces as well as blacking and polishing brushes. With so many fires lighting every day, dusting was a continuous activity, as was the need to keep a wary eye for flying sparks.

The splendid chandelier in the Drawing Room

To further reduce the risk of fire, chimneys needed regular cleaning. Chimney sweeps were employed to do this work but due to the narrowness of the flues, they employed small boys, some as young as six, as apprentices. Generally, the boys were sourced in the workhouses and, as the hiring of each child reduced the cost to the local parish or Board of Governors, such employment was encouraged. The nearest workhouse to Ardgillan was the Balrothery Union Workhouse at Ballough, a few miles north-east of Lusk. The initial meeting concerning the workhouse took place in Balbriggan in December 1839, with the Rev Edward Taylor among the many attendees. However, while the ex-officio guardians of the workhouse, elected at a subsequent meeting in April 1839, included his neighbours, George Hamilton and George Woods, the Rev Edward's clerical status rendered him ineligible for the position. The workhouse opened in 1841 with the expectation that the occupants, in spite of their weakened state, would be given work regardless of age. As for young boys and girls there, the only

The fireplace in the Library

employment offered to them was picking oakum, which was the unravelling of short lengths of old rope. The fibres were then mixed with pitch and used to seal ships' timbers. Some remains of the Balrothery Union Workhouse and adjoining Fever Hospital still stand while the enclosed graveyard, where so many deceased inmates are buried, lies in a field a short distance away just off the old north road towards Balbriggan. The site is marked with a stone cross.

Although an Act of Parliament in 1788 banned the employment of children under the age of eight, the law was largely ignored and the practice of using climbing boys continued. The smaller the child, the easier it was for him to climb up the dark, claustrophobic confines of a chimney to clean a blocked flue or extinguish a chimney fire, with the constant risk of becoming trapped. If this happened, the only way to free him before he suffocated was by breaking through the chimney's brickwork. But even finding the boy in the longer flues of a Big House was difficult, sometimes necessitating the sending up of a second boy.

The oak fireplace carved by the Guardorici brothers in the Dining Parlour complete with blackened andirons

Many of these young lads lived in filth, sleeping under their sacks, without the opportunity of a regular wash or clean clothes. Constantly breathing in choking, black, carcinogenic dust, the boys' eyes and lungs were affected, resulting in chronic illness and, frequently, early death. Although chimney sweeps' boys were romanticised from the late nineteenth century on, their lot was a particularly harsh one in a world where life for the poor was hard anyway. Regardless of who had to clean Ardgillan's many chimneys before rods and brushes became common, the task must have been an extremely dirty and unpleasant one.

While the Taylors enjoyed the warmth of several blazing log fires throughout the house, the servants had only the heat from a single stove to warm the attic area they occupied, a factor of life in a Big House then.

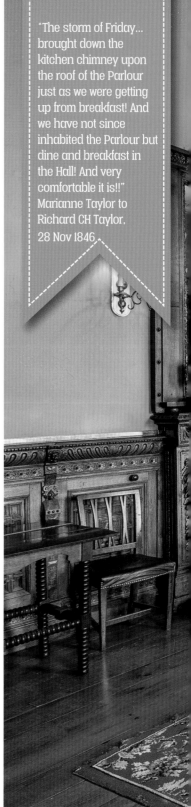

"The storm of Friday... brought down the kitchen chimney upon the roof of the Parlour just as we were getting up from breakfast! And we have not since inhabited the Parlour but dine and breakfast in the Hall! And very comfortable it is!!"
Marianne Taylor to Richard CH Taylor.
28 Nov 1846.

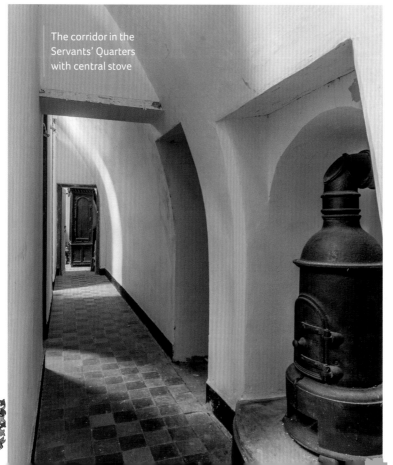

The corridor in the Servants' Quarters with central stove

A folding screen in
the Dining Parlour

THE DINING PARLOUR

In the absence of any detailed records of the manner in which the Taylors dined in the eighteenth and early nineteenth centuries, we can only assume from accounts of other similar houses that it was in keeping with the prevailing customs of the time. Since, at one stage, there were two dining tables in the parlour, presumably joined, and eighteen chairs, the Taylors must have entertained in a manner that was both elegant as well as wholesome, as Mrs Beeton recommended in her *Book of Household Management* (1861). Initially, perhaps, when Thomas Taylor of Headford House used Prospect as his summer residence, guests experienced service *à la française* when all of the dishes were brought to the table simultaneously in an elaborate presentation. From the 1800s on, with the Rev Edward and Marianne in residence, it would most likely have been amended to service *à la russe* with each course being brought to the table in sequence.

Some evidence of the daily routine in Ardgillan has survived. Notices left for guests informed them thus: 'Morning Prayers 9.20; Breakfast 9.30; Luncheon 2.30pm; Dinner 7.30pm'. In Victorian times, etiquette indicated that, when guests were present, places should be formally set, each with a card bearing a name. In a custom that has continued almost unchanged, thinly-sliced bread was laid on a napkin to the left of each plate while wine glasses were placed to the right. The centre piece of the Victorian table was the epergne, a silver bowl or basket designed to hold side dishes, fruit or dessert.

Disguised in the wall to the left of the sideboard is the jib door that connects the Dining Parlour with the Butler's Pantry beyond. Stairs lead from here to the Kitchen directly beneath. This proximity to the Kitchen confers two main advantages: firstly, the distance for carrying food from there

to the table was relatively short, ensuring that heat loss from each dish was kept to a minimum; and, secondly, the warmth from the Kitchen rose to the dining room above, adding to the heat coming from the wide fireplace. Adjacent to the jib door stood a leather folding screen used to afford privacy to family and guests as this door was left open while meals were being served from the pantry. The oak panelling and decorative fireplace were much later additions, being commissioned by Edward Richard Taylor in 1886 and carved by the Guardorici brothers from Italy. The two mirrors in the room are not the originals. One mirror, the larger of the two, was sold with the rest of the house contents in 1962, while the smaller now sits over the fireplace in the Tea Room of the Castle.

Left: The jib door to the Butler's Pantry

Below: The exquisitely carved double doors

As for the double doors, from the top down the panels display the Taylor coat of arms, the initials 'ERT' (Edward Richard Taylor) and the year of completion, 1889. Seemingly out of place, on either side of the fireplace, is a wooden knob. These are the disguised bells referred to earlier for summoning the servants.

In a Dining Parlour such as this, the combined effect of the high ceiling and sombre colours, the oak panelling and soft, cotton drapes, the family portraits and fine tableware, was designed to impress their guests and to reflect the status and wealth of the family.

Facing page (top left):
Wooden knob on fireplace,
a disguised bell for summoning
servants

*Facing page and this page (left
to right):*
Detail of the carved door
panels in the Dining Parlour

This page (right):
Detail of carved wall panel
to right of door

AFTER-DINNER ENTERTAINMENT

In Regency and Victorian times, after the formality of dinner, a typical social evening often ended at the piano for a sing-song or with listening to ladies playing the violin when it became fashionable for them to learn the instrument. Of course, dancing continued to be an ever-popular form of entertainment not just at events such as public balls but also at private

occasions in houses like Ardgillan. Among the most popular dances as the nineteenth century progressed were the Minuet, the Gavotte, the Bolero, the Tarantella, The Mazurka, the Cachucha and the Polka. Being able to dance well was an important advantage but if one could only dance badly, it was deemed wiser not to dance at all.

The pianoforte was a very popular form of entertainment

On other occasions, they turned to more lighthearted activities such as parlour games and cards. While most of these games were designed for children, adults adapted them for their own after-dinner amusement. When inhibitions were loosened by wine, the company could throw off the rigid, stuffy restrictions on social behaviour, especially if the game involved paying a forfeit, when the loser had to perform some frivolous stunt or action for the amusement of the others. Many of these games still survive today, for example, charades, checkers, chess and backgammon, or 'tables', as it was known.

Parlour bowling, a game that is no longer practical in the confines of a modern dining room, is described in one 1846 advertisement as 'truly delightful and exhilirating' (sic) but 'without causing over excitement'. It is further advocated as 'being an amusement in which the ladies can participate', (*Slater's National Directory*, 1848). But one after-dinner parlour game that may well have caused over excitement was 'Are You There, Moriarty?' in which two players lay on their backs on the floor, their heads about a metre apart, and held each other by the left hand. Having asked

'Are You There, Moriarty?' each tried to hit the other by swinging a rolled up newspaper or other harmless object over the head with the right hand without being struck oneself. Rolling aside was part of the game but the timing was all-important. A more raucous version of the game was enacted where the players were blindfolded but as soon as the contest began one of them removed the blindfold and proceeded to strike an opponent relentlessly much to the amusement of the spectators who knew the victim had been set up all along.

The Prospect House inventory of 1795 lists two card tables among the furniture in the Main Hall. While we cannot be sure which games the Taylors favoured, it is certain that all played chess skilfully and were equally adept at cards. Indeed, Harriet St Leger's diaries of her time in Ardgillan between 1817 and 1821 record evening activities such as music and dancing in the parlour with her nieces and nephews – 'the Chicks', as she affectionately called them. They also read aloud to each other from popular books such as Walter Scott's *Waverly* (1814) and *Rob Roy* (1818). The card games that Harriet lists include Whist, Loo (Lanterloo) and Piquet, all trick-taking card games, and these would have helped to pass the time on wet, winter days. Gambling was rife but it is unclear whether that was an approved activity within the Rev Edward's

An advertisement for Parlour Bowling from *Slater's National Directory* 1848 Edition

Below:
Two views of the reversible games table for card games and backgammon

89

household. A Victorian games table, on loan to the Castle, is a happy reminder of these family occasions.

The origins of board games such as chess, draughts and backgammon are unclear but they each have long histories. Chess is probably the oldest skills game on record, most likely first played in India although also known in China and Persia. Having learned the game from the Persians, the Moors then brought it to Europe when they invaded Spain. From there, it spread rapidly to every corner of the continent. As played today, the game is a perfect representation of the medieval world in feudal times where the various moves of pawns, knights, bishops and castles reflect their place in society.

Draughts, or checkers, also used a latticed board. While early versions were played in ancient Egypt, by the fifth century BC the Greeks knew it as the Five Lines Game, literally because they used a five line board with twenty-five spots. Unlike today's horizontal division, the Greeks had a diagonal divide, called 'the holy line', and each player started with twelve pieces. It was also popular with the Romans who called it, unsurprisingly, 'Twelve Pieces'. The centre spot was vacant until play commenced. As with modern draughts, the game progressed with a leap capture. The word 'draughts' derives from the Middle English, draught, which means to move or drag.

A game said to have originated in Mesopotamia at the time of the Persian Empire was known as The Royal Game of Ur, first recorded in 177 BC. The Romans enthusiastically adopted the game, bringing it with them to the furthest reaches of their empire, thus ensuring its popularity. Their version of the game was called *Duodecum Scripta et Tabulae* or 'Tables' for short. The Emperor Nero was known to be an avid player – one can only imagine the fate of those who played against him and won. It was by this name that Chaucer referred to it in 'The Franklin's Tale' in *The Canterbury Tales,* noting that 'They dauncen, and they pleyen at ches and tables.' Also Shakespeare refers to the game in *Love's Labour's Lost* when Monsieur the Nice 'plays at table.' Incidentally, this is how the phrase 'to turn the tables', meaning 'to reverse disadvantage to advantage' came about. Today it is known as backgammon, a name that did not appear in print until around 1640.

The backgammon board appears in many works of art, evidence of its continuing popularity though the centuries. In spite of efforts by the Church to have it banned because of its gambling element, the game continued to be part of Victorian and Edwardian after-dinner activities although, by the 1920s, its popularity had waned.

It is interesting to note that Spillikins, a simple game of uncertain origin that still appeals, was one of writer Jane Austen's favourites. Played in many parts of the world with slight variations in the rules, it was also commonly known as Pick-Up-Sticks and Jack Straw. Each player in turn tries to remove a stick, or straw, from a bundle without moving any of the others. Cheap to make and easy to play, it could be enjoyed in an elegant drawing room or in the most humble peasant cottage.

As for other more boisterous games that have survived until today, such as Blind Man's Buff, Hunt the Hare and Prisoners' Base, it is easy to imagine them being played around the house by the Taylor children and their young friends.

The games table in the Green Room, one of the main bedrooms in the original Prospect House

MASON'S IRONSTONE
CHINA COLLECTION

The Dining Parlour holds a special interest for enthusiasts of pottery as the Castle's extensive collection of Mason's Patent Ironstone China is on display here. Today, Mason is still perhaps the best known of the Staffordshire ceramic producers. The range of high-quality products from the Mason Works and the sheer, exotic nature of their designs ensures that the name will endure long into the future.

The company's origins go back to the latter half of the eighteenth century when Miles Mason was in the trade of 'Chinaman', buying porcelain wholesale from the Honourable East India Company. But as the easy supply of clay from China ceased in the 1790s, resulting in a severe shortage of earthenware products, Miles turned his hand to the manufacture of ceramics, with great success. Soon he had two factories up

Mason's Ironstone
China Collection
on show in the
Dining Parlour

and running, one for earthenware products and the other for porcelain. His three sons became involved but it was Charles James, the youngest, who most enjoyed mixing clay with his father from an early age. In time, the boy would go on to become a master potter while his elder brother, George, developed a flair for design.

But the Masons were not the only ones experimenting with clay at that time. By the early 1800s, more than one hundred and fifty ceramics manufacturers existed in Staffordshire, each trying to feed the insatiable demand for Chinese ware. Prominent among them were the two family firms of John Turner and Josiah Spode, whose granddaughter, Sarah, would marry Charles Mason in 1815. Many were producing pseudo-Chinese designs with soft-paste porcelain but these could not compare with the hard-paste porcelain products pouring in from the East. A dramatic change occurred in 1800 when the Turner

Close-up of Mason's Ironstone China Collection

93

family took out a patent on the first 'Stone China', only to go bankrupt in 1806. Then, some years later, Spode introduced fifty per cent calcined ox bone into a clay mix, and produced the first 'Fine Bone China'. This turned out to be a phenomenal success as it was very like porcelain. But the Masons were not far behind. Charles, in a stroke of genius, invented the name 'ironstone' for his new hard-paste, which he patented in 1813, calling it 'Mason's Patent Ironstone China'.

For all its success, though, ironstone china was a misnomer as Mason didn't actually use any China porcelain in its manufacture and chemical analysis revealed little evidence of an iron component in the product either, unlike Spode's bone china which actually contained bone.

However, this mattered little to his many competitors who were quick to capitalise on the 'ironstone' tag and responded with similar, snappy alternatives such as 'Imperial Ironstone' or 'Real Ironstone'.

The clay Mason used was a very dense earthenware containing a proportion of china stone. When finished, it resembled Chinese porcelain with its bluish tint and, following glazing, was easily decorated. This added to its attraction and, with George's exquisite designs, copying intricate Eastern themes, the Mason Works fed the insatiable popular demand for chinoiserie. Permits to incorporate a Royal Coat of Arms into their trademarks added further to their allure. Mason introduced slight variations to the mark over the years as his company output grew to a phenomenal level. But as time went on, competition became much harder especially when Mason's patent expired in 1827.

Top: Large platter from the Ironstone Collection in the Dining Parlour

Above: Mason's patent featuring the angular crown

The Ironstone Collection in the Dining Parlour in Ardgillan carries the patent mark used between 1830 and 1848, which features an angular crown. To cater specifically for the Irish market, Mason introduced a Dublin version of the trademark, retailing through Thomas Higginbotham & Sons, a China and Delph merchant of 106 Pil Street, now Chancery Street, and at 11/12 Wellington Quay, Dublin. Thomas Higginbotham must have been successful for, in 1846, he is also listed as retailing at 17, Upper Sackville Street.

GLASS, CHINA, EARTHENWARE, AND LAMP
ESTABLISHMENT,
11 & 12, Wellington Quay, Dublin.

THOMAS & HIGGINBOTHAM

Respectfully announce that, in addition to their Constant Stock, they have just imported some fine specimens of Art in ALABASTER and in MARBLE.

Dancing Figures, Medici Vases, Hebe Vases, Etruscan Vases,
CUPID & PSYCHE, AFTER CANOVA, &c. &c.

A general assortment of FRENCH BRONZES, selected from the first makers.

Wellington, Napoleon Crossing the Alps, Mameluke, French Guards, &c. &c.

NEW STONE DINNER SERVICES.

Porcelain, Dessert, Dinner, Tea & Breakfast Suits; Toilette Services, of the newest designs, and in great variety.

THE PATENT CATOPTRIC LAMP, THE CAMPHINE LAMP, AND EVERY LAMP OF MERIT.

The CHANDELIERS, for Drawing and Dining-Rooms, must be seen to be properly appreciated.

The largest and most select assortment in Ireland.

Families visiting Dublin can be supplied with every Article, useful and ornamental, all marked plainly at the Lowest Prices.

THOMAS & HIGGINBOTHAM,

But the same was not true of Masons. During the 1840s, Charles had made a number of strategically poor business decisions while competing manufacturers were making serious inroads into the market. Coupled with that, interest in the oriental style was waning and eventually he was forced into bankruptcy. The Mason Works was sold in 1848 and when Charles died in 1856 the golden era of their company was over. Incredible as it seems, the Masons unwittingly contributed to their own decline through the sheer durability of their ironstone product. And, as a happy consequence, almost two hundred years after manufacture, the extensive collection of Mason's Patent Ironstone China in Ardgillan can still be viewed in the Dining Parlour.

Higginbotham's advertisement in *Slater's National Directory*, 1848 Edition.

The Butler's Pantry

On stepping into the Butler's Pantry through the jib door, the visitor is struck by the austerity of this room in contrast to the grandeur of the Dining Parlour. Known also as the Serving Pantry, this is a functional room with its long worktops, numerous presses and glass cabinets all situated within easy reach of a busy servant working under pressure. An unexpected glass panel on the floor still sheds natural light on the narrow passage beneath leading from the foot of the servants' stairs to the kitchen. The word 'pantry' derives from the Old French form of the Latin word *panis,* meaning 'bread' but by the time the Taylor family engaged themselves in lavish entertainment, this room had assumed a more complex function, primarily being the place to store things used at table in the Dining Parlour. An architect's drawing from the mid-1800s shows the location of the original pantry adjacent to the north tower. Before the current pantry, located beyond the jib door, was installed, servants entered the the Dining Parlour from the passage by means of a door that is now blocked up.

When Prospect House was completed in 1738, the senior male servant in a house was known as the steward. Next in line was the butler – from the Old French, *boteille,* meaning 'bottle' – whose function it was to procure, store and serve wine and spirits for the use of the household. The proximity of the pantry to

The Butler's Pantry

the kitchen area below stairs meant that food arrived with the minimum of heat loss. Occupying the middle of the narrow room lay a large serving table onto which the various courses were delivered. In Big Houses, it was generally the butler's task to plate up, ensuring that the various courses were arranged to the highest standard before serving. At times, with a larger number to be served, the butler was assisted by a capable and presentable footman. During the serving process, silence reigned in the pantry as the flow of dishes and platters continued during the prolonged candlelit dinners, with a folding screen ensuring the privacy of those at table, from servants' eyes.

The Butler's Pantry is the only room in the Castle with barred windows. This was for security reasons as not only did the pantry contain all the wine and spirits from the cellar as they slowly came up to room temperature but it was also the store for fine glass and china, cutlery and serving pieces. In fact, the contents of pantries in some stately homes were often so valuable that an under-butler slept across the locked door as added security. It is highly unlikely that the Taylors ever had to take such precautions but it seems that the steward they had in 1852 was a very dutiful individual. On 9 November of that year at around four o'clock in the morning, the 'family

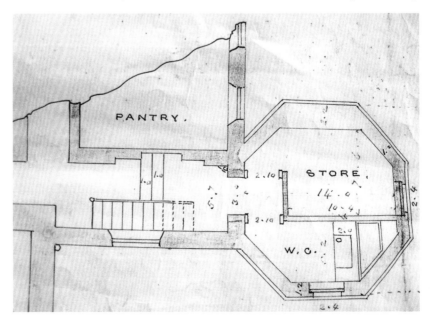

Plan of the original pantry, and tower with store and w.c.

awakened at Ardgillan Castle, and the steward fired a gun out of the window, fancying he heard housebreakers', (Sanders Newsletter, 11 November 1852) In fact, what had disturbed the trigger-happy steward was a significant earthquake that struck the east coast of Ireland and west coast of Britain on that night, prompting the Irish geophysicist Robert Mallet to record people's experiences of the event, including the above.

Reeve's Silver Enamel – silver powder mixed with water for polishing anything silver. Gold powder was also made available.

But not everything stored in the pantry was valuable. Cleaning agents for hated tasks such as the sharpening of knives and polishing of cutlery and silverware were kept close at hand here too. Eventually, certain innovations made the butler's life a little easier, especially when Spong & Co, manufacturers of kitchen utensils, produced a knife sharpener, an example of which can be seen on the pantry counter, its now-faded guarantee offering a word of caution. Spong only promised a sharp blade when the company's own powder was used inside the drum.

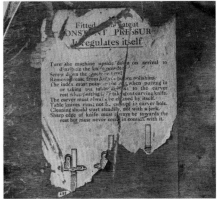

The Spong & Co Ltd knife sharpener. Spong's Guarantee: 'Only Spong's prepared knife powder to be used in this machine'.

Over the years the duties of the steward and the butler were combined and the latter survived to become the head male servant of a household. During the lifetimes of the Rev Edward and his son, Thomas, the Butler's Pantry was indeed a busy place. However, when Thomas died in 1883 and his son Edward took over, the occasions for entertaining must have been less frequent. Edward's duties with his regiment, the Grenadier Guards, meant he was absent for prolonged periods of time as was his brother, Basil, an officer in the Royal Navy who served overseas. In the 1901 Census of Ireland, Thomas Salmon, a widower aged sixty-four, is returned as caretaker; and by 1911, he is listed as both butler and domestic servant. As no Taylor was present in Ardgillan for either census, the exclusive services of a butler would not have been required and so servants' roles were combined.

Although Ardgillan was once said to have had up to twenty-five people employed on the demesne, the 1901 Census lists only seven. Their names are:

Rose Bradley, 40, Laundry Maid, Domestic; Mary Kerr, 40, Housemaid, Domestic; Thomas Salmon, 64, Caretaker; John Woodward, 51, Land Steward; James McCavish, 49, Lodge Keeper; Patrick Lacey, 56, Agricultural Labourer; and Peter Fedigan, 56, Wood Ranger.

In the 1911 Census, the names of the following seven employees were returned:

James McCavish, 58, Lodge Keeper; William Craig, 35, Head Gardener; Peter Fedigan, 72, Gate Lodge Keeper; Mary Kerr, 50, Housemaid, Domestic Servant; Thomas Salmon, 75, Butler, Domestic Servant; Annie Vanghey, 36, Laundry Maid, Domestic Servant; and Harry Cameron, 30, Land Steward.

Peter Fedigan, named in the Census lists for both 1901 and 1911, belonged to a family that was resident in the lodge at the middle gates for several generations. In her diaries, Marianne Taylor records dropping in to visit the Fedigans on her frequent walks around the demesne.

The Library

When Fingal County Council took possession of Ardgillan, the Library shelves were devoid of books. However, the collection now on display portrays a real impression of how it must have looked when the Taylors were in residence. The oldest books now housed here date back to the seventeenth century.

It was Edward, the Rev Edward's grandson, who commissioned the current arrangement for the Library including the doors disguised with faux books to create the impression of wrap-around shelving. A close examination of the false book spines reveals that each has the Taylor coat of arms – 'a naked arm embowed with an arrow proper' – embossed on it. Like many wealthy families, the Taylors may have commissioned custom-designed covers on books they were going to keep, making the Library in Ardgillan uniquely theirs. The preliminary sketches of the Library shelving that Edward ordered have been preserved as has the receipt for payment.

The Library has two hidden doors covered with faux books

Overleaf:
The Library as it looks today with its collection of antique books

Although the Church of Ireland churches in Balbriggan, Skerries and Balrothery had their own rectors, the Rev Edward also conducted services locally on occasion as well as further afield. It was likely that he prepared his sermons in the Library, drawing inspiration from the many books of religious tracts that continued to be published during his lifetime. As a member of the 'Association Incorporated for Discountenancing Vice, and Promoting the Knowledge and Practice of the Christian Religion', he

Also in the Taylor library were George Combe's *Essays on Phrenology* (1819) and Lord Clarendon's *Reflections upon Several Christian Duties, Divine and Moral, by Way of Essays* (1669 & 1670).

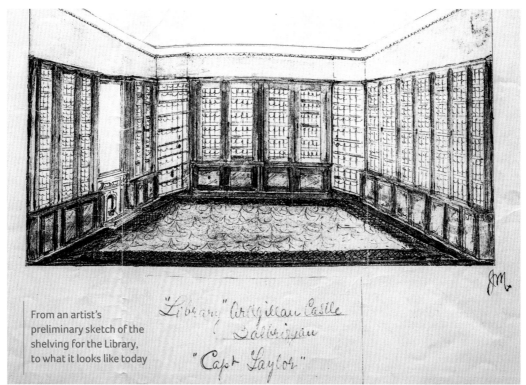

From an artist's preliminary sketch of the shelving for the Library, to what it looks like today

"Library" Ardgillan Castle
Balbriggan

"Capt Taylor"

104

attended the annual conventions in various Dublin churches, when a leading churchman addressed the assembled clergy with the Lord Lieutenant as invited guest.

Family diaries show that books were a valued part of everyday life in Ardgillan and a means of 'cultivating the mind'. Among the publications referred to are the writings of various renowned statesmen, essayists and men of letters including those of Horace Walpole, JG Russell and Edward Gibbon. Female writers were in evidence too – Madame d'Epiney's memoirs and the letters of Madame de Deffand, for example. The Taylors passed this love of books on to their children by listening to them read on a daily basis. In a house that once bustled with activity, the Library must once have been, as it still is, an oasis of peace.

"Wrote a note to ask Mr Hamilton to get me a book in Dublin. Taught Henrietta, heard Louisa read which ended at two o'clock. Read *Sketches of the Philosophy Life* with indolence till four." Harriet St Leger's diary, Ardgillan, 9 February 1826.

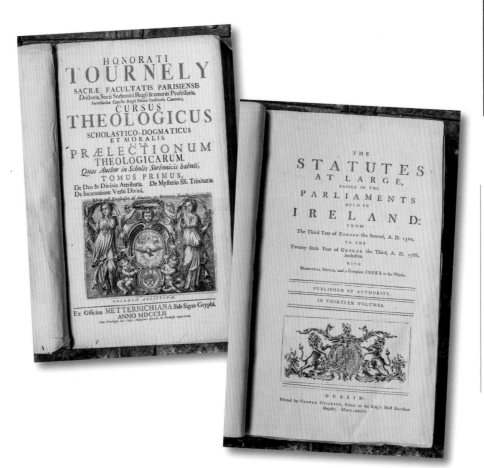

Far left:
Cursus Theologicus *Scholastico-Dogmaticus* by the eminent French Catholic Theologian, Honoré Tournély (1658-1729), published in 1752.

Left: *The Statutes at Large Passed in the Parliaments Held in Ireland*, published in Dublin in 1786.

THE MORNING ROOM

The Morning Room, overlooking the raised lawn to the rear of the house and radiantly bright when the sun shines, is generally associated with the family life of the Rev Edward and Marianne St Leger Taylor.

Two images of Marianne hang in this room: one is a small painting from 1808 and the other a photograph taken in her latter years (below).

The two pianos currently on loan were coincidentally manufactured by the same English company, Collard and Collard. Based on their serial numbers, the grand piano dates from between 1832 and 1850 and the upright piano, imported by Pigott of 112 Grafton Street, was manufactured between

The Morning Room

Right: The upright piano was made by the English firm of Collard & Collard and is dated between 1850 and 1875.

Below: The grand piano in the Morning Room was also made by Collard & Collard shortly after 1832.

1850 and 1875. A close look at the cartouche on the grand piano reveals that the company was previously known as Clementi, Collard & Collard. Muzio Clementi, an Italian who spent much of his life in England and who was greatly admired by Ludwig van Beethoven among others, died in 1832 – hence the change of name.

The word 'piano' is a shortened form of 'pianoforte', the original name for the instrument first made in Italy around 1700, as it was played *piano e forte*, i.e., 'soft and loud'. It differs from the earlier harpsicord, another keyboard instrument, in that the strings of the piano were struck with small hammers while those of the latter were plucked by quills.

The tall cabinet that now contains an antique china dinner set is actually a bookcase, with the extended front opening out into a writing desk. The dinner set on display was made by an English pottery company called Copeland in Stoke-on-Trent, Staffordshire, England. William Copeland took over his father's works in 1833 and went on to

make it one of the most prestigious makers of ceramics in Victorian Britain, while also finding time to be an elected MP and Lord Mayor of London. The set dates from January 1878 and shows one of Copeland's more popular designs.

This bright, beautiful room with its easy access to the lawn and the Yew Walk, allowed successive Taylor families to enjoy their beautiful surroundings.

Top: Close-up of cartouche on the grand piano showing Collard & Collard, late Clementi, Collard & Collard, London

Above: Strings of grand piano

Left: A Copeland plate from the set on display in the Morning Room

THE IRISH HARP

The harp has always been a potent and enduring symbol of Gaelic identity, tradition and expression but it was not until 1922 that the image was formally adopted for all state bodies and organisations, the national currency, as well as for the Presidential heraldry. This modern image is based on the Brian Ború Harp, also known as the Trinity College Harp, one of three Gaelic Harps still in existence. While reconstructions have been made, there is no guarantee that these replicas sound the same as the originals, now too delicate to be played. As for the Ardgillan harp, given its sad state of deterioration, it is unlikely that it will ever be heard again.

In the late 1700s, most companies of Volunteers used a version of the winged-angel harp topped with the royal crown as their crest but, due to its association with colonialism, committed nationalists rejected it, eventually settling for a gold harp on a green background. This was the variant carried by the 'Summer Soldiers', the rebels of 1798, often with an added slogan such as *Érin go Brágh,* which was the form used in 1803 by Robert Emmet. Although Emmet's rebellion was also brutally crushed, this flag continued to be popular during the 1800s as the de facto flag of pro-nationalists until it was superseded by the Tricolour.

The Ardgillan harp – strings attached. Still intact but its age is showing.

Shortly before these uprisings in Ireland, King George III had instigated the Illustrious Order of St Patrick in 1783 for members of the Irish

110

Ascendency. The Order's Star and Badge Regalia included a jewelled harp topped with a crown, shamrocks of emeralds and the red saltire Cross of St Patrick in rubies. Known as the Irish Crown Jewels, they were stolen from Dublin Castle in 1907 and have never been recovered. One of the founding fifteen members of the Order of St Patrick was Sir Thomas Taylor, 1st Earl of Bective (1724–1795), father of the Rev Edward. The painting of Sir Thomas by Gilbert Stuart shows the 1st Earl proudly wearing the Order's badge (see page 16).

The Ardgillan harp is also decorated with strands of shamrock, evidence of an early intertwining of these two iconic symbols of Irishness, and certainly predating their appearance on the Order of St Patrick's regalia. It stands 116cm high with fourteen strings remaining from an original thirty-six. Unfortunately nothing is known about the origin of this harp as no identifying marks are visible on the instrument and nothing is recorded about its history. However, legend has it that it was played by the famous blind harpist, Turlough O'Carolan. If true, that alone would make it priceless.

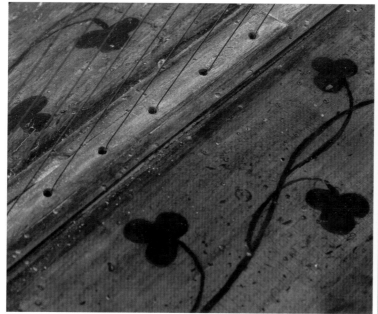

Detail of shamrock and strings on harp

FROM THE ART COLLECTION

High up on the walls of the main rooms, unobtrusively stretching from corner to corner, are long horizontal bars from which the Taylors' collection of paintings once hung. Old photographs of these rooms show how extensive and varied this once was but of course when the family vacated they brought all of the paintings away with them. In their place, Fingal County Council has put an interesting collection of its own on display. Although in some cases the artists and subjects are unknown, the images are ideally suited to their heritage house environment and include portraits, landscapes, seascapes and still life paintings.

Painting of Boy in a Red Dress – artist unknown

Of all the artworks in the Castle, perhaps the most curious is that of 'The Boy in a Red Dress with a Hoop' that hangs on the wall in the Morning Room. The ambiguously gendered figure that stares enigmatically out from the painting is a striking one with its mismatched head and body, long red dress, dainty black shoes and oversized hat lying to one side. Typical of a style of painting that was once common, it portrays aspects of the experience of childhood in Georgian times. One explanation was the fear of kidnap among wealthy, land-owning families. In order to keep property and estate intact, the bulk of an inheritance would go to the eldest boy. Smaller legacies would be settled on the younger sons while girls received a dowry on marrying. The eldest son thus became a potential target for kidnap for ransom. As a precaution against this, families tended to wait a few years before commissioning a painting of the eldest boy, then disguised his image by pairing his head with the body of a younger, different child. This resulted in the mismatch between the more mature facial features of the image and his chubbier, more infant-like, body and arms. As for the ambiguous attire, this was in keeping with the practice of dressing younger boys and girls alike in robes both prior to and during the Regency period. But, between the ages of four to seven, a boy was 'breeched', meaning that he was given his first pair of trousers, pantaloons or breeches. The ceremony of breeching existed as far back as the seventeenth century and marked the first significant step of a boy towards manhood. Being dressed like a mini version of his father, it was expected that he would fall much more under adult male influence. Many women attested that this change was a source of great distress to them as it often heralded separation, not just within the domestic situation but sometimes by them being sent to boarding school or elsewhere away from home. By the time of King George III, the concept of childhood had become more accepted and breeching happened at a younger age, from three to five.

Child abduction, or child stealing, was not uncommon at that time, fuelling a superstitious belief that such a disappearance was due to the malevolent act of fairies who would sometimes leave a troubled and unruly changeling in its place. Mostly, the abduction was for a short duration as the motive was quite simply theft. Well-dressed children were taken just for their clothes and footwear, as described by Charles Dickens in his 'child-stripping' scene in *Dombey and Son* (1848). Even the momentary distraction of a parent could result in the opportunistic disappearance of a small child. In a minority of recorded cases, children were taken to be pressed into employment, for example, as wandering street entertainers or chimney sweeps' boys or, more rarely, in response to a disturbed, emotional need. Although the limited records of the time show that most children were returned to their homes, the fear of child abduction persisted. As far as the law was concerned, until 1814, abduction was merely regarded as a misdemeanour but subsequently the taking of a child by force or fraud became a felony and led to more severe consequences including transportation for life.

> "I have got a charming crayon portrait of Edd. He had it done in London for me. It has its faults but the expression is quite his own."
>
> Marianne Jane Taylor writing about her brother, Thomas Edward, 4 September 1847

The Wreck of the Hesperus by Richard Brydges Beechey RN (1842)

Two paintings with marine settings by the Anglo-Irish artist Richard Brydges Beechey RN can be viewed in the Drawing Room on either side of the fireplace. One depicts a dramatic scene from Henry Wadsworth Longfellow's famous poem, 'The Wreck of the Hesperus' (1842), and the other shows a ship, HM Mailsteamer *Connaught*, entering Dun Laoghaire harbour in a storm. Brydges Beechey spent most of his life in the Royal Navy, eventually achieving the rank of Vice-Admiral. Like his father and mother, both of whom were accomplished artists, as were three of his brothers, Richard also became a skilled painter, specialising in wild seascapes and naval scenes.

Top left: Hercules Langford Taylor (1759 – 1790)

Top right: Francis Barry Boyle St Leger as a child (1799 – 1829), brother of Marianne Taylor

Above: Portrait of British actress Frances (Fanny) Kemble (1809-1893)

A partial inventory of the pictures that once hung in Ardgillan survives today. Dated 1912, it describes eleven paintings that were in the Dining Room and two in the Study, probably the room that is now the Library. All but two of the paintings are of members of the Taylor family and their relations, the exceptions being those of Jean Baptiste Massillon, Bishop of Claremont (1663–1742), and the actress, Frances Anne (Fanny) Kemble (1809–1893). While Kemble's portrait is understandable due to her close friendship with the family, the reason for the inclusion of a Catholic bishop's image is unknown. Perhaps it was because the Rev Edward, knowing the good bishop was a renowned preacher throughout his life, possessed a copy of Massillon's sermons translated into English in two volumes in 1803.

Close-up of
dramatic scene
from Brydges
Beechey's
painting,
*The Wreck of
the Hesperus.*

Pictures at ARDGILLAN. 1912.

Diningroom.

I. I. The Right Hon. Colonel THOMAS EDWARD TAYLOR. M.P. born 1811. died 1883.

2. FRANCIS ANN KEMBLE. daughter of Charles Kemble. born 1809.married 1834

3. Sir.Thomas Taylor. 3rd. Bart. M.P. 1st. Earl of BECTIVE. born 1724. died 1795.

4. MARIANNE. eldest daughter of the Hon. Richard St LEGER. 2nd.son of the 1st.
    Viscount DONERAILE (2nd. creation) married 1807 the Rev.the Hon. HENRY
    EDWARD TAYLOR. died 1859.

5. The Rev. the Hon. HENRY EDWARD TAYLOR 5th. son of the 1st. Earl of BECTIVE.
        born 1768. died 1852.

6. ANNE. daughter of CHARLES BLAKENEY of Holywell Co. Roscommon. married 1779
    the Hon. Richard St Leger. died 1809. (picture by Sir Thomas Lawrence.)

7. The Rev. ROBERT TAYLOR. Dean of Clonfert. 2nd. son of Sir Thomas Taylor 1st.
        Bart. born (circa) 1688. died 1744.

8. The Right Hon. HERCULES LANGFORD ROWLEY. M.P. married 1732.died 1744.

9. ANNE. daughter of Sir R.COTTON of Combermere Bart. married 1682.Sir Thomas
        TAYLOR. 1st. Bart.

10. The Hon. HERCULES LANGFORD TAYLOR. M.P. 2nd. son of the 1st. Earl of BECTIVE
        born 1759. died unmarried 1790.

11. JEAN BAPTISTE MASSILLON. born 1663. Bishop of Claremont 1717. Preacher at
        the Courts of Louis XIV & XV. died 1742.

Study.

1. HENRIETTA FRANCIS. 2nd. daughter of the Hon. RICHARD St LEGER. died unm.1878.

2. FRANCIS BARRY DOYLE. 2nd. son of the Hon. RICHARD St LEGER.born 1790.died
        unm. 1829.

A partial inventory of the pictures that once hung in Ardgillan, dated 1912

118

Part 3

DOWNSTAIRS
AT
ARDGILLAN

THE WINE CELLAR

t the bottom of the arched stairway of Prospect House, the dark basement wine cellar can be found. With its temperature and humidity maintained at a constant level, alcoholic beverages stored within its brick-lined walls were well protected. It was also well stocked, at one stage holding 'one pipe and one hogshead of port, half a hogshead of claret, four dozen bottles of Madeira, thirty dozen bottles of sherry, four dozen bottles of hock, twenty dozen bottles of cider and four dozen bottles of Alicanti, mead and different kinds of sweet wine'. (*Ardgillan Castle and the Taylor Family,* 1995) Bottles were taken from here to the Butler's Pantry where they were brought up to room temperature before being served. It was the butler's function to keep accurate records of all that went into and out of the cellar.

The liquid measurements listed above are no longer in use but the quantities indicate that Prospect House was adequately supplied. In today's terms, a pipe was a large cask holding 128 gallons; a hogshead was a smaller one containing 64 gallons; and a barrel held 32 gallons. The types of wine reveal that the regions then catering to the Irish market included Portugal, Bordeaux, Madeira, Spain, the Rhineland and Italy. The mead and cider would most likely have been home produced since mead has a long tradition of being consumed in Ireland and the making of cider was also well established here by the eighteenth and early nineteenth centuries.

Above:
A selection of bottles in the Butlers' Pantry

Facing page:
Inside the Wine Cellar

With the landed gentry's predilection for alcohol, as evidenced by the typical size of the Castle's wine cellar, perhaps the Rev Robert's plaque in celebration of being 'flushed with wine when the sun sinks beneath the ocean' makes sense after all. Although the cellar still contains a collection of old whiskey and brandy dispensers as well as hundreds of wine bottles, rest assured – they are all empty.

The Meat Larder with
slate counters

THE KITCHEN

The Kitchen is entered by way of the Meat Larder, an area that was permanently cool and dry with two ventilation shafts to keep it well aired. It was also kept vermin free. The Taylors maintained herds of pedigree livestock at Ardgillan providing them with meat of the highest quality while game shooting and fishing brought variety to the menu. Located beside the kitchen the larder was ideally placed for the preparation of meat, poultry and game for the table, and unused meat could conveniently be locked away until required. The thick slate counters were exceedingly cold to the touch and have been drilled through with many holes to allow blood to drip through.

Positioned directly under the Dining Parlour, the kitchen was the warmest room in the house and in many ways its heart. Step into it and you walk on the original limestone flags now worn and cracked with age. This 'great laboratory of every household', as Mrs Beeton called the kitchen (*Book of Household Management*, 1861), is not the original installed

Below stairs in the Kitchen

by the Rev Robert when Prospect House was completed in 1738 but belongs to a later period when the new wings containing the Drawing Room and the Dining Parlour were constructed. Beyond the kitchen lies the scullery and the various storerooms as well as the door leading to the outside fuel bunkers. For a period after the wings had been added, Ardgillan had the two kitchens in operation, the original for the servants and the new one for family and guests. However, at some stage, this doubling-up became impractical probably due to cost and the old one was dismantled. Its precise location is now lost due to the many modifications carried out below stairs.

Although comparatively small in size, the current kitchen is a good example of one from the Victorian era, a frantically busy place when guests were being entertained. Surviving features from the Taylors' time include the various cupboards, the built-in dresser, the serving hatch and of course the iron range. The house was largely self-sufficient in its day with herds of cattle and sheep fattening on the fertile grassland, a dairy in the courtyard, fresh fruit, herbs and vegetables available on demand from the Walled Garden, and flowers cut daily from the herbaceous borders.

The closed iron range was the most significant advance in cooking since the open fire. It marked the beginning of the kitchen as known today. The range currently installed, manufactured by Maguire & Son in Dublin, dates from around 1900 and replaces a more primitive model. Resting on a granite base, it is a highly sophisticated version with a closed central firebox and two generously sized ovens, one for roasting and the other for baking. The circulation of warm air could be controlled by the use of flues and dampers that helped to regulate the temperature. Circular openings of

The Kitchen counter and the meat larder beyond

different sizes over the fire allowed for pots with matching dimensions to be lowered directly onto the flames as required. The fire needed constant attention being stoked and fed regularly and ashes removed several times daily. The grate required a full cleaning out each morning with damp tea leaves being sometimes scattered on the ashes to keep the dust down and cinders retained for reuse. The oven interiors were cleaned too before the whole range and fire irons were rubbed with black lead paste and polished until they gleamed. All of this was done before it was relit and preparations for breakfast could commence. The same ritual applied to every fire grate in the house.

The cooking range with Maguire & Son Dublin nameplate

The additional hot plate over a small firebox to the side of the range allowed for simmering of pots, slow cooking or just keeping things warm. With a regular supply of fuel available from the woods on the demesne, the fires could be kept going as long as was necessary. Much later, coal became the fuel of choice and was stored in the bunker built under the south lawn. The introduction of the range led to the development of a wide variety of implements and utensils, many examples of which are on display in the kitchen. Copper became popular as a suitable metal for saucepans and was soon in widespread use.

The hot plate

Occupying the central space in the kitchen is a large, rectangular, softwood table used primarily for the preparation of food for cooking. Only when all their duties had been completed did servants finally get to sit down for their own meal. As displayed in Ardgillan's kitchen, most servants sat on a long bench, or form, instead of a chair, while bolting down their meal before the large tavern clock on the wall called them to duty once again.

The wooden counter top, complete with a slate insert for rolling dough and pastry, stretches the length of the kitchen under two large windows. Many kitchens in Ascendency residences had high ceilings with windows placed near the top to allow smells to escape. These high windows had the added advantage of depriving the cooks and kitchen maids of any visual distraction that would take their minds off their work. In Ardgillan, however, with the kitchen's low ceiling and eye-level windows, the external servants' passageway that extends the whole way around the castle is visible from inside. It is said that a passing gardener spotted a young kitchen maid at the pastry counter and took to calling by. But the budding romance ended with dismissal. Relationships between servants who worked within a Big House at that time were not encouraged. Of the employees previously named in both the Census of 1901 and that of 1911, the butler/caretaker was listed as a widower and the female domestic staff were all recorded as single. However, the male staff who worked outdoors on the estate or who lived in the lodges were mostly married.

Wooden churn with butter-making equipment and utensils

The kitchen clock

The serving hatch

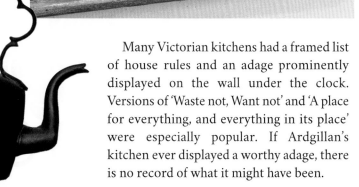

A kettle from the cooking range

Butter pats and seals – detail

Many Victorian kitchens had a framed list of house rules and an adage prominently displayed on the wall under the clock. Versions of 'Waste not, Want not' and 'A place for everything, and everything in its place' were especially popular. If Ardgillan's kitchen ever displayed a worthy adage, there is no record of what it might have been.

THE KITCHEN DRESSER

On departing Ardgillan in 1962, the Taylors sold off all of the furniture that had adorned their home for over two hundred years, with just a single exception – the imposing dresser in the kitchen. This beautiful piece was custom built to fit around the ceiling beam that supports the Dining Parlour directly above it. And so the dresser remains exactly where it has always stood.

Dressers have been a feature in homes large and small throughout Ireland for generations. In the traditional rural cottage, the hearth was the social centre of the home but the dresser took pride of place. It is most likely that dressers were copies of the type of furniture originally found in medieval castles, which became very popular from the eighteenth century on, when people could afford them. These dressers were usually made to order on site by journeymen carpenters. Pine was the wood most commonly used and when funds were available the finished product was painted to give it a rich, attractive appearance. The upper section was generally comprised of racks and shelves on which decorative plates and dishes were stored, while cups and small jugs were suspended from hooks. It was on the dresser too that the faded letters from

The Dresser, an essential
piece of kitchen furniture

loved ones long emigrated to faraway places were kept and to be read aloud in the evenings when neighbours out 'a-rambling' called by. The lower section was deeper with the top being used as a work base or stand. Underneath was generally a cupboard for storing bowls, pails, utensils and butter-making equipment but older versions, like the one in Ardgillan, were left open. Food items such as tea, sugar, meal and flour were not usually stored in the dresser but in drum-like containers near the fire to keep them dry. The coop dresser was different in that the bottom compartment was used to keep hens conveniently close by and to ensure their safety from predators at night. The added benefit was that fresh eggs were handily available for the family throughout the year. With all these advantages, the dresser became the most valued item of furniture in the rural cottage.

A typical example of its kind, although larger in dimension than most others, the Ardgillan dresser would also have been seen as a functional kitchen necessity along with the cupboards, the large pine table and the benches for servants. Distinguished guests of the Taylors would have paused to admire the ornate furniture in the main rooms of the Castle, the paintings on the walls, the contents of the library and the souvenirs of the latest Grand Tour abroad. Perhaps they even visited the spotlessly clean dairy, as was common in Victorian times. However, it is unlikely that they ever went down the stone stairway to see what is now the only remnant of Taylor furniture – the kitchen dresser, the epitome of traditional craftsmanship, beauty and function united in one unique piece.

Front view of the dresser cleverly built around the ceiling beam.

Inset image:
The dresser – detail

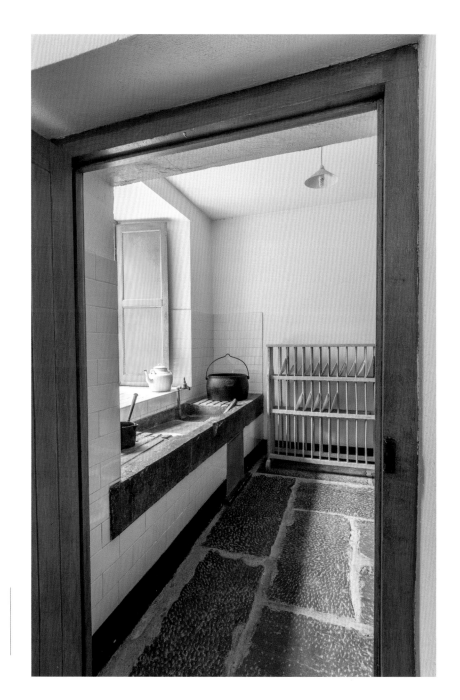

Entrance from the Kitchen to the Scullery, showing sink and drying rack

THE SCULLERY

Ardgillan's kitchen may present an impression of homely cosiness but stepping into the Scullery is a stark reminder of the hardship and austerity of the lives of the domestic servants who worked there. The word 'scullery' is from the Old French *escullerie* meaning 'office of the servant in charge of the dishes', a grandiose way of indicating that this is where the plates were washed and stacked. It was in rooms like this, with their drab walls, bare flagstones and solid limestone sinks, that most young girls began their Big House service as scullery maids who, along with the laundry maids, were the lowest grade of below stairs employment.

Predating the glazed stoneware 'Butler's Sink' that came into vogue in the 1700s, Ardgillan's shallow limestone sink comprises three sections, and is set low off the ground to allow for the smaller stature of the young women who worked here. It acted as a base for the bucket or basin of hot water in which the small pots and pans were washed. A discoloured, circular patch inside the sink indicates where these buckets would have rested over years of use. The washing up of glazed porcelain tableware required more delicate handling, often being done in a basin on the floor while the butler tended to the glassware upstairs.

Discolouration of the limestone sink

Initially, the great quantity of water needed in the house was sourced from nearby spring wells and heated on the fires. The drying rack, loaded from the top down, was used to allow plates and dishes to drip-dry as drying cloths were not in use then. Pots and pans had to be scrubbed, then scoured with sand and dried, before being stored on the wide shelves – no wonder that scullery-maids constantly suffered with sore hands. Cleaning cutlery, especially knives, was also such a difficult task that when Spong & Co produced a knife cleaning machine that could take up to ten knives at a time, it became known as 'The Servant's Friend'. Much later, with advances in plumbing, the installation of a single tap in the limestone sink must have brought great relief to the poor scullery maids who previously had to manage with buckets.

The Scullery in Ardgillan also contains a collection of sundry items including a washing board, a collection of old kettles and a number of laundry irons. The two long ironing boards, wrapped in their Foxford blankets, were retrieved from a Magdalene Laundry in Dublin – poignant reminders of the hardships endured by so many women in dreary laundry rooms elsewhere.

THE LAUNDRY

The austere
Scullery at Ardgillan

The servants' basement-level passageway leads to a series of rooms that housed the Laundry. No longer in use, they still retain many of their original features from the days when the Castle was in its prime. It was here that the various laundry tasks were performed out of sight, a general practice then that gave rise to the adage that people 'should not wash their dirty linen in public'. This of course meant that the unfortunate laundry maids were invisible too, their work being deemed to be of low status in a class-conscious society, even among servants.

It would not have been unusual to have hundreds of separate items for washing each week in a Big House, depending on how many people were in residence. In Ardgillan, the wash load would have been heavy enough when it was just for the Taylor household but, when relatives and distinguished guests came to stay, the pressure on the laundry staff must have been tremendous. To make matters worse many guests may well have brought their own servants with them, adding to the burden. Keeping track of separate personal items throughout the wash and then returning each, pristinely clean, to its owner must have been a huge challenge. It was little wonder that servants hated to see guests arrive as it meant much more work for them. And considering that the whole wash incorporated up to eight different processes, it was exhausting, repetitive and thankless labour.

A laundry maid's day started as early as 3am when the metal tubs of water were put on the fire to boil. Soft soap or ash lye was added to the hot water and then the main laundry was soaked for hours. Extra soap was used to remove awkward stains while fabrics like lace or velvet had to be treated with the greatest of care. Then followed the process of pounding and scrubbing using a broomstick contraption that looked as

The disused
entrance to the
Laundry

if it had a small milking-stool at the end. This was called, among other things, a dolly, a peggy or a ponch (as in 'punching the laundry'). After more boiling, the load was repeatedly rinsed in cold water and finally wrung by hand. While most Big Houses had enclosed drying areas outside where exposure to sunlight enhanced the whiteness, all of the laundry in Ardgillan could be dried in the drying-room. Here, lengths of wood high on the walls were grooved to hold a series of iron bars from which the washed items could be hung, with warm air flowing around them through openings in the fireplace wall.

Above:
A selection of old irons

Below left:
Imperial box iron

Before the 1800s, hard soap would have been homemade or bought in the form of large blocks. This was grated into flakes and mixed into a lather. But, by the end of the 1800s, it was possible to buy commercially wrapped laundry soap at a reasonable price. Soap powder was also widely available in response to a growing concern for cleanliness coupled with a fashion for whiteness in clothing items and linen. The use of vinegar, baking soda and oil of vitriol to preserve or restore colour was widespread while various recipes existed for removing stubborn stains. Stale urine and a solution of

chicken dung had an added bleaching effect on linen but left the material anything but sweet smelling. The subsequent application of herbal extracts was essential before the process of starching the clean laundry took place. Items that had to be unstitched before being washed were carefully sewn back together. Then came the ironing. It was customary for plain, delta-shaped flat irons, known as smoothing or sad irons (from the Middle English *'sad'* meaning 'solid') to be used in rotation – one in use, the other reheating on the laundry stove. The iron base had to be kept immaculately clean, sand-papered and polished. Later irons, called box irons, were shallow boxes into which slabs of red-hot metal called 'slugs' were inserted. Regardless of the type of iron used, the work was invariably arduous. A collection of these irons is on display in the Scullery.

Imperial box iron with 'slug' inside – open

The names of two of the women who once worked in the Laundry in Ardgillan are known. Rose Bradley – listed in the 1901 Census as a forty year-old laundry maid and domestic, Catholic and single – must have moved on sometime after that for her place had been taken, according to the 1911 Census by Annie Vanghey, 36, an unmarried Catholic also from County Meath. Perhaps these forgotten women laboured over the same, antiquated Pioneer Washer dated 1889 that is still rusting quietly in the now idle Laundry.

The Pioneer Washer dated 1889

Laundry fireplace wall with vents

THE SERVANTS' PASSAGEWAY

When Prospect House was completed in 1738, it could not have functioned without the presence of a number of people to provide a range of services to its owner, the Rev Robert, who lived there until his death in 1744 at the age of fifty-five. The names of those who were originally employed there are lost in time but the design of the original house, and later extensions, made provision for the accommodation of many servants. In the inventory drawn up in 1795, there is reference to a servants' barracks, or sleeping quarters, for five men as well as a separate room each for the steward, housekeeper, cook, maid, manservant and coachman.

A collection of disused machinery in the Laundry

When grand mansions assumed excessive proportions in the eighteenth and nineteenth centuries, the question of how to plan for the co-existence of two widely different but mutually dependent social classes under the same roof became a real problem. One solution proposed by architects was to add wings to the side of the house but, as these would have to match the grandeur of the original structure, some saw it as wasteful extravagance just to accommodate servants. It was also deemed impractical as it situated servants far from their place of duty.

A simpler solution was to put servants' living quarters either below the ground level of the house or at the very top, where they could be kept out of the way unless they were on duty or were, literally, waiting to be called upon. Housing servants underground ensured that the warren of rooms they occupied would provide a layer of insulation for the living space above them, making life upstairs in a large, draughty house so much more agreeable. The planned, systematic way in which architecture addressed this rigid separation of wealth and service in stately homes now seems callous and calculated yet it was just another manifestation of how a socially divided society operated then.

The underground walkway at Ardgillan Castle, invisible at ground-level, evolved with each new extension allowing servants unseen access to all parts of the house. The slope on the south lawn forms the curved roof of the walkway underneath, which leads to the now defunct laundry area. Ingeniously, the glass panels set into the slope shed light on to the passageway beneath. Meanwhile, iron grills at the front of the house spill light not just onto the area below but also into the kitchen.

In the attic of the Castle, the series of rooms known as the Servants' Quarters consists of six partitioned bedchambers accessed from a tiled corridor. Two are modest-sized rooms and the other four are simply cubicles, all with small, shared roof windows that provided a minimum of light for the servants' personal needs. These roof windows also had the advantage of catching the first light of dawn, thus waking the servants early. Warmth for these six rooms came from a single recessed stove halfway along the corridor.

In their present state, the Servants' Quarters are stark reminders of the type of austere conditions endured by men and women during their lives in service.

Two views of the servants' below ground-level passageway

Door leading from the Servants' Passageway to the rear lawn

Part 4

LETTERS
FROM AFAR

BATTLEFIELD TOURISTS, 1821

Among the various documents donated to the Castle by the Taylor family were copies of letters, journals and diaries from the 1800s, some of which give real insight into significant events in their lives. One of the documents was a travel journal from 1821 written by Marianne Taylor's younger brother, Francis Barry Boyle St Leger (1799–1829), an aspiring writer. After a short stay with relatives in England, Barry had embarked with a companion whom he names only as Hotham on a ten-week 'journey through the Netherlands, the Rheinish provinces and parts of France'. It is possible that Barry's friend was Beaumont Hotham, 3rd Baron, an officer in the Coldstream Guards.

Ten Weeks

on the

CONTINENT.

Being Notes made on a journey through the Netherlands, the Rheinish Provinces, and Part of France, in the Summer of 1821.

___

1.

___

"—Rapporter la moisson d'idées que j'ai recueillies dans ce voyage."

Mme. de Staël.

Written in a clear hand, Barry's daily entries record their journey through the Low Countries, stopping off at a number of places including Antwerp and Ghent. He presents a colourful and touchingly personal description of their progress and the people they encountered on stopovers until their arrival in Brussels on 15 August. On that evening, he wrote: 'A visit to Brussels, that is a first visit, includes as a matter of course a visit to Waterloo'. Although Barry admitted in his journal to not having 'much interest' in going to the site of the famous battle, Hotham was very keen to see it so, like many others in the intervening six years, they became battlefield tourists.

Barry St Leger's Journal: *Ten Weeks on the Continent*

Incredibly, their guide at Waterloo was none other than Jean Baptiste La Coste, the same man who had guided Napoleon's troops as they took up their positions in the early hours of 18 June 1815. La Coste must have regaled them with breathtaking stories as he conducted them around the

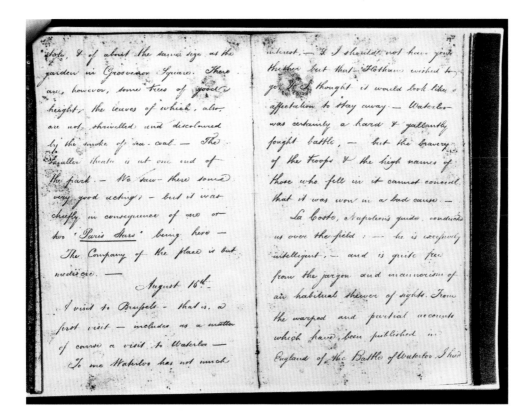

main positions of the battlefield, including the buildings at La Belle Alliance and Hougoumont. Barry recounts that contrary to the 'wretched calumnies that were spread in England' about Napoleon not leading the charge of the Old Guard himself as the battle reached its climax, La Coste explained that the Emperor expected to be victorious 'in a few minutes'. And he nearly was, except for the late-afternoon arrival of Field Marshall Blücher and his Prussians onto the battlefield. At Hougoumont, on seeing evidence of the English 'mania for writing their names everywhere', Barry spotted the familiar signatures of Lord (George Gordon) Byron and Sir Walter Scott who had visited Waterloo on separate occasions. La Coste observed to Barry that Scott 'took many notes in going over the field. Lord Byron none'.

It is well known that Scott had been fascinated by the battle from the beginning. In late July 1815, freed of pressing obligations, he hastened to Waterloo where he was allowed onto the battlefield and feverishly collected many discarded objects including helmets, weapons and breastplates. He

16 August 1821 – Arriving at Waterloo

> pour un grand ... je suis tout ce
> moment, les têtes étaient trop troublées
> "pour penser a moi." — This is
> exactly as the case was, and now
> but the most pitiful & malignant
> misrepresentation could place it in
> any other light. — Still as La Coste
> was the sufferer, he deserves praise
> for viewing and speaking of the matter
> with such fairness. — We went
> round the different positions, La
> belle Alliance, Hougoumont &c —
> At Hougoumont (whose real name,
> by the way, is Goumont) the English
> have plentifully indulged in their
> mania for writing their names every
> where. — Among multitudes of every
> sort & degree, appeared two which
> are pretty widely known,
>
> Lord Byron & Walter Scott — By the
> side of Lord Byron, there was some
> writing scratched out with a pencil,
> which, La Coste said, was some
> "badinage" which he had written
> of his wife, which made every body
> laugh excessively till some of her
> family came & scratched it out—
> I had no idea that Lord Byron,
> who really is a gentleman, could
> be guilty, of such a piece of vulgar
> taste & bad feeling — It is curious
> what a medley he is, for just after
> having done this act of petty malice
> he wept, La Coste told me, on being
> shewn the spot where his friend & relation
> Major Howard fell. — Walter Scott
> (& John Scott also) took many notes

Journal
reference to
Byron and Scott

also managed to procure four regimental banners with bullet holes in them, three French and one British. These rare banners were stored away in Scott's home, Abbotsford, near Melrose, unknown to anybody until family trustees discovered them in 2008. As for Lord Byron, he viewed Napoleon as a hero so his presence at Waterloo was unsurprising. But what disgusted Barry was La Coste's story about the renowned poet, prompting him to refer to Byron as a 'curious medley'. According to La Coste, Byron had written his name then immediately added some badinage (teasing comments) about his wife, which made everybody with them laugh until her family scratched it out. Shortly after 'that act of petty malice', Byron wept at the exact spot where 'his friend and relation, Major Howard, fell'. Byron's tears were for Major Frederick Howard whose grandmother was a Byron, hence Barry's reference to him being related to the poet. Interestingly, the account of Howard's last moments at Waterloo was actually recorded by various eyewitnesses. As the battle was ending, Major

Howard led the 10th Hussars, nicknamed The Prince's Dolls, in a cavalry charge against a retreating French Imperial Guard square when he was shot in the mouth. Falling from his horse, he was killed when a Guardsman stepped out from the square and crushed his skull with his musket butt. A plaque, dedicated to the memory of Major Howard by his brother officers, can still to be seen on the wall of the church in Waterloo.

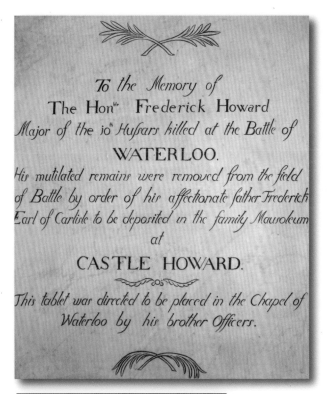

All in all, Barry was very impressed with La Coste's 'candid manner' while claiming that he only accepted one napoleon (a coin) for all his trouble on the night before the battle. But he was far from impressed with Henry Paget, 2nd Earl of Uxbridge who had eight horses shot from under him while leading successive charges against the French during the Battle of Waterloo. As he sat on a fresh mount beside the Duke of Wellington, a cannonball hit his right leg, leading to the famous exchange: 'By God, sir, I've lost my leg!' to which Wellington is said to have replied 'By God, sir, so you have!' Uxbridge's shattered leg was later amputated by Wellington's personal physician, Surgeon John Hume, and ceremoniously buried in

Above:
Memorial plaque to Major Frederick Howard in the chapel at Waterloo.

Left:
John Robert Hume, Surgeon to Wellington (c.1781–1857)

the garden of the house belonging to Monsieur Hyasinthe Paris. A lengthy inscription had been placed on top of the 'grave', much to Barry's annoyance. He thought the 'inflated and bombastic panegyric' dedicated to the Earl's severed limb was vanity carried to 'an absurd and miserable pitch' compared to the more modest dedications to the brave soldiers who had fallen. Added to this 'wretched silliness and egotism' was the fact that Uxbridge had actually brought his wife and family 'to contemplate and sigh over the tomb of his toes'.

On leaving the battlefield, Barry was further irritated to find that sellers were still hawking relics to passing tourists a full six years after Napoleon's defeat. The only way he could get rid of them was by buying some buttons of the Old Guard 'with the eagle on them'.

Imperial Guard button found at Waterloo

Journal reference to the Earl of Uxbridge's memorial to his leg

Back in Brussels, his time in the city was made much more enjoyable by the services of a *laquais de place,* a local guide, who escorted them around. He observed that this *laquais* (perhaps the origin of the word, 'lackey') went by the romantic name of Léonard Rousseau and was 'exactly the sort of servant who makes one agree so completely with Matthew Bramble that it is better to be served by a clever rogue than by an honest simpleton'. Here Barry was quoting a fictional character, Matthew Bramble, who appears in *The Expedition of Humphrey Clinker,* written by Tobias Smollett in 1771.

While Barry's continental tour lasted ten weeks, his three short days in the Brussels area provide some extraordinary insights into happenings at Waterloo just six years after the guns fell silent, and would have provided great material for conversation in the Drawing Room at Ardgillan. Francis Barry Boyle St Leger died unexpectedly of an epileptic seizure on 20 November 1829, much to the distress of his two sisters, Marianne and Harriet, who had been very close to him.

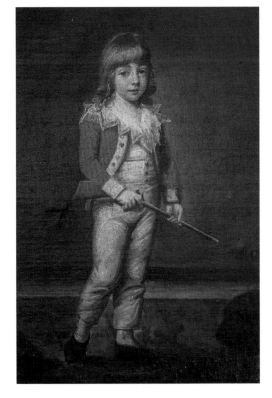

Barry St Leger with
toy gun – detail

INTO THE VALLEY OF DEATH

On 27 October 1854, Richard Chambre Hayes Taylor of the 79th Regiment of Foot, the Cameron Highlanders, younger son of the Rev Edward and Marianne, wrote to his older brother Thomas Edward about a military action he had witnessed two days before in Crimea.

Richard had joined the 79th in 1835, probably in Richmond Barracks, Dublin, at the age of sixteen. He had enlisted in the Scots regiment instead of following Thomas into the 6th Dragoon Guards, of which their uncle, General Robert Taylor of Dowdstown, was Honorary Colonel. His initial overseas posting was to Gibraltar in 1846 but it was not until 1854, when he had been promoted to Major and appointed to the staff of Sir Colin Campbell, Commanding Officer of the 79th, that he saw action for the first time when the regiment was ordered to Crimea. The troops embarked at Portsmouth on 4 May of that year and sailed for Turkey on the steamer *SS Simoon*. On the morning of 25 October, Richard was on the heights overlooking a broad valley near the port of Balaclava. It was from this elevated position that he observed the Light Brigade going into

Envelope addressed to Capt Richard Taylor, 79th Highlanders, stationed in Gibraltar

Officers of the 79th Camerons at Crimea – Richard CH Taylor is on the left of the group; Sir Colin Campbell, CO, is in the centre

action. Like other experienced officers, Richard must have been astounded at the deployment of light cavalry in this manner, their usual function being to act as the eyes and ears of the army, to carry out reconnaissance and picket duty, and generally to make nuisances of themselves by harrying the enemy. A full-scale charge such as this was a task for heavy cavalry.

In his letter, Richard vividly described the unfolding action. Lord Raglan (Fitzroy Somerset, 1st Baron Raglan), Army Commander, had ordered the Light Brigade to be held in readiness for an assault as soon as sufficient infantry support should arrive. On seeing that guns captured earlier by the Russians were being removed, Raglan sent the following order: 'Lord Raglan wishes the cavalry to advance rapidly to the front – follow the enemy and try to prevent the enemy carrying away the guns. Troop of horse-artillery may accompany. French cavalry is on your left. Immediate.' The vagueness of this order, carried by Captain Louis Edward Nolan, would lead to catastrophic consequences. But if Raglan's intention was unclear, what was beyond doubt was the courage of the cavalry led by Lord Cardigan (James Brudenell, 7th earl of Cardigan) as they set off on the mile and a half ride towards the Russian guns.

The Light Brigade at Balaclava consisted of five Light Cavalry regiments. The 11th Hussars, the 17th Lancers and the 13th Light Dragoons formed up in a two-deep line while just behind them came the 4th Light Dragoons alongside the 8th King's Royal Irish Hussars. From his vantage point, Richard reported seeing 'a mass of infantry open out, unleashing a heavy battery of artillery which opened grape and canister on them, whilst infantry attacked their flanks and Cossacks closed on their rear'.

Captain Nolan, hit almost immediately by a shell splinter, was the first cavalryman to die. By the second minute of the charge, the Brigade was taking ferocious fire from both flanks. By the third minute the line had contracted, with the 11th slotting in behind the 17th and 13th. The Russians continued to pour shot into the exposed horsemen, leaving a trail of dead and dying men and animals along the valley. By the time the surviving cavalry reached the Russian gun positions, the longest seven minutes in those men's lives had elapsed. But still worse was to follow. Waiting for them were more of the feared Cossacks.

Above:
Pte Gregory Jowett,
11th Hussars, who
saved 2nd Lieutenant
Roger Palmer's life
at Balaclava

Below:
Pte Jowett's Crimea
Medal and Ribbon

Richard must have had a special concern for the 11th Hussars because riding with them was his friend and neighbour, Lieutenant Roger Palmer from Kenure House, Rush. Palmer led from the front and was one of the first to reach the Russians before more Cossacks counter-attacked. At that stage, the charge had broken down into a melee, a heaving mass of bodies cutting and slicing at each other, with every man for himself. In the confusion, Palmer failed to notice the Cossack who took aim at him with a carbine. But Private Gregory Jowett of the 11th Hussars saw him. In a split second, Jowett cut the Russian down with a slash of his sabre, saving Palmer's life.

There is a fascinating dimension to this brief moment in battle. A few nights before, Private Jowett had been on picket duty and was found asleep in the saddle by the officer in charge of the watch, Lieut. Roger Palmer. Appreciating how exhausted his men were, Palmer upbraided the guilty cavalryman instead of having him flogged, this being the prescribed punishment. So, a few days later, as Palmer saw the Russian fall, Jowett must have felt he had paid back the officer's leniency towards him. Shortly after that, Palmer captured a high-ranking Russian artillery officer who thought his position had been overrun and surrendered his sword to him. But, in fact, the Light Brigade had taken so many casualties it was all but destroyed as a fighting unit. Almost immediately, bugles sounded the Retreat and Palmer withdrew with the remnants of the Brigade.

The return journey was just as harrowing as the charge. Wounded men who had lost their own horses had to be helped into the saddles of riderless mounts in an effort to get back; others had to hack their way on exhausted animals through swirls of Cossacks who kept trying to cut them off until they reached the safety of their own lines. The closest estimates of casualties on the day were 118 killed, 127 wounded and 60 taken prisoner. In addition, 335 prime cavalry horses were lost. After regrouping, only 195 men were still in the saddle out of the 670 or so who had started the charge.

A contemporary French observer thought the cavalrymen were mad, Russian observers believed they were drunk, and Tennyson's famous poem written three weeks later, immortalised them forever as the 'Noble Six Hundred'. Richard concluded in his letter that the Light Brigade had been 'led into a snare...the consequence was, nearly the whole of the Light Brigade was annihilated.' It is easy to imagine the effect his testimony from the battlefield of Balaclava must have had on being read back at Ardgillan.

Roger Palmer survived the Crimean War, returned to Kenure House with the Russian officer's sword, and lived there with his wife, Lady Gertrude Millicent Palmer, until he died in 1910, fifty-six years after his unforgettable charge with the Light Brigade. Sadly, all that is left now of Palmer's magnificent Kenure House in Rush is the portico.

Details of Private Gregory Jowett's birth and death are unknown but the part he played in saving Palmer is officially recorded in the annals of the 11th Hussars. A photograph of Jowett survives, as does his Crimea Medal that was offered for sale at auction in 2016. As for Major Richard CH Taylor, his leave home was to be unexpectedly cut short. He would soon find himself India bound.

Richard Chambre
Hayes Taylor

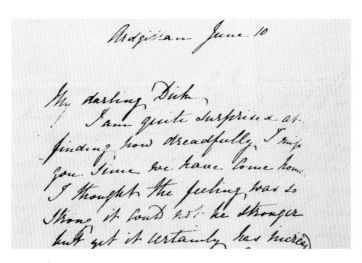

Letter from Marianne to her son,
Richard (Dick), after he had
departed on service overseas

made in Benares in 1850
for Shah Jehan.

He fled to Bareilly in 1852
(during the Mutiny) after Shahjehanpur
had been taken by British Troops.

Shah Jehan was routed
at Bareilly & himself killed.

Uncle Dick took toilet set
in brass-bound Indian mahogany
box as loot from Shah Jehan's
personal possessions.

The silver tops to toilet
Articles were made in Exeter in
1838 to Shah Jehan's order.

Box made in 1837, also
glass portions.

{ Ivory handled screwdriver }
{ " " nail file }
{ Steel Button Hook/Boot drawer }
All made in Benares in 1850
(also other missing articles)

1838 - 50

Above left: Description of Toilet
Set that once belonged to Shah
Jahan

Top right: Contents made to
order by Shah Jahan

Centre: Lid of mahogany box with
RCH Taylor's name inscribed
and inscription - detail

India – The Journey Out

'Soldiers of the old Highland Brigade', began Sir Colin Campbell, CO of the 79th Camerons, addressing the regiment at Kamara, Crimea, on 8 May 1856. 'I have now to take leave of you. In a few hours I shall be on board ship, never to see you again as a body – a long farewell. I am now old and shall not be called on to serve any more.' As events turned out, he was wrong on both counts.

Listening to him was Lieutenant Colonel Richard Chambre Hayes Taylor. He too was looking forward to a long period of leave after a hard-fought campaign in the Crimea. A month later, he departed Balaclava on board the Steamship *Victoria*, arriving at Portsmouth on 3 July. Having attended the inauguration of the Victoria Cross by Queen Victoria in London, Richard and his regiment were transferred to Dublin and he immediately went home on leave. However, he was not destined to enjoy the reunion with his family or the comforts of Ardgillan for long as news of the Indian Sepoy Mutiny arrived. (To Indians today, this conflict marks the beginning of their War of Independence.) Newspapers also provided dramatic accounts of the massacres of Europeans – women and children included – at Delhi, Jhansi and Cawnpore. These acts of brutality followed a number of atrocities already committed by General George Neill of the Honourable East India Company against alleged 'mutineers' when many innocent 'natives' were also butchered. Informally called 'John Company', it had effectively ruled British India since 1833. As a result of these barbarous incidents, Sir Colin Campbell was recalled to duty with

Lieut Col Richard CH Taylor

the 79th. Thus Richard Taylor, within days of arriving home at Ardgillan, was summoned to rejoin Sir Colin, his old friend, again. The regiment was bound for India.

The 79th Camerons sailed from Dublin for Calcutta on 1 August, 573 bayonets strong, on board the vessels *Louisiana* and *Tyburnia*. Richard, meanwhile, sailed from Southampton on 3 October on the SS *Ripon*, a side paddle steamer belonging to the P&O Line, bound for Alexandria, Egypt. Although early steam ships were a faster means of transport than sail, life on board was equally tedious, the time being taken up with sleeping, eating, reading and conversing. And of course there was written correspondence at which Richard continued to be prolific. His long letters home detailing sea voyages, the horrendous two-year campaign and Indian Colonial society as he experienced it, provide a fascinating insight into Anglo-Irish and Empire mindsets as well as lifestyles.

Ship's barometer in oak case that belonged to Basil Richard Taylour RN

Coming so soon after the Crimean campaign, he found separation from his family hard, especially from his mother to whom he was devoted. Yet, something more mundane pre-occupied him at first on leaving Southampton – the opera glasses he 'had stupidly forgotten in London'. His brother, Thomas, responded immediately and posted them on. Richard describes his fellow passengers as 'Officers of the Queen's service going to join all the stations, Company officers, Military, Naval and Civil Engineers, telegraph men, chaplains, three priests, merchants, indigo planters; in fact, representatives of nearly every class.' He added that there were 'several ladies on board – three of them married', and deemed that the trip must have been 'a most unsatisfactory honeymoon'. What particularly disturbed Richard was the fact that these women were going to India at a time of serious unrest and uncertainty although they were travelling in comparative style.

Actually, it wasn't unusual for young ladies to arrive in India on P&O ships during the autumn season, either before the Mutiny or after it, as it coincided with the 'cold weather' period when the heat in the Colonies was more tolerable. They stayed with relations or with close family friends as their protectors in the hope of meeting eligible young men with a view to marriage. This was not quite straightforward though, as career-focused men had to remain single for years following their arrival until they established themselves in the Indian Civil Service or in their regiment and, even then, could only marry with permission from their superiors. As for the girls, on the voyage out from England they were known as the 'Fishing Fleet', while those who returned home in the spring without having found a match were unkindly referred to as 'Returned Empties'.

Apart from 'a larky widow' who kept him amused at dinner, by the time the *Ripon* neared Malta, Richard was unimpressed with the other passengers, considering them to be 'a decidedly uninteresting lot, and on the whole snobbish, with the thorough English manner, distrustful of everyone, and each looking with suspicion and sullenness on the other'. With great relief, he arrived in Alexandria and during a brief stopover managed to see the Pyramids, which appeared to be 'quite close, although in reality, some fifteen miles off'. He noted that 'the heat was great and the dust tormenting, a strong desert wind blowing.' The next stage of the journey was across the desert to the Red Sea by rail as the Suez Canal was still under construction. A week later, then on board the SS *Alma* in the Red Sea, he recalled the desert crossing thus:

'The entire distance was through dreary sandy stones, real desert, the very desert I had long heard of, and in which I was not disappointed. It appeared endless, one continuous water of sand, flat except in some few places where the sand had been drifted by the wind into hillocks like snow drifts; the only evidence of life being an occasional dromedary slouching along with an Arab seated aloft, looking with disgust at the smoking engine and its long train of unbelievers.'

Model of *Brigantine* donated by the Taylor family on display in the Main Hall

But, he added: 'Nevertheless, I must say that a railway train in the Great Desert does look out of place.' Twenty-eight miles short of Suez, the track ended and the party took to horse-drawn 'vans', arriving in Suez, 'a vile place', at 4am. Back at sea again, on the SS *Alma* steaming towards Aden, Richard wrote:

'I have been quite well throughout the voyage, but feel as if I were terribly in need of exercise. What with the heat, the crowd on the decks and the rolling, I do not think my walk amounts to more than 100 yards a day. I live very temperately, read a good deal and smoke perhaps rather more than I intended.'

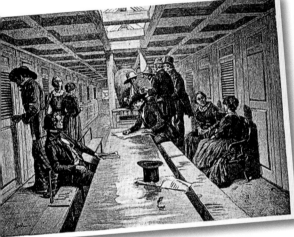

Preparing for dinner on board a steamer

Long meals helped to pass the time on these interminable voyages but still Richard complained about the inconvenience caused by frequent dining. He grumbled: 'I am being turned out of my place to lay the cloth for one of our innumerable meals.'

His spirits must have flagged on occasion for, in a later letter dated 28 October 1857 from the Indian Ocean, he wrote that he 'was never before so sick of a voyage. Time hangs heavily and really there is scarcely a person on board that I care to fraternise with. They are a stupid, uninteresting lot, and, without quarrelling, all seem heartily sick of each other. A few youngsters making their first trip into the world are the only exceptions to the general rule.'

Richard's long journey ended when the SS *Alma* finally dropped anchor at Calcutta. On 1 November 1857, he told his mother: 'Here I am at last arrived at the end of a stupid, tedious voyage. We came to anchor yesterday about 12 o'clock, having thus been just one day under the six weeks making the passage from Southampton.'

His war in India was about to begin.

31

Calcutta – November 1st /57

My dearest Mother

Here I am, at last arrived at the end of a tedious stupid voyage. We came to anchor yesterday about 12 o, having thus been just one day under the six weeks making the passage from Southampton. During the latter part of the voyage, we had had weather, after leaving Madras, it rained almost constantly, & the wind & sea being sufficiently high to oblige us to close the ports, one may imagine the discomfort caused by the combined effects of heat, damp, stench & suffocation. – I am told there is an extra chance of a mail to England to-day, as a steamer (the Oriental) sails for Suez, with widows, orphans, & sufferers of all sorts; returning, I believe, with troops. Possibly the mail she carries, may be detained at Alexandria, but I'll embrace the oppor-tunity to write a line, on the chance of its reaching you before the regular mail which starts this day week. — I am at present inmated with "my aunt" Mrs Fagan! Before I had left the steamer yesterday, her husband came on board, & hurried me off at once to his house, assuring me that there was not a hole

Richard CH Taylor's letter to his mother with news of his arrival in Calcutta

A Hard-Fought Campaign

On 22 November 1857, Lieutenant Colonel Richard CH Taylor watched from the dockside as part of his regiment, the 79th Camerons, at last arrived in Calcutta, after a long voyage around the Cape. By this stage, he had grown weary of the social life of the city and was anxious to get, in his own words, 'up country', to the North Western Provinces where the Sepoy Mutiny was spreading throughout the territories.

Richard learned that the unrest festering for years had many causes including land annexation by the Honourable East India Company, increased taxation, issues of religion and the loss of army privileges for Indian troops, the Sepoys. The unrest came to a head with the introduction of the cartridge for the new Enfield Rifle, issued in 1853, which was greased with beef and pork fat. As the cartridge had to be bitten to release the ball, this was regarded as consuming forbidden meat, an insult to the religious beliefs of the Muslim Sepoy (pork) and the Hindu Sepoy (beef). The mutiny began in Meerut on 10 May 1857 and spread rapidly throughout central India and the upper plains of the Ganges. On 1 December 1857, as Richard set off towards Benares, he wrote to his mother, Marianne, that 'not a single native was to be trusted.'

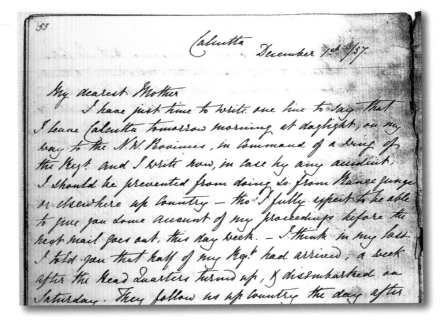

Richard CH Taylor's letter home with news of his imminent departure for the North West Provinces, 1 Dec 1857

The route the regiment took was called the Grand Trunk Road, sometimes known as the 'Long Walk'. Famously described by Rudyard Kipling, this ancient road starts in Bangladesh, crosses upper India and ends in Kabul, a distance of approximately 2,500 km. In a letter home, Richard explained that the daily march had 'commenced by 3pm and the stage is completed by 10 (o'clock) of the following day so that we have five hours for rest and provant.' On 8 December, in a letter to his sister, Eliza, he described his accommodation while on the road: 'We are put up in mat huts calculated to hold fifty men each – there is nothing in the huts but some straw – officers and men are accommodated alike. I screened off a corner, put up a native *charpoy* or bedstead...and have made myself very cosy and comfortable.' From Benares, he wrote to his mother on 20 December: 'A permanent gallows has been erected in the Artillery Parade Ground but has not been used for some days. In action no prisoners are taken, all wounded are finished off...this is a sad state of affairs, but I believe it cannot be avoided.'

The Grand Trunk Road

Writing to his brother, Thomas, on 4 January 1858 from Camp Allahabad, Richard stated: 'My opinion of this country does not improve with acquaintance. One is pestered with servants and attendants and followers of various sorts, amongst whom one feels completely helpless from ignorance of the language...The sun is very hot by day and the nights are bitterly cold...Provisions are dear and bad; (officers') mess a scramble and horses unattainable.'

Settled in Camp Allahabad on 14 January and newly-promoted as temporary Brigadier General, Richard briefly described an encounter with the enemy: 'We had an expedition last week which lasted only one day; across the Ganges in the Oude direction some fourteen miles off. We cut up a good many rebels, burnt several villages, and hung and shot some prisoners. My regiment lost none. We had a long day, having gone over fully 40 miles – men tired and footsore.'

According to the Official Records of the Regiment, this march by Richard and his men, forty-eight miles in twenty-three hours, may well be the longest ever completed within the British Army during that timeframe. Furthermore, Richard received a commendation for bravery in this action by the Governor General, one of many he would attain during the campaign. On arrival in Cawnpore on 3 February 1858, he described the sombre scenes that awaited them, stating that the buildings were 'perfectly riddled with shot and shell...no wonder they capitulated...The scene of destruction is complete'. The deep well into which the bodies of the dead Europeans had been thrown was 'bricked over and filled up.' He also told of finding 'daily little relics of the unhappy garrison amongst the ruins – bits of women's and children's sundresses, trinkets, scraps of letters and music, etc.' He further commented that '...the view altogether is not calculated to make our people inclined to be merciful to any of the enemy they meet.'

By the time the column reached Lucknow on 28 March, Richard had grown weary of the fighting, declaring 'I don't care how soon it is over, for it is a barbarous system of warfare – no prisoners whatever are taken, everything and everybody is destroyed.' Execution of prisoners was the norm, the most horrendous method being 'blown by cannon', a horrific practice first used by the Moghols in the sixteenth century. Graphic eye-witness descriptions exist of prisoners being tied to loaded cannon, their backs to the muzzle, which were then fired, literally blowing them away. The phrase continues in use today, with a happier meaning, of course.

People back home did not just read about the fighting in India – they saw pictures too. Some of the first images of the devastation caused by war were taken in the Crimea by a Venetian photographer named Felice Beato (1832–1909). When Beato arrived in Calcutta around February 1858, he made his way towards Lucknow. Unlike others of his profession who arranged individuals or groups in formal poses, Beato may well have been the first ever to show corpses. It is believed that in at least one photograph he had the skeletal remains of Sepoys strewn in front of a ruined building for dramatic impact.

Richard's force finally succeeded in lifting the siege of Lucknow, after much bitter fighting. On entering the ruins, he wrote to his mother on 20 March 1858 stating that it must have been 'a magnificent city, far the finest I have seen in the East; a mass of gorgeous palaces of enormous extent and elaborate architecture, with gilded domes and minarets, quite realising my boyish ideas of eastern magnificence.' While he was in Lucknow, a disastrous explosion occurred. Extensively reported as an accident in the newspapers back home, Richard describes it differently: 'Behind a mosque a large quantity of powder was stored. Whilst workmen and soldiers were taking measure for its removal, the whole exploded, fired, it is said, by a Sepoy lying concealed who, of course, lost his own life. A great number suffered; I scarcely know how many. I lost a very good smart Sergeant...he was completely peeled and roasted.' Among the reporting journalists present was William Russell of *The Times*, with whom Richard 'shared sandwiches and cigars'.

Richard's numerous Indian letters conclude when his application for leave to come home was finally granted. On 15 April 1859, he wrote to his sister, Eliza: 'I cannot help feeling a pang of regret at leaving the old regiment after passing twenty-three happy years in it.' But Richard's campaign would continue for another eight months before his dream of going home would be realised. He was still in Cawnpore when the Honourable East India Company ceased to exist with the passing of the Government of India Act in August, 1858, marking the beginning of the British Raj (literally, 'rule; in Hindustani), yet, he makes no reference to this historic event in his letters.

The Raj would last from then until July 1947, when Independence for India was finally achieved.

Sir Colin Campbell, Lord Clyde

HOME THOUGHTS FROM ABROAD

Throughout the two long years he spent in India, Richard's perpetual concerns had been for his mother, Marianne. Due to her advanced age – she was seventy-seven when he departed – she was constantly on his mind, as was Ardgillan. He was only a week in Calcutta when he wrote on 8 December 1857: 'I have a craving for news from home.' On receipt of a

letter from his sister, Eliza, updating him with family news, he replies on 14 December: 'It is just those little details that are so valuable to the wanderer at a distance; they bring him back in mind to the well-remembered scenes of home, and in fancy, he pictures to himself all that is so graphically described.'

More alarmingly for one so far away, he heard again probably from Eliza of an accident that had befallen Marianne. Reputed to have been caused by a fall from a horse, it must have been serious because on 14 March 1858, while camped near Lucknow, he wrote to his brother, Thomas:

'I am much distressed to hear of the sad accident to our poor, dear Mother, and I cannot conceal from myself that the effects of such a shake to her system must cause great anxiety to us all. Indeed, my dear Edd (the family name for Thomas Edward), you put it in the true light when you prepare me for the worst, and I begin to feel that even if I pull through this business, I can scarcely expect to have the intense satisfaction of meeting my dear Mother again in this world.'

Thomas Edward
Taylor MP

In a further letter to Thomas dated 27 July 1858, from Futtegurh, he despondently wrote: 'The accounts of poor dear mother are better than I expected but nevertheless it is a sad thing to feel that any day may bring me bitter News, for I know the end cannot be far off.' Referring to her impending death, he realised that 'The breakup at Ardgillan will, I fear, be very sorrowful and for the first time I feel that my youth is really past. We should be very thankful that we have hitherto formed such a happy and united family.'   In a humorous aside, Richard revealed that the soldiers had a new name for Sir Colin Campbell, CO of the regiment: 'The nickname they have given him, I am sure it must have been invented by a Dublin wag, is "Crawling Camel".'

Extract from RCH Taylor's Indian Campaign diary

As a touching act of kindness towards her brother, Eliza later enclosed a lock of Marianne's hair in a letter that he received while still in Cawnpore. He responded on 27 August 1858, saying: 'Nothing you could have sent could have been half so acceptable. The colour of the hair is wonderfully little changed.'

Left: Richard CH Taylor's letter to his sister, Eliza, dated 26 May 1858

169

The low wall that Richard CH Taylor enquired about in his letter

Dating the various developments at Ardgillan is almost impossible now due to incomplete records but Richard's letters offer tantalising clues to some of them. For instance, his letter to Eliza of 18 September 1858 dates the installation of glass greenhouses and 'the low wall in continuation of the terrace, in front of the laundry'. The low wall referred to here is the boundary between the lawn at the rear of the house and the Yew Tree path. The grounds and woodlands were also on Richard's mind for, from the chaos of Cawnpore, on 28 September, he wrote to Thomas: 'I am glad to hear you are getting on so well with your improvements by the garden – Ardgillan will really be an improved place. How did the plantings push forward this year?' In the sweltering heat of the Indian sun, the thoughts of Ardgillan must have reminded him of the more temperate climate back home, for he stated: 'I quite long for a good Irish day, cloudy and still, and to see a tree without leaves.'

Richard's letters show him to be a man of moderate habits, confining himself to 'tea and ginger-beer' but, as for the soldiers of the 79th, he reports that they 'have been behaving anything but well – Scotsmen are the devil at New Years time; I believe they consider it a religious duty to get drunk at that epoch.' He also showed a keen sense of wit as well as the ability to laugh at himself. He once described Marianne as 'the darling mother of the chubby boy'. Much later, in a letter to Thomas on 31 March 1859, again alluding to his girth, he humorously concludes by saying: 'That is my palanquin waiting, and the bearers are scanning my proportions with a despondent look.' A palanquin is a boxlike litter on long poles carried on the shoulders of four men. At last, in a letter to Thomas on 15 April 1859, he confirmed that his longed-for leave had finally been granted but finding a passage home presented huge difficulties as, with the Mutiny finally declared over, the sudden demand for space meant every ship was full to capacity. Eventually he managed to get a berth on the P&O Paddle-Steamer *Indus* and sailed, homeward bound from Bombay, on 23 April 1859.

In the present world of instant communication, it is impossible now to understand the significance of these hand-written letters between 1857 and 1859, whether those at home read his in the Morning Room or he read theirs in the stifling heat of an army tent somewhere on the North West Provinces of India. With disease and death all around, Richard would not have known daily whether he would still be alive by nightfall but it is abundantly clear that in reading these letters, full of news

Gen Richard CH Taylor shortly before his death in 1904

and gossip from Ardgillan, he derived great comfort and pleasure. Regretfully, he did not get to see his mother alive again. After a prolonged illness, Marianne St Leger Taylor died on the 22 March 1859 while Richard was still somewhere on the Grand Trunk Road marching back to the coast. Nearly two months later, then just some forty miles from Marseille, and on board the P&O Steamer *Nepaul*, a distraught Richard wrote to Thomas: 'The very painful intelligence of our dearest Mother's death reached me while still on the *Indus* – from a newspaper I first heard of it.' It was a cruel blow for the returning soldier.

Lt. Col. Richard CH Taylor went on to have a glittering army career, finally retiring as Governor of Sandhurst in 1886 with the rank of General. He died on 6 December 1904 and was buried with full military honours in the family vault under St George's Church, Balbriggan, beside his parents. Copies of his letters home from India, now fully transcribed, are preserved in Ardgillan Castle.

Military drum in
the Main Hall,
1938

Part 5

MILITARIA

THE DONARD INFANTRY SNARE DRUM

The Donard Infantry snare drum, part of the Ardgillan Collection of Militaria, is a typical example of a late eighteenth-century militia instrument. With a shell measuring sixteen inches by sixteen, a snare drum was usually made from a thin layer of ash, rolled and fastened with tacks in an elaborate pattern that became known as the 'nail board'. It was covered at both ends with calfskin or sheepskin, leading to the drummer's nickname of 'calfskin fiddler' or 'sheepskin fiddler'. Two hoops, one smaller and one larger, press down on the calfskin at each end and keep it in place. A continuous length of cord runs through holes in the larger hoops, zig-zagging up and down, with moveable leather braces that can draw the loops together, or slacken them as desired, to elicit variations in the notes produced. One loop of the cord stretches across the drumhead and acts as a snare to increase the reverberations when struck. Thus it became known as a snare drum but, as it was often played to the side while marching, it was also called a side drum.

A military snare drum was elaborately decorated with an emblazonment representing the regimental coat of arms, name and motto. Second only in symbolic value to the colours, or flags, of the regiment, the drum was also venerated by the troops who protected it with their lives. In battle, the colours, or flags, were sent to the rear for safety. Not so with the drums. Unarmed, the drummers beat the pace for the rank and file soldiers as they marched towards the enemy and then controlled their deployment into battle formation. Transmitting an officer's orders in the presence of the enemy by the different beats of the drum was a task that required cool heads, steady hands and real courage.

Idealised images of military drummers during the time of Wellington and Napoleon depict them as small boys valiantly beating their drums amidst the chaos of the battlefield. Perhaps this impression stemmed from the presence of boys, known as 'barrack rats', in each army depot, many of them sons of soldiers or orphans raised among the men. Too young to bear arms, some opted for the drum but, as the snare drum was of a standard size, no consideration was given to the relative stature of the drummer, hence the frequent portrayal in art of the diminutive drummer boy with the unwieldy instrument slung on his hip. Despite this romantic image most drummers were in fact adults. At Waterloo, for example, the vast

Opposite page:
The Donard Infantry Militia Drum preserved in Ardgillan Castle.

Above:
The drum emblazonment – detail

majority were mature men, many of them in their thirties. Whatever their age, all were expert musicians, adept at both fife and drum. Their lively playing maintained morale and kept the men's spirits high on long, dreary marches and in drab, austere depots.

Becoming a drummer must have been an attractive option for a young recruit. The pay was higher than that of the common soldier and drummers were quickly promoted to the rank of corporal. Notwithstanding that, in addition to learning music, they still had to train every day with the rank and file. Long years of practice resulted in a highly regulated standard and quality of playing, whether drumming lively marching songs or beating the various orders for complicated military formations during exercises in the field. The 'long practice' had but one aim, to ensure that the drummer performed his duty to perfection, especially in the presence of the enemy.

It was not only the drum that made the drummer stand out. His uniform was distinctive too, consisting of the reverse of the regular rank and file soldier's – hence, 'reverse colours'. Easy to spot in the line, as were officers, the drummer too was considered a legitimate target for enemy sharpshooters in order to disrupt battlefield communications. The 27th Inniskillings was the only Irish Regiment of Foot under Wellington at Waterloo. Although they were exposed to the most withering fire from the French at the climax of the battle, of the seven named drummers present, three were wounded but miraculously none were killed. The uniform had other positive advantages too as the drummer was also a prime target for the ladies. It was said at the time that because of his musical skill and his elaborate peacock's dress, the drummer 'always got the girl'. Perhaps that is why there was never any shortage of volunteers to take up the drum!

Title page for the *Manual for Volunteer Corps of Infantry,* 1804

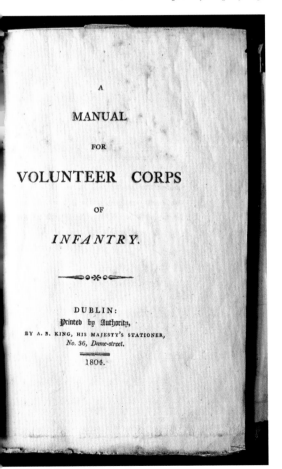

A

MANUAL

FOR

VOLUNTEER CORPS

OF

INFANTRY.

DUBLIN:
Printed by Authority,
BY A. B. KING, HIS MAJESTY'S STATIONER,
No. 36, Dame-street.

1804.

Now faded with age, and not looking at all military, Ardgillan's snare drum once belonged to the Donard Infantry from Wicklow whose captains in 1798 were George Heighington and William Heighington. The instrument's artistic emblazonment has now lost its magnificence and the lettering speaks of a bygone age. Doubtless, the unknown hands that played the Donard Infantry drum would have been familiar with the instructions from *A Manual for Volunteer Corps of Infantry* published in Dublin in 1804.

or

ave
the
rch
take
1.

great
take
as to
n all
yards

ast be
very

SIGNALS TO BE MADE BY THE DRUM.

The signals.—To advance, *Grenadiers March ;* to retreat, *Retreat ;* to halt, *Troop ;* to cease firing, *General ;* to assemble, or call in all parties, *To Arms ;* are to be always considered as fixed and determined ones, and are never to be changed.

All of those signals made from the line or column are to convey the intention of the commanding officer of the line to the officer commanding the batalion, who will either communicate them to the several companies or detachments by word or signal.

IT

Left: Excerpt from the manual – drum signals

Below: The drumsticks, calfskin top, hoops and chords of the Donard Infantry drum – note the snare across the top of the calfskin

For centuries, the drum dictated every aspect of the soldier's daily life until the bugle finally replaced it in early Victorian times. Even today, the stirring beat of the snare drum remains an essential feature of all military ceremonial displays. While the sound of the venerable Donard Infantry drum which once carried across the Wicklow Hills will be heard no more, its preservation in Ardgillan is a unique reminder of the existence of the militias in Ireland and the infamous part they played in putting down the Insurrection of 1798.

The 'Brown Bess' Musket

The invention of gunpowder heralded the gradual introduction of a range of new weapons and tactics to the battlefield. After the more primitive wheellock and firelock guns came the flintlock, so called because it was fired when a flint struck against an ignition system which in turn fired a ball. Collectively these weapons became known as muskets, from the Middle French *mousquette,* meaning 'a kind of sparrowhawk', following a fashion of the time to name weapons after beasts.

The flintlock was the main weapon that crushed Bonny Prince Charlie's (Charles Edward Stuart) Jacobite dream at Culloden in 1745; it was the standard musket during the Seven Years' War from 1756 to 1763 and later was used on both sides during the American War of Independence. It decimated the pike-carrying Insurgents in 1798; and in the capable hands of the 27th Inniskillings at Waterloo it was instrumental in holding the centre of Wellington's line against Napoleon's forces in 1815. In short, it was the dominant battlefield musket for well over one hundred years and helped to create an Empire.

Ardgillan's collection of flintlock weapons includes the musket that became affectionately known as the 'Brown Bess'. Mass-produced from 1722, this musket was manufactured with continuous improvements until the 1830s and remained in use until much later. Prior to 1700, the manufacture of muskets was totally uncoordinated. Individual gunsmiths all over Europe and in the New World Colonies were making a wide variety of flintlocks, some more effective than others, using barrels of different lengths and calibres (the calibre of a gun is the internal diameter of the barrel). This meant that the size of the ball, or bullet, had to be different also to suit an individual piece. Interestingly, both 'bullet' and 'ball' have the same Middle French root, *boule,* meaning 'ball', and the diminutive, *boulette,* a 'bullet'.

This chaotic situation was addressed when the Royal Board of Ordnance was set up in London on 15 September 1714 with the task of standardising and controlling gun manufacture. The introduction of the Long Land

Left:
Firing mechanism
Brown Bess musket.

Centre:
Crowned GR stamp
– detail

Bottom left:
Dublin Castle stamp
– detail

Bottom right:
Firing mechanism of
musket manufactured
by Dixon of Dublin

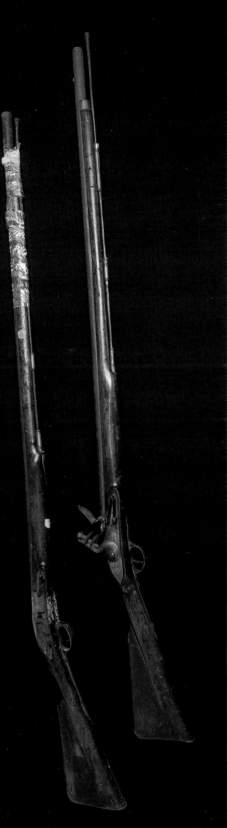

Pattern Musket was the result of their deliberations. It was 159cm in length and weighed a hefty 4.7kg but later versions of the musket were shorter such as the unsurprisingly named Short Land Pattern Musket from 1740 and the India Pattern from 1797. While most surviving muskets are stamped 'Tower', indicating that they were made in the Tower of London, the Ardgillan examples are marked 'Dublin Castle' where some 60,000 were manufactured under licence. In a display of national bias, contemporary comparisons published in London favoured the Tower musket, stating that it was more reliable than the Dublin Castle version.

The origin of the name 'Brown Bess' is still uncertain but by the second half of the eighteenth century it seems to have been in common use, being first recorded in 1785. One theory is that it got the name from the walnut wood used for the stock, although another suggests that it was because of the browning applied to gun barrels around that time. This is unlikely as the redcoat army did not 'brown' their barrels, preferring them to be bright metal instead. Alternatively it could have stemmed from Arquebus or Blunderbuss, weapons that predated the musket. To 'hug Brown Bess' became a euphemism for enlisting but army training manuals of the period never referred to the weapon by its colloquial term, invariably using the proper name of 'firelock'.

The musket was a smoothbore, muzzle-loaded weapon, unlike the rifle that had a grooved barrel. To load it, both the gunpowder and the ball were rammed down the barrel using a metal ramrod although earlier ones were of wood. The ball had to be slightly narrower in order to fit so,

Earlier and later Dublin
Castle versions of the Long
Land Pattern Musket
– the Brown Bess

when fired, it rattled down the barrel before being propelled out in the general direction in which it was aimed. In the chaos of the battlefield with thick, black smoke obscuring everything, the most effective way of using the Brown Bess was 'firing by volley'. At long range, as few as one ball in ten struck home so soldiers had a relatively good chance of surviving the first volley unscathed – but at close range volley-fire was devastating. When that was followed by a frenzied, bayonet charge, it was a brave opponent who stood firm.

Veteran soldiers preferred to die rather than be wounded as they all dreaded the surgeon's knife. The musket ball flattened on impact with the body, tearing flesh and bone apart, resulting in horrific wounds. With the primitive standard of surgery available then, amputation was the common, painful consequence. Many didn't survive the procedure due to loss of blood, trauma or gangrene but, after the battle of Metz (1793), Napoleon's brilliant and innovative surgeon, Dominique-Jean Larrey, organised medical teams with specially designed 'flying ambulances' to be positioned near the front lines to carry the wounded off the battlefield for immediate emergency treatment.

It is interesting to see how much of our current figures of speech had their origins in old military terminology. For example, the term 'lock, stock and barrel' refers to the main parts of a musket, implying wholeness and totality. And again, prior to commencing an amputation, it was common practice to put a lead musket ball in the wounded soldiers's mouth so that he could clench his teeth on the soft metal as the surgeon's saw did its work. Hence, 'bite the bullet'.

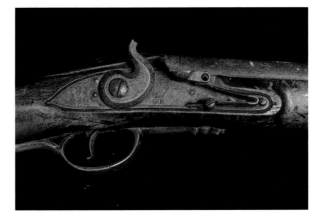

Old musket
Dublin Castle

The Carbine

From the start, it was envisaged that arming a mounted trooper with a musket would allow him to engage the enemy long before he could use a sabre or lance. But it was immediately obvious that the Brown Bess, due to its length, was an impractical weapon on horseback. The answer was simply to shorten the barrel. The resulting carbine was identical in all respects to the longer musket but its use in battle did little more than cause some disorder in the ranks of inexperienced troops. It was a much more effective weapon however when used by dismounted cavalry to fill a gap in the line, for example, or when guarding horses, even though its shorter barrel made it more inaccurate than the Brown Bess.

Mounted troopers were trained to clean and reload the carbine on the move, stopping only to fire the weapon. This was some feat on horseback considering that, like all muskets, it had to be loaded through the muzzle. To make matters more difficult it was regulation for the trooper to have his drawn sword hanging from a lanyard on his right arm when using his carbine. The weight of a sword swinging from his wrist made accurate aiming almost impossible. It was standard practice for cavalry when within the presence of the enemy to keep on the move in order to avoid becoming a target. They stopped only to discharge their weapons.

As all muskets had their ignition system on the right – no musket had a left-handed version – the trooper fired to the right of his own horse's head with the weapon tilted upwards so that the explosive discharge would be diverted away from the next horse. Cavalry mounts were accustomed to the sound of the gun blast but the sudden flash could cause a startled horse to throw its rider. It was the standard wisdom of the time that cavalry should never receive a charge standing at the halt as the sheer impetus would sweep all before it. But on one atypical occasion, volley fire from the saddle by the French 20th Chasseurs à Cheval brought the massed Russian cavalry charge crashing down at Eylau in 1807.

Thomas Edward Taylor MP joined the 6th Dragoon Guards (DG) in 1829 at the age of eighteen, and retired in 1846 with the rank of captain in order to devote himself to a career in politics. The appellation 'Guards' with 'Dragoon' conferred a higher status on a cavalry regiment and allowed them to have their own numbering system. The 6th DG were called 'The Carabiniers', from the word 'carbine', a title bestowed upon them in 1691. By happy coincidence, the Ardgillan carbine is stamped DG.

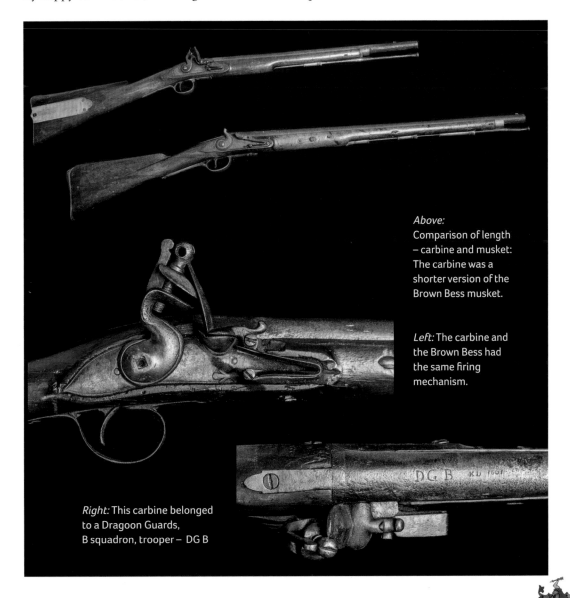

Above: Comparison of length – carbine and musket: The carbine was a shorter version of the Brown Bess musket.

Left: The carbine and the Brown Bess had the same firing mechanism.

Right: This carbine belonged to a Dragoon Guards, B squadron, trooper – DG B

The Blunderbuss

The blunderbuss, forerunner of the shotgun, was also a feared musket of the period. It was a firelock with a short, stubby but wider barrel, flared at the muzzle. Its name probably came from the Dutch, Donderbus, meaning 'Thunder Pipe'. As with all muskets, it was muzzle-loaded except that it could take a number of lead balls at one time, unlike the single shot Brown Bess and shorter carbine. When fired, the flared muzzle allowed the shot to spread making the blunderbuss truly devastating at close range. It became a favourite weapon for sailors, especially pirates, being ideally suited for fighting in the confined spaces of a ship. If the skull and crossbones flag did not strike fear into a passing ship's crew, coming face to face with the open mouth of a blunderbuss usually did. Its short length made it easy to handle. Once loaded, all one had to do was point and fire. It was so versatile that it could take almost any sort of projectile that would fit into the barrel including stones, nails, shards of metal, and even sand. Some, like the Blunderbuss in Ardgillan, had a quick-release blade, folded back on the barrel when not required so that the weapon was still effective even when it had been discharged. While the blunderbuss did not often appear on the battlefield, George Washington promoted its use by the Dragoons in his Continental Army, arguing that it was a much more effective weapon than the carbine.

With the expansion of the coach network in the eighteenth century, security of passengers and mail became a major issue. To counter the scourge of highwaymen, the driver's escort was armed with a blunderbuss rather than a carbine. Up close it was a deadly deterrent to the 'Gentlemen of the Road' and was the origin of the phrase 'to ride shotgun'. One wonders how many times the notorious Michael Collier, (Collier the Robber) a highwayman from the Hill of Bellewstown who plied his trade mostly on the roads of North County Dublin and Meath, faced a loaded blunderbuss as he robbed the mail coaches on the Dublin to Dunleer Turnpike. Although many of Collier's gang ended up on the scaffold, he himself survived to die of natural causes in 1849 at the age of sixty-nine.

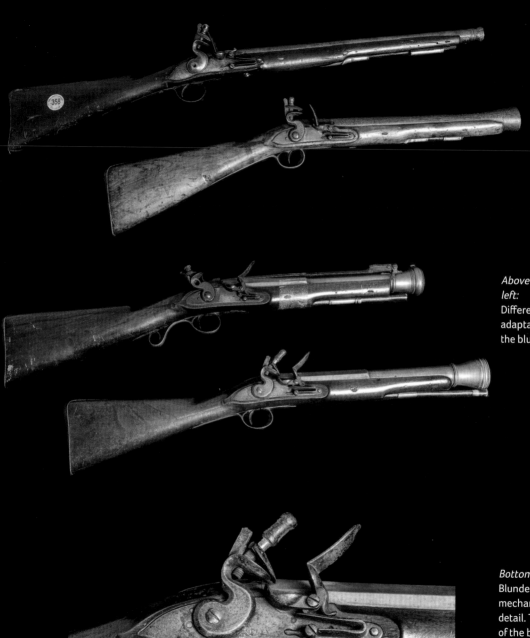

Above and left: Different adaptations of the blunderbuss

Bottom left: Blunderbuss firing mechanism – detail. The exterior of the barrel is octagonal

PISTOLS AND FOWLING PIECE

Cavalry also used a pistol as a close range weapon, keeping a brace of them in saddle holsters. Troopers in action were known to fire them and then throw them away as it was impossible to reload them with the enemy milling around. Although the Ardgillan collection lacks a single barrel pistol, it includes a double-barrelled version, a four-barrelled one, and numerous pocket specimens. These were tiny but deadly weapons, easily concealed until needed.

The most impressive firelock in the Castle is the elegant and beautifully decorated fowling piece. The weapon got its name from the fowler, an individual who hunted wild birds, or fowl. A much lighter weapon than the sturdier Brown Bess of the military, its extended barrel allowed for greater muzzle velocity and accuracy. Records show that these guns were in use as far back as 1688 to shoot at flying birds.

From the earliest version of the unwieldy Brown Bess to the delicately crafted fowling piece, each weapon in the Ardgillan Collection of firelocks could be described as an object of lethal beauty.

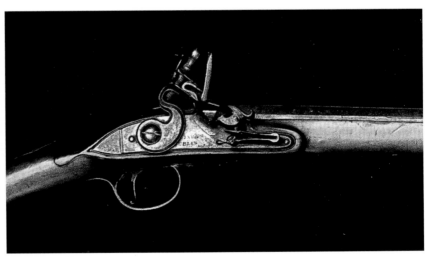

The fowling piece.

Firing mechanism on the fowling piece – detail

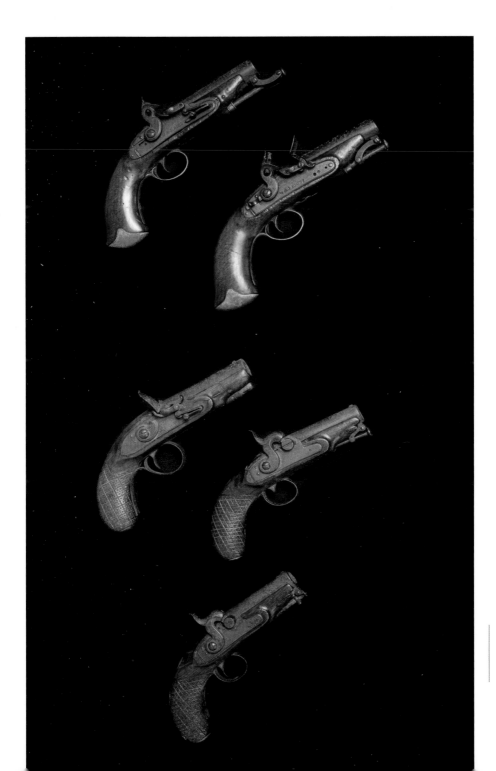

Flintlock
pistols from
the collection

The Engraved Powder Horns

Initially set up in 1778 as Ireland's response to the threat of French invasion, the Volunteers were local militia units raised in place of the regular army regiments dispatched to the American War in the Colonies. As the numbers of Volunteer militias grew, some of their leaders adopted a more political stance and, with the formation of the Irish Patriot Party under the leadership of MPs William Flood and Henry Grattan, they forced some concessions from Westminster for the Irish Parliament sitting in Dublin. However, the party's influence waned due to disagreements among the leaders and, with the passing of various Acts of Parliament, the Volunteers were effectively curtailed militarily. At the same time, the Militia Act (1793) was rushed through the Irish Parliament and in a striking change of policy Catholics were finally allowed to bear arms and enlist. In a country previously devoid of employment opportunities for Catholics, joining the militia provided some element of security with each parish providing a set quota of men.

Essentially, the function of the militias was to act as a kind of riot squad in quelling disquiet in the country in the absence of regular troops and, as previously with the Volunteers, to assist in repelling the expected French invasion. To avoid conflict of interest, a militia could not serve in its own county, nor was it permitted to serve overseas. As recorded in many eyewitness accounts, militias are mainly remembered for the savage brutality with which they and their British counterparts put down the Rebellion of the 'Summer Soldiers' in 1798.

As reminders of that fateful period, two engraved powder horns are preserved in the Castle. Cattle and oxen horns, naturally hollow when removed from the bone underneath, were most commonly used as waterproof containers for gunpowder until they were replaced first by paper cartridges and later on by bullets. The gunpowder was poured in at the wide end while the narrow end allowed small amounts to be tipped out to prime and load a musket. A stopper at each extremity kept the powder dry and a long strap allowed it to be carried slung over the shoulder. In the American Colonies, some frontiersmen carved their

Engraved images
- details

Engraved militia powder horns
Detail of artwork on horn
(below)

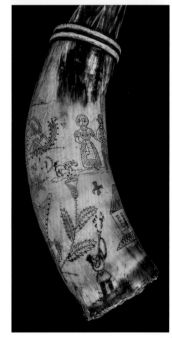

powder horns with significant features of the terrain marking the locations of mountains, passes, lakes, rivers and crossings as a handy form of map. In Ireland, some horns had a different purpose during the Insurrection of 1798 – they were used to warn of approaching militia or yeomanry. The loud moaning sound they created when blown through the narrow mouthpiece carried for miles across mountains and valleys. However, the penalty for being caught in possession of such a horn was immediate death.

The unique gunpowder horns in Ardgillan, one of which belonged to a soldier from the Fartullagh Rangers, County Westmeath, are engraved with symbols associated with the Volunteers: the maiden harp, winding strands of shamrock and the Royal Coat of Arms. The delicate etching on these horns has transformed these mundane pieces of military equipment into works of art.

THE SWORD COLLECTION

Since its first appearance during the Bronze Age as a larger version of the dagger, the sword has been continually refined and adapted to suit the changing nature of warfare throughout the centuries. But whether it was on the battlefield of Thermopylæ, Cannæ, Clontarf, Hastings, Agincourt or Culloden, the sword consisted of the same basic parts, a handle and a blade, with the same aim of inflicting brutal injury on the human body. However, while the two elements remained constant, each successive modification since the Roman Army first employed the *gladius* was designed to deliver a tactical advantage over an enemy.

The Ardgillan swords date mostly from the late eighteenth and early nineteenth centuries, a period when Irish society was highly militarised and talk of revolution and invasion was widespread. The collection includes both straight and curved bladed swords of varying types as well as some of eastern origin. The most common straight sword then was the 1796 pattern backsword so called because it had one cutting edge while the other, the 'back', was thickened to provide strength. Used by heavy cavalry, they charged with the weapon pointed and stiff – the thrust method – but close-up it could be used as a bludgeon. The scabbard was engraved with the boast: 'Guaranteed Never to Fail'. By contrast, the broadsword was double-edged.

Light cavalry, such as the Hussars, favoured the sabre with its wickedly curved blade that was ideal for cutting and slashing from the saddle. After the 1798 Rebellion, most of the wounds inflicted were recorded as being to the head, shoulders and upper body, the consequence of downward

Heavy one-edged, sabre with metal scabbard

sabre blows by Yeoman cavalry. It was this contrasting use of cavalry swords that gave rise to the phrase, 'cut and thrust'.

Overlooking the deadly purpose for which they were made, the Ardgillan swords could be seen as works of art with beautiful, intricate craftsmanship apparent not only on the handles and guards but also extending down the blades. As was the custom with sabres, the upper part, the *forte*, was 'blued' before gilt ornamentation and inscriptions were added. Two of the sabres carry the name of the officer to whom each was presented and their company. They were made by Dublin swordsmiths; one by Archers, with warranty still clearly legible and the other by John Read of College Green. Many European swords carry Latin inscriptions such as *In Nomine Domine* and *Benedictus,* but the French *Dieu et Mon Droit,* 'God and My Right', popular in the Georgian era, was the preferred choice of most late eighteenth century Irish militia officers.

In contrast to the longsword and the sabre, the beautifully balanced smallsword in the collection possesses a triangular blade, narrow at the point but lacks a cutting edge. More like a rapier, this light sword was carried by officers as part of their dress uniform. This was also the weapon of choice in duelling as a means of settling affairs of honour until pistols became more common. This was a progressive development as there was more likelihood of escaping injury in a one-shot pistol exchange than in a prolonged

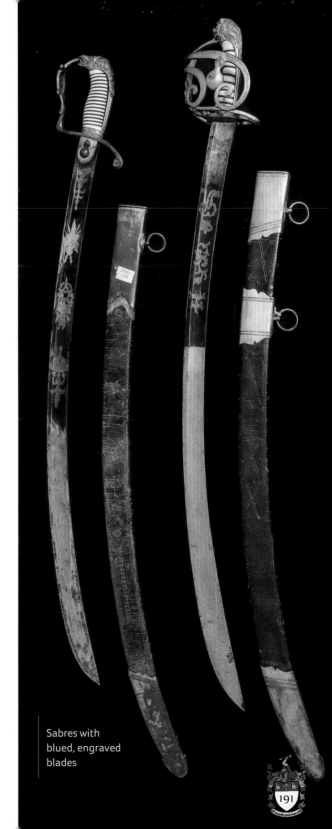

Sabres with blued, engraved blades

Sabre blade engraving
dated 1st May, 1804

Sabre and scabbard locket –
Archers, Dublin

with D-hilt
and blued,
aved blade

sword fight which ended in bloodshed. Although there was a growing popular concern about duelling in Ireland and elsewhere during the eighteenth century, it was not until the mid nineteen-hundreds that it finally became acceptable for gentlemen to settle their affairs by other means.

For thousands of years, the sword has been considered to be an honourable weapon in both eastern and western societies. The carrying of one was a sign of noble birth, elevated military rank or social status, a privilege bestowed by royalty, or earned the hard way – on the battlefield. The practice continues in today's modern armies with the bearing of a ceremonial sword by commissioned officers.

Sabre basket-hilt with lion pommel

Sabre pommel – detail

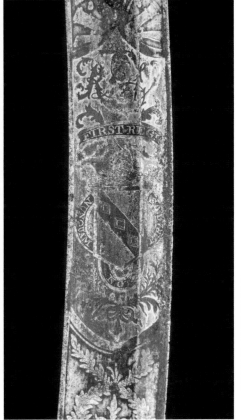

Basket-hilt detail – the angel harp

Sabre blade engraving with gilt

MILITIA BADGES AND MEDALS

The names of many volunteer, militia and yeomanry companies from the late eighteenth century are long forgotten. However, a unique collection of shoulder belt plates, medals and officers' gorgets – preserved in Ardgillan – serves as a reminder of that turbulent time when invasion by France was a real threat, and depots had been stripped of their soldiers for services overseas in the colonies. The belt plates could be attached to the crossed white shoulder belts by means of two prongs at the back, or to the soldier's shako, the tall headdress that was prevalent then. The officers' gorgets were worn round the neck, vestiges of the suit of armour once worn by knights.

While the belt plates and gorgets do not identify the names of their owners, the medals were presented to named individuals or units for excellence in the performance of specific military skills.

Of the hundreds of militias created in the last decade of the eighteenth century, few are remembered today but the belt badges in the collection in Ardgillan are a reminder of some of them, including the Carberry and Grand Canal Legion, the Dartrey Yeomanry, the Linen Hall Corps, the Oyster Haven Infantry and the Gorey Dismounted Infantry. Most of the belt badges portray the angel harp topped with a crown, surrounded by the name of the unit etched in a curved scroll. The Lawyers Artillery, the Volunteer unit that Daniel O'Connell joined, includes its motto *Fulmina Belli,* 'Thunderbolts of War', as does that of the Belfast Merchants Corps, *Quis Separabit,* 'Who Shall Separate (us)?'

Badge for Lawyers
Artillery

During that period, members of the Taylor family were active in the militias. When the Royal Meath Militia was raised in 1793, Thomas Taylor, 1st Earl of Bective from Headford House, Kells, was appointed as Colonel, as were successive Taylors in turn. The word 'Royal' was permitted in the title since Meath was once a kingship in its own right. The Royal Meath was stationed in Cork in 1796 and was present at Bantry Bay when the French attempted a landing there. In 1798 the unit was engaged in Wexford where it suffered heavy casualties.

Bective wasn't the only Headford Taylor active in 1798. Brigadier General Robert Taylor, a career soldier, served with the 5th Dragoons during the Insurrection. After the French Revolutionary Wars in Flanders and Germany, he had returned to Ireland with the rank of Colonel and was second-in-command to General Lake on 8 September 1798 at the Battle of Ballinamuck where the French surrendered and the Irish prisoners were slaughtered. Lake later commended Taylor in dispatches. He retired with the rank of General in 1819 and was made Hon Colonel of the 6th Dragoon Guards in 1821, the regiment that his nephew, Thomas Edward of Ardgillan, would later join.

When the General died in 1839, he left his house in Dowdstown, Navan, to Thomas Edward, who resigned his commission in the 6th Dragoon Guards two years later to enter politics. Although Thomas was an elected MP from 1841 until the end of his career, he also served as Hon Colonel of the Royal Meath Militia.

But the Taylors' connection with the militia was not just with the Royal Meath. By sheer coincidence, a framed commemorative list of Officers of the South Cork Regiment of Militia Light Infantry is preserved in Ardgillan Castle with Hayes Viscount Doneraile as Lieutenant Colonel. He was uncle to Marianne St Leger Taylor. Furthermore, her father, Richard St Leger, served as a Lieutenant in the South Cork Militia when it was formed in 1793.

Belfast
Merchants
Corps

Gen Robert Taylor
(1760 – 1839),
younger brother of the
1st Marquis of
Headford

Officer's Gorget
– Ballymahon
Volunteers

The Irish Militia, consisting of 38 regiments, was raised in 1793 to supplement the understrength regular army in the face of the threat from France. A few counties, including Cork, had two regiments, the North Cork and the South Cork. Hayes St Leger, 2nd Viscount Doneraile, uncle of Marianne (St Leger) Taylor, was appointed Lieutenant Colonel of the South Cork Light Infantry. Its Colonel was William Tonson, 2nd Baron Riversdale, of Rathcormuck, Co Cork. In 1881, the South Cork became the 3rd Battalion of the Royal Munster Fusiliers, joining two former Bengal Fusilier battalions transferred from the East India Company as well as the militias from Kerry and Limerick County. The illustration lists the names of all of the officers appointed upon its formation.

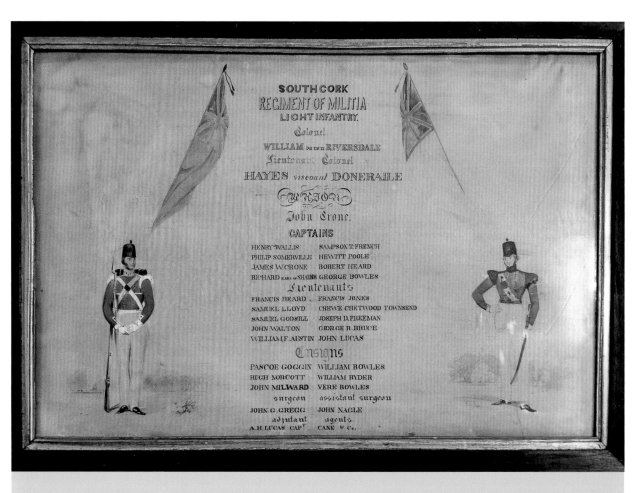

List of officers of the South Cork Infantry Militia – from an original print. They were nicknamed the 'Long Corks' due to their tall stature. Hayes St Leger 2nd Viscount was appointed Lieutenant Colonel upon its formation in 1793.

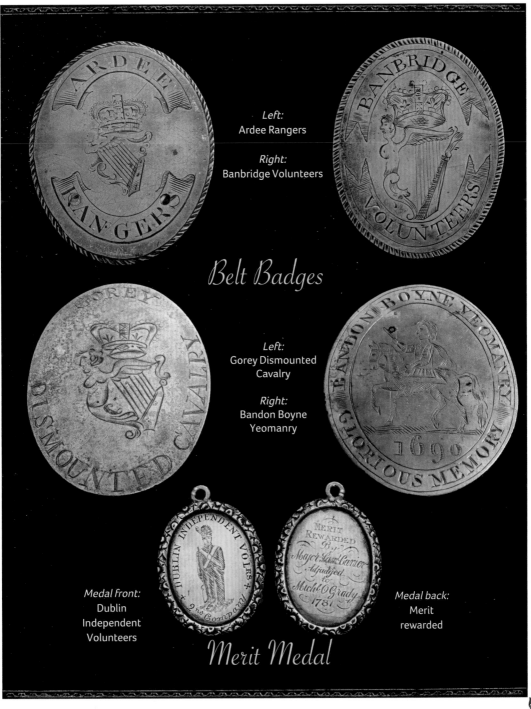

Left:
Ardee Rangers

Right:
Banbridge Volunteers

Belt Badges

Left:
Gorey Dismounted
Cavalry

Right:
Bandon Boyne
Yeomanry

Medal front:
Dublin
Independent
Volunteers

Medal back:
Merit
rewarded

Merit Medal

Militia Belt Plates – Ardgillan Collection

Ardee Rangers
Armagh Volunteer Yeomanry
Banbridge Volunteers
Bank Infantry *Pro Aris et Focis*
Belfast Merchants *Corps Quis Separabit*
Bellaghy Rangers
Brandon Boyne Yeomanry Glorious Memory 1690
British Band Major Sth. Cr. Rd. Iy.
Carberry and Grand Canal Legion 1796
Carton Cavalry 1796
Castlewellan Rangers
Cooleystown and Warrenstown Cavalry
Coolock Cavalry
County Dublin Light Dragoons
County Louth Rifles (Maltese Cross Design)
Dartrey Yeomanry
Dublin Volunteers
Dundalk Infantry
Dunemoney Volunteers
Gorey Dismounted Cavalry
Lawyers Artillery *Fulmina Belli*
Linen Hall Corps 1796
Loyal Donagore Infantry For Our King and Country
Loyal Limerick Rangers
Myroe infantry
Oyster Haven Infantry
Portaferry Yeomanry
Richhill Volunteers
Stewartstown Infantry

Gorgets

Ballyeaston Volunteers
Ballymahon Volunteers
Independent Dublin Volunteers

Other Plates

For Our King and Country 1796
Giants Causeway
King and Constitution
Rebels Lie Down
Tam Marti Quam Minerve 1797

Merit Medals

1. T. Leary Band Sgt. Kildare Militia for merit by Col. John Wolfe 17/06/1799
2. Pte. M. Garron Dunlavin Independent L.D. For horsemanship and lance drill 17/03/1799
3. Jas. Kelly Stokestown Light Horse for skill at arms by Maj. G Conry 1779
4. The Volunteers 2nd Batt. By Col. The Earl of Breadalbane - to suppress rebellion and to aid in repelling a French Force which had invaded the Kingdom 1798 AG&C
5. Patk. Whelan Longford Light Horse a Reward of Merit 18/10/1779
6. Fermoy Cavalry No 1 Merit 1799
7. Sergt. Maj. Keegan Carlow Legion as a token of regard for his many virtues and for the great sacrifices he has made on their behalf - by The Members of the Legion 1780 non nobis solum

8. Robert Corrigan Delvin Volunteers A Reward of Merit to a Voluntary Defender of his Country by Col. Thos. Smithe - Volunteers of Ireland in omnia paratus 1780
9. Major Sam Canier 2nd Company dublin Independent Volunteers Merit ... Adjudged to Michl. O Grady 1781

Part 6

THE HUTTON COLLECTION
OF
CARRIAGE DESIGNS

John Hutton & Sons Coach Builders

The extraordinary collection of carriage design plates on display in the Castle once belonged to John Hutton & Sons, premier coach-builders in Ireland since the company was set up in 1779. The first of the Hutton family, Thomas, arrived along with the Taylors during the time of Cromwell. As an army officer, he was given a grant of confiscated land in Ulster following completion of the Down Survey.

A century later, the descendants of Thomas Hutton had relocated to Dublin where they owned a tanyard and a boarding house. Robert and Sarah Hutton had sixteen children, nine of whom survived to adulthood. Their third child, John, was born in 1757. On his father's death in 1779, John went into business for himself, setting up as a coach builder in Great Britain Street, now Parnell Street, Dublin. Prior to this period it was unusual for a gentleman to travel by carriage but it had since become common practice, resulting in a rapidly expanding market for wheeled transport. Young men-about-town readily took to the curricle, a light, two-wheeled vehicle drawn by a pair of horses. It was later replaced by the similar cabriolet (from which the word 'cab' derives), although drawn by a single horse. The growing demand of an expanding social, commercial and professional class for light carriages resulted

Coach and carriage in front of Ardgillan, 2016

Hutton paper
borders for
carriage
decoration

in a corresponding increase in coach and wagon manufacturers in Dublin, among them Matthew Tone, father of Wolfe Tone. With the development of improved turnpike roads after 1729, the market for better carriages continued to expand and young Hutton seized the opportunity.

His immediate success was due in part to his employment of Rudolph Ackermann, originally from Stollberg, Saxony, as coach designer. Although always in great demand, Ackermann had time to plan a state coach for the Lord Lieutenant in Ireland in 1790, a state coach for George Washington and was involved in the decoration of the existing coach of the Lord Mayor of Dublin that was constructed in 1791 by William Whitton of Dominic Street. Ackermann also designed the funeral coach for Horatio Lord Nelson as well as the coach in which Pope Pius VII travelled to the self-coronation of Napoleon as Emperor. Most significantly though, he was the inventor of a moveable system for steering a carriage. Instead of a central 'turntable' where both wheels spun around a single pivot, Ackermann used a double pivot, one for each wheel, thereby eliminating the 'wheel slide' effect of old. His geometric knowledge, coupled with his flair for design, made him invaluable to his employer.

Hutton's big break had come in July 1788 when he was commissioned to build two mail coaches for the Irish Post Office, which had become an independent service in 1784. Three months later, the first new mail coach was delivered to great public fanfare. It was so successful that, from then on, all mail coaches were based on the Hutton design, a huge personal triumph that gave him a virtual monopoly on the mail coach contract.

By 1789, Hutton had moved from Great Britain Street to a new premises in Summer Hill (now Summerhill) then on the outskirts of the city. He was warned that the gentry would not travel that far for a coach but he confidently believed that if the coaches were good enough they would come – and they did. Lavish illustrations of the most comfortable, elegant and desirable two- and four-wheeled vehicles enticed even the most pampered of the gentry into the company showrooms where up to fifty completed carriages were on display. They could also view the fitting-out department where colour schemes could be discussed and the interior linings, silks and lace could be chosen. Hutton's insistence on staying at the forefront of design, using the best of materials and the latest machinery, ensured the continuing success of the company. By 1811 he had been joined by his two sons, Robert and Thomas.

When King George IV came to Ireland in 1821, Daniel O'Connell travelled to meet the King in a Hutton coach. He would later use another of the company's splendid carriages for his triumphant parades through Dublin. It was as a result of the King's visit that John Hutton was granted his first Royal Patent. With the passing of time, though, Thomas took over the company while Robert became a Liberal MP for Dublin, along with Daniel O'Connell.

Business fell in the late 1830s even though the company had been granted another Royal Patent, this time from the newly crowned Queen Victoria in 1837. A few years later, the Great Famine saw a collapse in orders. At this stage many potential purchasers were unable or unwilling to flaunt their wealth in the face of such horrendous suffering by the masses. Hutton stockpiled finished carriages and awaited the increase in demand for new vehicles using his own wealth to cushion his employees from hardship, but the market was slow to recover.

In 1851 when the Crystal Palace was erected to house the Great Exhibition in London, Hutton & Sons booked a stand in

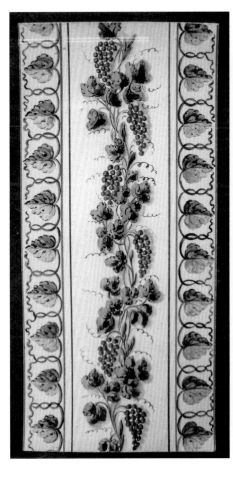

Above: Hutton paper borders for carriage decoration

Left: The Hutton Family crest

the opulent venue but the official catalogue of the Great Exhibition offers no information or detail regarding the vehicles that Thomas had on display. It merely categorises Hutton & Sons as Class V at Stand 884, presenting 'machines for direct use, including Carriages, Railway and Marine Mechanism'. But whatever Hutton had on show, Queen Victoria was impressed with what she saw. Two years after the London exhibition, the Great Industrial Exhibition was held in Dublin from 12 May to 31 October 1853. Sponsored by William Dargan, Ireland's greatest railway engineer, the exhibition was housed in a single, massive building on the lawns of Leinster House with a frontage opening onto Merrion Square. The National Art Gallery was later built on the same site with Dargan's statue erected in front of it. Along with a collection of art shown to the public for the first time was the 8th century Tara Brooch that had just been discovered in 1850. To encourage greater attendance from the provincial towns and cities, all of the railway companies offered reduced fares to Dublin.

Queen Victoria, accompanied by Prince Albert, attended the exhibition on 29 August and viewed admiringly the exquisite coach that Hutton had on display on Stand 462. Described in the catalogue as 'a dress coach, fully appointed for town use, built for Her Majesty, the Queen', its construction marked the high point of Hutton's career. Known ever since as the Irish State Coach, it became the Queen's state carriage of choice instead of the Gold State Coach following the death of Prince Albert in 1861. This coach is still in use by the reigning monarch for the formal opening of each new legislative session of Parliament.

1853 Great Industrial Exhibition Catalogue entry for Hutton at stands numbered 462/3/4

> screw by which the balance can be adjusted for or without a driver.
>
> **462** HUTTON, J. & SONS, Summerhill, Dublin, Manu.—A dress coach, fully appointed for town use, built for Her Majesty the Queen.
>
> **463** A chariot; and a barouche, on C and under springs.
>
> **464** An outside car with lancewood and whalebone shafts.
>
> **465** KILLINGER, C. 20 Westland Row, Dublin, Des. and Manu.—Killinger's Irish jaunting car (regi-

But if 1853 was the year of Thomas Hutton's greatest coach-building triumph, it also brought great personal tragedy. His young daughter, Annie, had fallen in love with Thomas Davis, writer, politician and chief organiser of the Young Ireland movement. Together with Charles Gavin Duffy and John Blake Dillon, Davis had founded The Nation, a nationalist weekly newspaper that first appeared on 15 October 1842. Davis first met Annie at Elm Park, her father's country house on Goose Green Road, now Grace Park Road, which the Dublin *Penny Journal* of March 1834 describes as being free of 'the suffocation or the annoyance occasioned by the driving of the jaunting cars, jingles, etc. on the opposite side of the city – the danger of being overrun by a drunken jarvey from Baggot Street'. It was in these elegant surroundings that they fell in love at first sight, as Annie later recorded. Thomas Davis was twenty-nine

Thomas Davis
(1814 - 1845)

years old at the time and she was eighteen. The progress of their relationship was not smooth at first largely due to parental disapproval. Because the young writer had forsaken a career as a barrister to pursue his nationalist, political aims, Hutton was so unimpressed that he forced a separation by sending his daughter abroad on a number of occasions. But young love won through in the end and consent was granted to an engagement in July 1845. However, the lovers were never to be united as Thomas Davis died of scarlet fever shortly afterwards on 16 September 1845, at the age of thirty-one. The author of 'The West's Awake', 'A Nation Once Again' and 'Annie's Song' would write no more. Annie Hutton never recovered from the shock of this loss. Tragically, and in a cruel twist of fate, she died almost eight years later on 7 June 1853, just three months before the magnificent coach her father had built for the Queen met with Royal Approval. An original graphite sketch of Annie Hutton, signed by the artist, Frederick

Sketch of Annie Hutton who died in 1853 in her twenty-seventh year.

William Burton, hangs in the Castle.

Despite this, the Hutton firm continued to thrive and constructed all types of carriages to the highest standard of craftsmanship until the end of the nineteenth century. By then the motor car had begun to make an appearance and coach-building was forced to take a new direction. Ahead of the field as usual, Hutton invited John Fallon Colohan, credited with being the first person to drive a car in Ireland, a Daimler, to join the Board of Directors of the company.

By the early 1900s, Hutton & Sons were the leading importers of cars in the country, opening new showrooms on Dawson Street, Dublin. They concentrated on selling to wealthy clients who, being used to high-quality coach interiors, insisted that the body of the motor car should match the excellence of the engine and chassis. The company became renowned for the exquisite Daimler models that emerged from their workshops. However, the unwise decision to stay with exclusive models for the wealthy purchaser while rejecting the offer of the agency for Ford, would in time lead to the demise of the firm. Business gradually lapsed and Hutton & Sons eventually closed their doors in 1925. The manufacturing premises were purchased by the Dublin United Tramway Company. The site is now the Summerhill depot of Dublin Bus.

Along with Rudolph Ackermann's carriage designs, five hardback journals in which the company's artists sketched the armorial arms of their many clients (from 1807 until 1895) are preserved in the Castle. The list of names within them forms a veritable who's who of political, ecclesiastical, military, professional and social life of the nineteenth century. Most pages in the journals are quartered, with a rough sketch of an individual's coat of arms in each quadrant but the more significant clients such as members of the aristocracy and landed gentry, archbishops, bishops and several lord mayors, occupy a full page with a detailed rendering of their family's crest and motto. Noted also are the types of vehicle that clients

Cartoon Napoleon from Hutton's journal

A Curricle with the Patent Security Reins.
Invented by P.I. Meyer Jun.r 91 G.t Portland Street.
London Published April 2 1802 by R. Ackermann N.o 101 Strand and Bey gang Leip 219.

Left:
Ackerman's 1802 design for a curricle

More sketches from Hutton's journal

ordered, the most common being the landau, brougham, wagonette, clarence, phaeton and stanhope.

A few of the most significant heraldic sketches from the journals are those of the Marquis of Wellesley, brother of the Duke of Wellington in 1822, Daniel O'Connell in 1825 and 'Her Majesty the Queen' (Queen Victoria's Irish State Coach) in 1853. Amusingly, the sketch artists also had time to indulge in the drawing of cartoon-like caricatures.

Sketches of the heraldic emblem of the

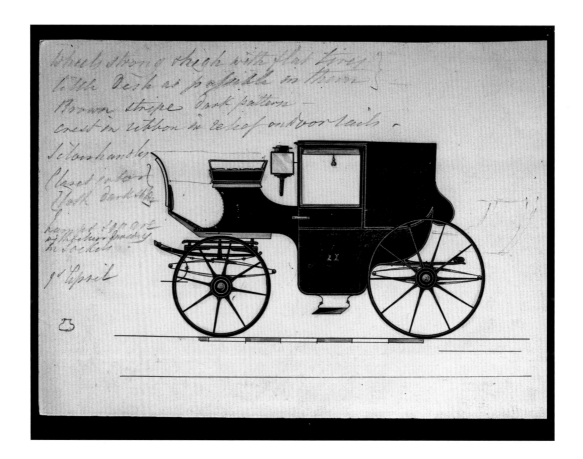

Another Hutton carriage design with contemporary notes

Taylors – 'on a wreath, the naked arm embowed, with an arrow proper' – appears several times in the Hutton journals. First to appear was General Robert Taylor of Dowdstown who purchased a carriage in 1812 while the Headford branch of the family were Hutton clients throughout the nineteenth century. Clotworthy Taylor, who changed his name to Rowley on getting married, incorporated the family arms into those of Langford and Rowley and had it emblazoned on the coach he ordered in January 1826. And, yes, the Taylors of Ardgillan also attended the Summerhill premises of Hutton & Sons as clients. When the Rev Edward died in 1852, he left a carriage of her choice from the coach house to Marianne along with two black horses. Perhaps it was the Hutton that she selected.

Coach in front of
Ardgillan

Arms: Her Majesty The Queen

Arms: Marquis Wellesley (Duke of Wellington's brother)

Arms – Daniel O'Connell

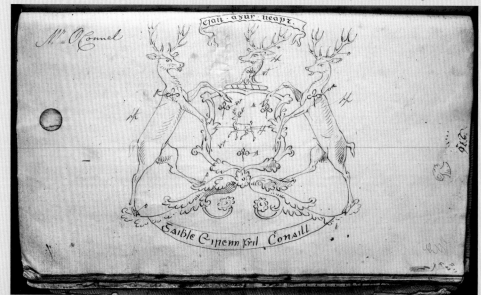

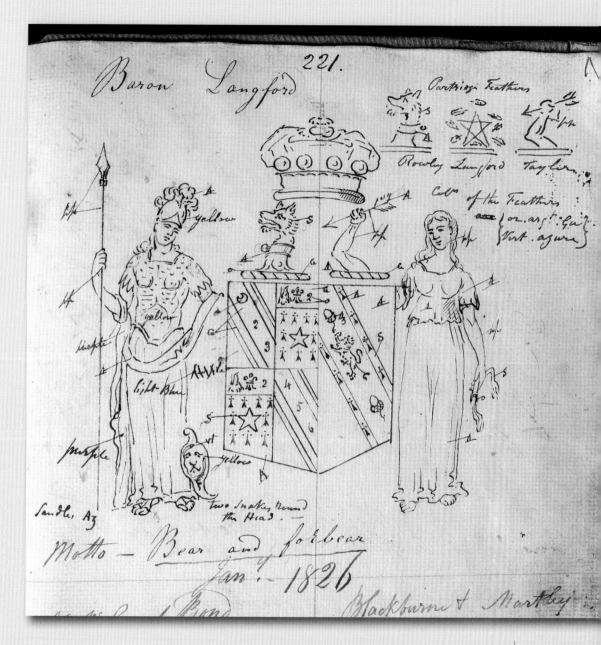

Coat of arms of Baron Langford (Taylor) - note the Taylor arms (the naked arm clutching an arrow) on the top right, and under the crown. The family crests of Rowley, Langford and Taylor are incorporated into this 1826 design.

The Hutton Family

Top:
The Hutton family photographed in April 1910

Right:
Names of those included in the photograph

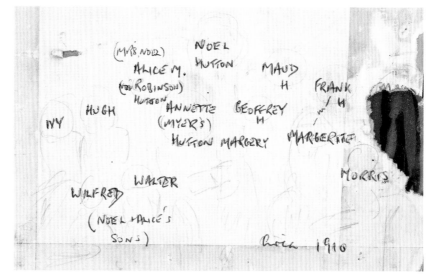

On Display in The Tea Room

With so much to absorb on a visit to Ardgillan Castle and its beautiful grounds, it is worth taking a few minutes in the Tea Rooms overlooking the South Lawn and the Yew Walk to relax and let it all sink in. But even here there is much to be seen.

Tea Rooms
at Ardgillan

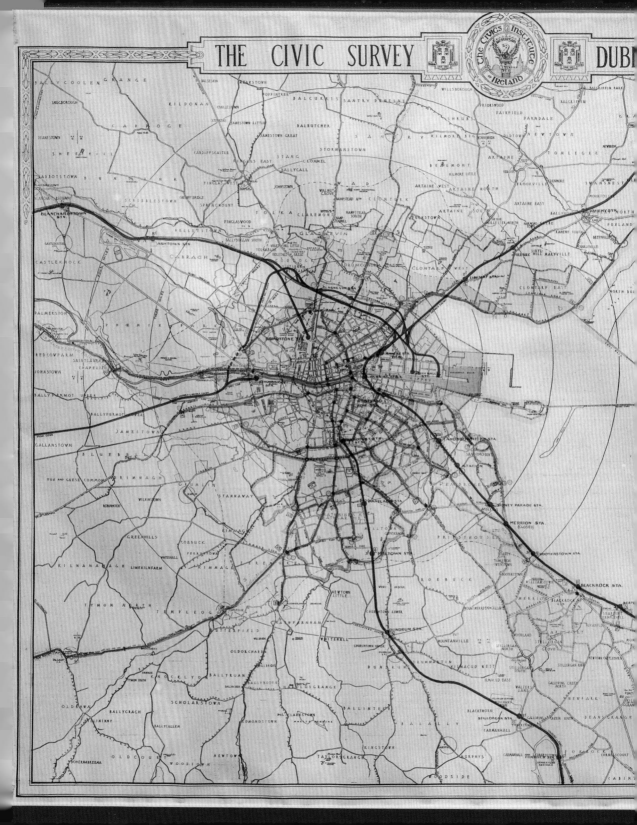

DVBLIN BAY

INDEX
TRAFFIC

TRAMWAY SYSTEM
WITH FARE STAGE

TIME ZONES
FROM NELSON PILLAR

1º FARE BOUNDARY
DUBLIN

RAILWAY LINES & TIME
FROM DUBLIN STATIONS

MOTOR BUS ROUTES

POINTS OF CONGESTION
VEHICULAR TRAFFIC
CANALS & LOCKS

In the first room a series of fascinating framed maps dated 1925 hang on the walls. They were published as part of the Civic Survey of Dublin and Environs Volume 2 in the series entitled 'Dublin of the Future' – Volume 1 consisted of the prize design of the 1916 Town Planning Competition. The maps show that Dublin then was still largely confined within the boundaries of the Grand and Royal Canals as well as by the two circular roads. Almost unrecognisable today, the city was on the cusp of the urban sprawl that would absorb so many of its outlying villages in the following decades. This set of maps, each depicting a different aspect of civic information, was presented to Ardgillan Castle by Lady Dunsany of Dunsany Castle, County Meath, in May 1995.

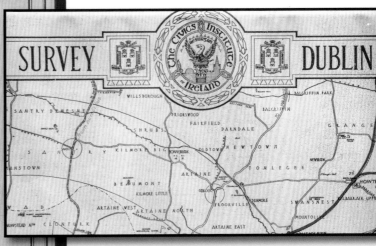

Dublin City North prior to development

One of the Civic Survey maps from 1925.

In the other room, the resplendent mirror with the beautifully carved frame is the original that once hung over the fireplace in the Dining Parlour, a last vestige of the time that the Taylors were in residence here.

Finally, on leaving the Castle grounds at the top of the hill, take a moment at the middle gates to savour anew the magnificence of Ardgillan's dramatic setting in the landscape with the tossing sea and the distant mountains as backdrop. It is certainly an image that endures.

This is the original mirror that once hung over the fireplace in the Dining Parlour

Main image (below centre): Capt Edward Richard Taylor (1863–1938), Grenadier Guards. Known within the family as Uncle Ned, he was the last resident Taylor to be born in Ardgillan Castle.

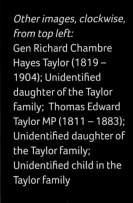

Other images, clockwise, from top left:
Gen Richard Chambre Hayes Taylor (1819 – 1904); Unidentified daughter of the Taylor family; Thomas Edward Taylor MP (1811 – 1883); Unidentified daughter of the Taylor family; Unidentified child in the Taylor family

The Taylor Family

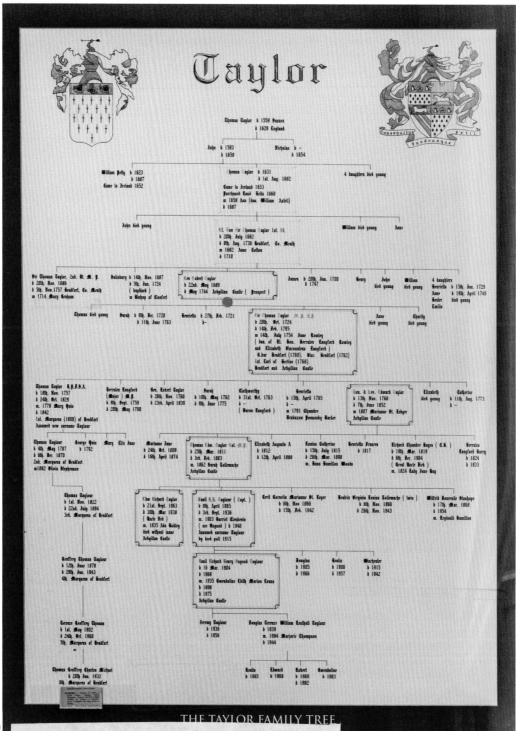

Taylor

THE TAYLOR FAMILY TREE

EPILOGUE

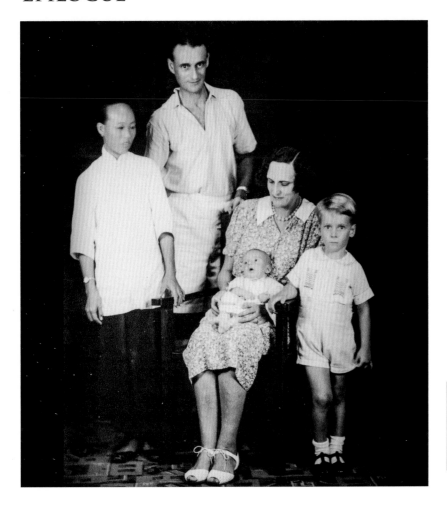

Richard and Gwen Taylour, with their children, Terence and Jeremy (standing), and their *amah*

TERENCE AND LINDY TAYLOUR

Terence Taylour (it was Terence's grandfather, Basil, who had the 'u' added to his surname) was born in Singapore and was brought to Ireland as an infant when his father inherited Ardgillan in 1938. He spent all of his childhood and early adult years there until his father finally had to sell the estate in 1962 due to rising costs. In January 1967, Terence and his wife

Above: Terence Taylour

Left: Family photo of Gwendoline Taylour's marriage to Michael Cotter. Back row L-R: Zack, Jenny and Chloe Taylour. Front row L-R: Kenlis, Terence and Gwen Taylour, Michael Cotter and Lindy Taylour. *Elisha Clarke Photography.*

Lindy moved to South Africa where they lived for seventeen years. At first, they ran a haulage business but, in a change of direction, they farmed in the very South of the Cape near Bredasdorp for the last six years before returning to Ireland in 1984. Since then, they have resided in their present home in the midlands. However, Terence and Lindy still retain a strong attachment to Ardgillan and take a keen interest in its preservation.

On a number of occasions, they have returned to their ancestral home for various occasions both cultural and commemorative. However, the most significant event they attended was the marriage of their daughter Gwendoline to Michael Cotter on 3 October 2015. The ceremony was held in the same Drawing Room that had witnessed so many happy family occasions over a period of two hundred years. What more fitting place could they have chosen?

Rose Garden

Select Bibliography

Adkins, Roy & Lesley. (2014) *Eavesdropping on Jane Austen's England,* Abacus (London)

Allen, Charles. (1975) *Plain tales from the Raj* Abacus (London)

Ardgillan Castle and The Taylor Family, (1995) Ardgillan Castle

Arthur, Max. (2006) *Lost Voices of the Edwardians* Harper Perennial (London)

Cobbe, Frances Power (1894) *Life of Frances Power Cobbe as Told by Herself* Houghton Mifflin & Co (Boston and New York)

Collins, Sinéad. (2005) *Balrothery Poor Law Union, County Dublin, 1839 – 1851,* Maynooth Studies in Local History: No 59 Dublin

Flanders, Judith. (2012) *The Victorian City, Everyday Life in Dickens' London* Atlantic Books (London)

Grimes, Brendan. (2016) "Skerries Building Company" in *Time & Tide 10* Skerries Historical Society

MacMillan, Margaret. (1988) *Women of the Raj* Thames & Hudson (London)

Musson, Jeremy. (2010) *Up and Down Stairs* John Murray (London)

Geraghty, P.J. (2013) "The Dublin and Drogheda Railway, the First Great Irish Speculation" *Dublin Historical Record,* Vol. 66, No.1/2 (Spring /Autumn 2013)

Prendergast F. (1992) "The Down Survey of Ireland, An Appreciation of Sir William Petty and Thomas Taylor", Commissioned by the Management Committee, Ardgillan Castle 1992.

Prendergast F. (1997) "The Down Survey of Ireland" *Survey Ireland*, 14

D'Alton, John. (1844) *Introductory Memoir of the Dublin and Drogheda Railway*

MacKenzie, T A, Ewart, J S & Findlay, C. (1887) *Historical Records of the 79th Queen's Own Cameron Highlanders* (London)

Many of the quotations selected for this book were transcribed from the family letters and diaries by Geraldine McQuillan.

The author gratefully acknowledges the kind permission granted by Terence and Lindy Taylour to reproduce extracts from their family letters, documents and diaries.

Acknowledgments

I would like to thank Paul Reid, CEO of Fingal County Council; in particular, special thanks must go to Coilín O'Reilly and Kevin Halpenny FCC, and to Gerry Clabby; to Mary Godwin FCC and to the Board of Directors of Ardgillan Castle. My thanks also to David and Emily Diebold of the *Skerries News* for publishing the original series of articles, *Hidden Gems of Ardgillan Castle*; and to their readers whose generous feedback encouraged the idea for this publication. A special word of acknowledgement is due to Michael Lynch (Senior Parks Superintendent, FCC, Retired) for the central role he took in ensuring that Ardgillan Castle and Demesne would be preserved for future generations and to William Kearney who was responsible for many of the collections of artefacts that are featured here. Thanks also to Tom Reilly, Manager of Ardgillan Castle, and to Danielle Wilson-Higgins, former Heritage Officer, for their unfailing enthusiasm and support. Grateful appreciation is also due to Geraldine McQuillan who transcribed many of the Taylor family letters and journals that are quoted in this text. And a special word of thanks must go to Sinéad Mallee, Graphic Designer, not only for her creative flair and meticulous eye for detail but also her endless patience in dealing with our many amendments and revisions.

The warmth and generosity of Lindy and Terence Taylour is especially appreciated. They kindly gave us full access to their family archive during the researching and photographing of original material for this book.

Aidan J Herron: I wish to thank my family for their unfailing belief in me; Amy, my daughter, who has edited the book; her professionalism and expertise have kept me on the straight and narrow during the writing process; my son, Brian, who always urges me to push the boundaries of what is possible; and Anne Marie, my wife, who has patiently lived with the book from the very beginning and whose critical input has been inestimable throughout.

Eamon O'Daly: I wish to gratefully acknowledge the support, assistance and in particular the patience of my wife Christine and our daughter Maureen in the production of this book. Their help and encouragement have been invaluable.

The Taylor family motto and coat of arms – detail

This recently rediscovered carafe that belonged to the Taylor family is now on display in the Castle

holiday for all Poblanos – a lot of res
have to close their doors. As it is, the
(Cinco de Mayo), half the cooks in Am
that in mind.

Fifteen or twenty years ago, we'd ha
cheap labor. You know, the old 'wetb
unskilled immigrant labor, toiling away f
menial jobs, paid cash under the table at mi
Things have changed somewhat for the better   nave yet
to see as many mestizo-looking chefs with Spanish-sounding last
names running high-end French kitchens as we should, all those
dishwashers and porters didn't simply settle for spending the rest
of their lives cleaning up after the rest of us. They watched, they
learned, they trained on *garde-manger* and grill and prep and
sauté – usually on their own time – and when some flighty white
kid decided he wanted the winter off to go skiing in Colorado,
they were ready to step in. When the French sous-chef appeared
to be unable to work without a long, lingering two-hour lunch
with his socialist comrades in the front of the house and the chef
had finally had enough of his clock-punching, lazy prima donna
act, the Poblanos were ready. Now, many areas of Puebla are
like a talent pool of free-agent or draft picks in professional
sports – pursued, protected, sought after by chefs who'd rather
snip off a pinkie finger than lose them to the other team. They've
been trained by a procession of French, American, and Italian
chefs – most of whom come and go, turning over quickly, but
who each leave behind a little knowledge, a new technique, a few
more nuggets of information, some new ideas. So now, ask
Carlos to do something with the soft-shell crabs and with that
old asparagus and you can have a reasonable expectation that he
will whip right into a salad of soft-shell crabs with asparagus and
citrus vinaigrette in classic French nouvelle style. Stuck for a
monkfish special or a soup? Don't worry, Carlos is all over it,
remembering some long-gone French chef's preparation. (Old
Henri-Pierre may have been a lazy Communist ratbag, but he
could cook like an angel.) A lot of times, I'll walk into an
unfamiliar kitchen to say hello to the cooks – or to thank the chef

and I'll see the familiar posse of white-clad
istening to the Spanish station down by the dish-
area, and of course I'll say hello, then casually inquire
re, exactly, they hail from.

'¿ Poblanos?' I'll ask, pretty sure of the answer.

'¡ Viva la rasa!' will come the reply.

My cooks are almost all from Puebla, and not just from
Puebla but from the same small area around the towns of Izúcar
de Matamoros, Atlixco, and Tlapanala, situated downwind
from the famous volcanoes of *Under the Volcano* fame. If there's
an epicenter of fine French cooking, it appears to be Tlapanala, a
sleepy little village surrounded by sugarcane fields and mango
trees, about three miles outside of Izúcar. That's where my sous-
chef, Edilberto Perez, was born. It's where Isidoro, my veteran
grill man, hails from, and Antonio, my roundsman, and other
cooks, runners, prep cooks, and dishwashers, past, present, and
future. Their families still live there and they visit whenever
possible. Over the years, I've heard a lot about the town, about
Eddie's house, his ranch, about his uncle, the *heladero*, who
makes ice cream the old-fashioned way, about Antonio's family,
who live next door, about my prep cook Bautista's former street
gang, the terrifying Vatos Locos, whose distinctive tag I often
find scrawled on locker room walls, and whose hand signs (a 'V'
and an 'L', signified by turning the right hand and making a sort
of open-thumbed peace sign) I recognize. I heard about my prep
guy Miguel's family's *pulquería*, Isidoro's family's candy store. I
heard a lot about the joys of *barbacoa* (Mexican-style barbecue),
mole, *pulque*: I wanted to go. I wanted to go very badly. I told
my cooks how I'd visit their parents and tell them all what
desgraciados their sons have become, now that they're living
that *vida loca* in New York. So, when I first started putting
together my '*Borrachón* Abroad' pitch for my publisher, I knew
one of the places I absolutely had to go. I huddled with my sous-
chef and said, 'Eddie, I want to visit your town. I want you to go
with me, to show me your town. I want to meet everybody's
families. I want your mom to cook for me, if she's willing. I want
to drink *pulque* and *mezcal* and eat *menudo* and *pozole* and real

mole poblano – like from Puebla – and *barbacoa* like you been tellin' me about all these years. I want to wear a cool-looking cowboy hat, ride a horse, find out where that serial killer Bautista really comes from. I want to go down there with you and have a really good time. We'll get the TV people to pay for it.'

'Let me call to my wife,' said Eddie, inspired. 'I send her down first to making the preparations.'

Which is how it happened that I found myself sitting by the *mercado* in the small central square of Tlapanala on a languid late afternoon, the sun slowly setting, watching as the women and children of the village lined up at the telephone kiosk, waiting to receive prearranged calls from kitchens in New York and apartments in Queens.

The streets were quiet and dusty, kids kicking around old soccer balls, shooting hoops in the court by the *mercado*, where old women sold chilis, squashes, *chayote*, yucca, and vegetables. Occasionally, an old man passed by, driving a few head of cattle, a herd of goats, a few donkeys down Tlapanala's tidy streets. A stray dog wandered over to see if I had any food. Young mothers sat with their babies. Children, still in their school uniforms, played on the back steps of the kiosk, the afternoon's silence broken now and again by the singsong music from a propane truck, playing along to the unforgettable chant of '*Gaaazzz! GaaaaAAAaazz!*' and announcements over a loudspeaker describing the products on sale at the *mercado*. At four o' clock, the peal of the bread alarm informed residents that fresh bread, hot out of the oven, was now available at the bakery.

A few yards behind me were the railway tracks. The train to Tijuana and beyond. Nueva York. The road out, the starting point, where generations of Tlapanala's young men began their long, hard climb out of poverty to become cooks in faraway America.

There were few young men left in the village. I saw only women, children, and much older men. In Tlapanala, you can tell the homes of families with a son or a father standing behind a stove in New York: They're the houses with the satellite dishes on the roofs and metal rebars still protruding from the top of new additions and annexes (instead of capping or removing the extra lengths, they keep them sticking up out of the concrete; should money come, they can more easily add a second floor). I sat on my bench, contentedly watching and listening, an object of curiosity, a lone *gabacho* drinking *cerveza* Modelo, grinning for no apparent reason. Looking down the street, I spied my sous-chef taking an evening stroll with his wife, new baby propped on his arm, young daughter trailing behind, holding her daddy's other hand. Thirteen years ago, Eddie took that train behind me to Tijuana, swam and waded across the border, then hopped a train to New York. He slept on the subway for his first few weeks, slept on the floors of friends' apartments when he could, until he got a job as a night porter. Now he's a sous-chef, a title inadequate to describe his importance. He's opened and worked at every restaurant in the company – Washington, D.C., Miami, Le Marais – and, of course, for me – at the mothership in New York. Long before I arrived on the scene, he'd been the go-to guy for every chef who walked in the door. Now he's a fully documented permanent resident (and soon-to-be citizen) of the United States of America, and a newly enrolled student at the French Culinary Institute, where he hobnobs with culinary luminaries like Jacques Pépin and André Soltner. (He's learning where all that French food he's been making brilliantly for years really comes from – and why. Eddie knows how to make a *gastrite*, he just didn't know what to call it. I wish I could watch him in class, when they show him glaçage or how to make a liaison, or explain the principles of déglacer. He'll say, 'Oh, that! No problem. Same like for the ravioli at Les Halles.') Eddie rents an apartment in Park Slope, owns both a house and a small ranch in his home town of Tlapanala – and considerable livestock. He's an employer in Mexico, a role model and leader in New York. And he's my friend. I wish I could take even the slightest credit for the Edilberto Perez story. But I can't. He did it all. Watching him walk the streets of the place he was born, though, I was filled with pride just for knowing him, and for being lucky enough to have worked with him. Before visiting

Eddie, however, I'd had a grim duty to perform. Yet another forced march to television entertainment. 'Tony . . . Tony . . . listen. It's a food show. It's going on the Food Network. We need some variety! We can't just show you hanging around in Puebla, getting drunk with your sous-chef! Don't worry! We're on it. We've got some really special ideas.'

That's why I went first to the state of Oaxaca. So I could be force-fed iguana.

Reasons Why You Don't Want to Be on Television: Number Four in a Series

I was in Puerto Angel, a fishing village on the Pacific coast, staying at a remote, kooky, overgrown retreat built around a ravine on the slopes of a mountain overlooking the sea. The only other residents were Martin, my driver; two shooters; a burned-out geriatric hippie known as 'Quiet Dave,' who spoke in a spacey whisper; the proprietor and his wife and assistants; and a former CIA chief of base for Nha Trang during the Vietnam War and his Chinese girlfriend. As I'd just been to Nha Trang, we had a lot to talk about.

Here's what I hoped for in Puerto Angel: a neglected stretch of beach, a near-empty, far from luxurious hotel, a few straggling eccentrics. Down the road a ways was the resort town of Zipolite, a sort of Last Stop for well-toasted surfers, backpackers, beach bums, fugitive dope pilots from the seventies, the itinerant jewelry/handicraft set. It's the sort of place you wake up in – after dropping one hit of acid too many at your 112th Grateful Dead concert – not having any idea how you got there, and far from caring.

We shot a whole-roasted-snapper scene in Zipolite, watched the fishing boats come in at Puerto Angel, the whole town running to meet them as they skipped full throttle through the waves and onto the beach, hulls loaded with fresh tuna. We drove to Huatulco, about twenty miles away, with the idea of doing some snorkel fishing. It was one of those ludicrous, pointless exercises in television artifice so beloved by people who look at life largely through a lens: 'Get some cool underwater shots of Tony! We can have him fish with a local! Cut to medium shots of Tony, looking hunky in a Speedo, in chef mode, grillin' and chillin' on the beach, sun setting dramatically in the background!'

Video gold.

After two hours of useless and unproductive floundering in the sea, the underwater camera rig having filled up with water – after about six miles of footage of my concave chest wheezing on the beach while Leo, our hired fishing guide, continued, without success, to catch even a stunt fish for a faked shot – we gave up. Matthew settled for frozen fish at a nearby tourist strip, and the always popular 'Tony gets drunk on local beverage, then sits in sullen silence, hating himself and everybody to do with this production scene.'

I never wanted to eat iguana. 'Yes you do,' insisted the TV masterminds. I had no particular curiosity about iguana. I knew from talking to my cooks that people eat iguana when they can afford nothing else. It's cheap and plentiful. Even Leo, talking about how he went out a few times a week with his dog to sniff out iguana, admitted he did it only because he had no money for real food. I had no expectation that a big lizard would taste good – and I was not anxious to have one killed so I could find out for sure. But Matthew seemed to feel that the 'iguana scene' would be must-see TV, a guaranteed cable Ace for Best Reptile Scene in a Continuing Cable Series.

Now, maybe somewhere they're making delicious marinated, then barbecued iguana with crispy skin and well-grilled but tender meat. Maybe if you sear it and then braise it long enough and infuse it with enough other flavors, it might make a meal interesting to adventurous palates. Maybe. I didn't see it.

The owner of our hotel was dispatched to wrangle up a nice plump example of iguanadom at its very best. But after three or four hours of investigation, he came up as empty as Leo's fishing line. Instead, he decided to sacrifice the poor hotel mascot, a ten-year-old wrinkly, leathery, liver-spotted thing – he looked paralytic – with a bifurcated tail and a troublingly agreeable nature. I took one look at the creature and tried very hard to weasel out of the meal.

'Matthew! Jesus Christ, man! He's a pet, for fuck's sake! Let the thing live! How good can he be? Just look at him!'

The hotel proprietor was no help. Stroking the iguana's belly, he insisted, 'Look! He is ready. He wants to die.' I was appalled.

What arrived later were iguana tamales: the hotel pet, boiled, sectioned, then simply wrapped in corn husk with *masa* and sauce. Next to *natto*, it was maybe the worst thing I'd ever had between my teeth. The iguana was undercooked. When I unwrapped my tamale, I found that I had been honored with the head and a forearm – still on the bone. The texture was like chewing on GI Joe – if Joe had been resting at the bottom of a long-neglected turtle tank. There was almost no meat to speak of, just tough, rubbery skin, knobby, slimy little bones. When I managed now and again actually to winnow out a little meat from between bones and skin, I was sorry I had. It was dark, oily, and viscous, with the pungent aroma of steamed salamander.

In the thankfully brief scene you see in the edited version, I look like I'm eating at gunpoint.

I hit the city of Oaxaca next, a place justifiably famous for its food. It's a beautiful town: lovely hacienda-style hotels, exquisite Spanish churches and cathedrals, a picturesque *zócalo* where you can sit at a café table and watch the world go by, a fabulous *mercado*, nice people. It is also, unfortunately, a magnet for the world's ugliest tourists. Herds of squinting, sun-blotched fanny packers in black socks and sandals shuffled by, snapping pictures. Extravagantly pierced backpackers, filthy from the road, sat in the park, ineptly strumming old Dylan tunes on clapped-out guitars. Thick-ankled German women looking for love, and hordes of doddering tour groupers and serial shoppers, fanned out to buy the inevitable tonnage of papier-mâché figurines, hammered tin, cheap silver, ponchos, serapes, funny hats, T-shirts, and pottery. College kids, fresh from the donkey show in Tijuana, sulked noisily on benches, broke and frustrated, waiting for a Western Union money order from mom and dad. But as it got late and the tourists drifted off and the locals began showing up in clean white guayaberas and frilly dresses, filling the café tables around us, Martin, my driver, and I started to enjoy ourselves.

Mezcal was served like tequila, in shot glasses, accompanied by chasers of *sangrita*, a spicy tomato juice concoction. With the de rigueur wedge of lime came a mix of salt and dried, powdered, chili-roasted maguey worms – an unexpectedly delicious accompaniment. Martin and I sat in the café, nibbling on *tortas* (sandwiches) of fresh cheese and ham, drinking beer and *mezcal*, a mariachi band strolling from table to table. Behind us, a man in his fifties, with a face scarred by a youthful bout with smallpox and the fists and brows of a former pugilist, sat alone at his table, drinking Modelo Negro, his straight black hair plastered down over his forehead, staring into space with a look of infinite sadness. After a long while sitting in silence with the same brooding expression, he motioned the mariachis over to his table, handed them a few pesos, and made a mumbled request. They played beautifully, and when they were done with the song, the man, though outwardly unmoved, handed them more pesos and asked for another. Again, his demeanor remained impassive as he monopolized the six-piece band.

Then suddenly, mournfully, without raising his eyes from the table, he began to sing. Still seated, looking at no one else, he sang of love and loss and broken hearts, his voice rich, deep, and beautifully modulated. Every customer in the café listened with rapt attention. More pesos, another song. The sad-faced man in a guayabera shirt, eyes almost shut now, sang and sang, the crowd cheering wildly after each song ended. He seemed oblivious to their roars of approval, focused through slit eyes on some point far away – or deep inside his battered skull – his voice carrying over the now-empty *mercado* and into the night.

I ate well in Oaxaca. I had chocolate *atole*, a thick hot chocolate beverage with the texture of Cream of Wheat, made from local chocolate, cinnamon, and cornmeal. I tried an ice cream made with *leche quemada* (burned milk), which is surprisingly delicious. I sampled the mysteries of the seven *moles*, watched *queso fresco* being made – a fresh farmer cheese – saw how one batch can be taken along to make a drier, aged variety, and a soft-curd version. At the *mercado*, I bought *morcilla* and chorizo sausages from one of the butchers, had them grilled with the garnishes and tortillas available from the many 'make your own' taco stands. I had a marvelous *menudo*, a spicy tripe and offal soup/stew, returning later to try *pozole*, a similar dish with chick peas. Outside the *mercado*, I found a busy taco stand, packed with Oaxaqueños sitting on benches. A cook and an assistant were hard at work hacking up a freshly cooked pig's head, rolling up still-warm portions of tender pork in corn tortillas, then drizzling them with *salsa verde*.

I squeezed in between some locals and ordered a few. Best tacos ever. I could have sat there forever under a naked light-bulb, surrounded by enthusiastically eating Mexicans and their children. But there were people waiting for a spot. I returned the next night, and the next.

Off a dirt road in the farmland around Oaxaca de Juárez, the state's capital, Dominga made me tamales. She cooked in a small outdoor kitchen: a charcoal fire, clay saucepan, steamer, a *comal* for toasting, a mortar and pestle, and a stone rolling pin. Chickens and roosters wandered around the dusty back lot and small garden, near the pigpens.

We were going to the *molino*, the community mill, where for centuries Mexicans have gone, often every day, to grind their dried corn for *masa*, their dried chilis for *mole*, and their chocolate and their coffee beans on stone wheels. Dominga was a short, wide woman with mestizo features and strong arms and hands, which had seen a lot of work over the years. The corn soaking in a plastic bucket in one hand, a tub of chilis and garlic in another, she walked the few blocks in the hot sun to a small shed with a tin roof, where a line of women in similar frilled dresses and aprons waited for one of the two generator-powered machines to become available. Inside, the *molina*'s owner carefully fed handfuls of chilis into one machine and corn into the other, a rich, smooth paste issuing from both. *Mole, masa, atole, café* – made fresh every day by mom.

You may think you've tried Mexican food. Unless you've been to Mexico and eaten in a home, you haven't. Mexican food is not that sour two-day-old sludge foaming and fermenting in the center of your table next to a few stale corn chips, a little limp cilantro turning to slime among the long-gone onions. It is not graying or packaged guacamole, whipped in the food processor until it achieves the consistency of baby food. It is not heaped with cheddar and Monterey Jack cheese (you won't see any of that in Mexico) and served with allegedly refried beans. In Mexico, everything is fresh. Dominga owns no Cuisinart. She doesn't have a freezer. Her salsas do not arrive in jars, and her recipes are not faxed from Central, portion-controlled for multi-unit use. Mexican food is not particularly hot and spicy. It is not soggy, frozen chimichangas, already haemorrhaging ingredients into the deep-fat fryer. It is not the dull, monochromatic slop you see all over America and Australia and the UK.

Dominga made me Oaxacan-style chicken tamales – instead of wrapping the chicken and *masa* and sauce in a corn husk, as is usually done all over Mexico, she wrapped them in banana leaves. When she returned from the mill, Dominga removed a simmering freshly killed chicken from a pot and pulled the meat off in shreds. (*Pollo pelado.*) She mixed and kneaded her fresh *masa* with some rendered pork fat (packets of which are an essential ingredient around here), lightly toasted the banana leaves on the *comal*, and stirred her intoxicating-smelling *mole negro*, which had been simmering for hours and hours.

Proximity to livestock and animal feces, I have found in my travels, is not necessarily an indicator of a bad meal. More often than not, in recent experience, it's an early indicator of something good on the way. Why is that? It might have to do with the freshness question. Still living close to the source of your food, you often don't have a refrigerator or freezer. Equipment and conditions are primitive. You can't be lazy – because no option other than the old way exists. Where there are freezers and refrigerators, laziness follows, the compromises and slow encroachment of convenience. Why spend all day making *mole* when you can make a jumbo batch and freeze it? Why make salsa every day when it lasts OK in the fridge? Try a salsa or a sauce hand-ground with a stone mortar and pestle and you'll see what I mean.

Dominga's tamales were marvelous. I ate them hot out of the steamer under a small *palapa*, among the flies and the chickens and the pigs – and it was damn near a religious experience.

Martin, Eddie, and I stopped at a *pulquería* outside of town. It was a sky-blue hovel with a distorting jukebox and a lone addled drinker. The *pulque* – the fermented sap of the maguey cactus – sat in fifty-five-gallon vats behind the bar, smelling sweet-sour. The bartender ladled the thick, viscous, milky-looking sap into two plastic beach pails – the kind kids make sand castles with. We sat down at a weatherbeaten picnic table and poured ourselves drinks in tall, not particularly clean glasses. 'Ewww!' said one of the TV crew, watching Martin enthusiastically insert and withdraw a finger into the *pulque* to check consistency, a long mucuslike strand coming along for the ride. The finger test wasn't doing much for my stomach's sense of well-being, either. I'd dined earlier on generous portions of fried worms and sautéed ant eggs – a specialty of the area. The worms had been OK – buried in enough guacamole and *salsa roja*, and the ant eggs had been . . . well, OK, nutty-tasting, with a mealy feel and a lingering woody aftertaste. But the order of *chiles en nogada*, the national dish of Mexico – stuffed *poblano* peppers, loaded with ground beef, walnuts, dried fruit, and cinnamon, served with two sauces (the colors of the nation's flag) – had been terrible beyond words. I don't like beef with cinnamon, particularly accompanied by a sauce. Sitting in the *pulquería*, swilling bucket after bucket of the mildly hallucinogenic low-rent beverage of choice for Mexicans in need of an affordable buzz, I was all too aware that underneath the roiling hellbroth of *pulque* even now beginning to bubble in my belly was a less-than-solid foundation of ant eggs, worms, and that horrible *chiles en nogada*. The ride back to my room in Izúcar de Matamoros was agony.

Eddie's house in Tlapanala was a neat, clean one-story building – two bedrooms, living room/dining area, large kitchen – with a nice backyard and an outer kitchen and shed. When I arrived, Eddie's wife, mother, children, and baby-sitter were sitting on a couch and in chairs, watching satellite television. In the kitchen, a table was covered with the makings of *mole poblano*: *poblano* peppers, plantains, chocolate, nuts, herbs. In the outside kitchen, the mother of my *tournant*, Antonio, was making tortillas, while next door, the mother of my former salad man, Gilberto, looked on. I knew I was in trouble when I stepped into Eddie's well-tended backyard and saw a twenty-four-pound turkey still strutting around energetically. Eddie smiled and informed me that, as guest of honor, it was up to me.

'*Matelo!*' he said, handing me a machete. I'd never whacked an animal before. I was decidedly squeamish at the prospect. But the pressure was on. I was, after all, Eddie's boss. If I looked like a punk, he'd look like a punk for working for me. I was well aware that any one of the women – and probably most of the kids – could easily step in and take out that turkey like they were brushing their teeth. I eyed him carefully. He was huge and lively. Brandishing the machete, I stepped forward and, with Eddie's help, managed to restrain him. Eddie tilted the turkey's head back and poured a shot of *mezcal* down his throat. His wife dragged the turkey over to a bench, gave his neck a turn so he was pinioned flat to the board, and let me take over.

Now, I knew that turkeys are stupid. I knew that when you chop the head off a chicken, for instance, it takes some time for it to die, that it flaps around the yard for a while, too dumb to know it's dead. The phrase 'running around like a headless chicken' comes to mind. And I knew that I should expect the turkey to be no smarter than a chicken. Turkeys drown, sometimes, looking straight up into the rain, forgetting to close their mouths (kind of like Bon Jovi fans). I knew all this. I intended – as the gentle and sensitive soul I am – to dispatch this particular bird to turkey heaven as cleanly, quickly, and painlessly as possible. I would not waver, hesitate, or falter. I raised the machete over the struggling bird's neck, absolutely resolved to whack clean through, to end his life with one firm stroke. I came down with a resounding chop, the blade going *Thunk!* into the wood.

The turkey's body went insane, flapping and flailing and bouncing around! Oh my God! I thought, I've missed! I've botched it! Convinced that I'd somehow missed a major artery, cruelly and ineptly only wounding the animal, I began swinging the blade again and again in a terrified frenzy, like a novice serial killer, hacking blindly at a tiny strip of connecting skin that still held head and body together. A gout of blood erupted onto Matthew's lens – a shot, by the way, that he missed. Spray decorated me from forehead to sandals. I looked down and saw that the contorting head was in my hand, but the body, still flapping wildly, had been taken by Eddie, who nonchalantly hung it from the shed ceiling to be plucked. I was now a killer. I sat next to my victim for a long time before pitching in and yanking feathers from the still-warm body, wondering what the hell had happened to me.

It was a long, sleepy afternoon while the food cooked. Relatives showed up for the meal; a table was set up in the backyard. We eventually sat down to a very fine *mole poblano de qua jobte*, accompanied by enchiladas, salsas, salads, and beer. I looked around at the faces at the table and saw the faces of my cooks back in New York.

'Welcome to my little rancho,' said Eddie.

He'd arranged for a Mexican Woodstock at his little ranch in the foothills outside Izúcar. It looked like it would be the biggest thing the town had seen since they'd risen up and slaughtered the French – the Triumphant Return of Eddie Perez. He'd hired mariachis, a pop band, a singing vaquero with dancing palomino, a lariat act. A soundstage was in the finishing stages of construction in the dusty, sun-washed lot behind a row of low structures. Chickens, roosters, cattle, pigs, donkeys, and goats roamed freely among the accordion cactus in the surrounding hills. He'd invited the whole town: the mayor, a representative of the local criminal fraternity, notables of every stripe. He'd hired the entire off-duty police force of the neighboring town to act as security, and an army of women had been pressed into service. Rancheros dug a pit for *barbacoa*. Little boys in button-down shirts and little girls in Communion dresses ran messages and shuttled cooking equipment to and fro. Cases and cases of beer, tequila, and *mezcal* had been laid on. Gallon upon gallon of fresh-fruit *ponche* was in the works. Long tables had been set and arranged under the thatched roof of a *palapa*. This was going to be some party.

Meanwhile, I was having my own Marlboro Man moment. It's one thing to wear denim and cowboy boots in New York; it's quite another to kick dust and dung off your Tony Lama boots, sit back in a shady corner against a plain adobe wall, tilt back your chair, and put your feet up on a post. A cowboy hat, in New York, is a fashion accessory never, ever to be worn – unless you're a Chippendale's dancer. In Puebla, in the midday sun, however, it's a necessity. I tipped the brim of my spanking new hat down over my eyes to provide shade for my already-roasted nose and felt pretty damn cool. Sauntering into a spare outbuilding where some rancheros were already free-pouring tequila into dirty shot glasses, I brushed the dust off my hat and rasped, '*Tequila . . . por favor.*'

Sitting with Eddie and Martin – all of us in full ranchero dress with our hats and boots – watching a woman with Antonio's face making tortillas on a *comal* a few yards away, recognizing the features of people I worked with and had worked with in the faces of the women cooking rice in a clay pot over an open fire, the girls cleaning cactus for *ensalada de nopalitos*, the old *heladero* hand-cranking fresh lime sorbet over ice in an old wooden churn, I had never felt so happy to be part of my strange dysfunctional family thousands of miles away, back in my kitchen in New York.

The big event began with the digging of a pit the size of a large grave.

A fire was built at the bottom and allowed to burn down to glowing coals. When it was ready, some rancheros lowered big pots of goats' head soup into the pit, the stripped skulls dropped into the liquid at the last second by their horns, a pile of avocado leaves arranged around them. Sheep's stomachs, stuffed with blood, spices, and mint – a sort of Mexican version of *boudin noir* – were carefully placed inside. Then five whole goats, cleaned and butterflied, were stacked one on top of the other and covered with more avocado leaves. (The goats had been slaughtered earlier in the day. Their skins were even now stretched and drying on Eddie's roof.) The pit was then covered with a woven straw mat, which had been soaked in water, and carefully shoveled over with dirt. The various components would cook like this for about three and a half hours.

All over the arid lot, the pace quickened. From a sleepy, sun-drenched space, the ranch was quickly becoming a hive of activity. Everywhere, things were coming together, guests beginning to arrive. The mariachis began to play; pop singers drank beer and tuned their instruments; a kid I recognized as a former busboy in New York arrived with floral arrangements. Couples began to dance. Kids played tag. Men sat down at the long tables, women and children to the rear on folding chairs. Eddie, who never touches a drop back in New York, was already drunk – doling out the already-lethal *ponche*, he insisted on floating another inch of raw tequila on top. The rancheros, too, seemed well on their way, and the party had only just begun.

'Don't worry about nutheeng,' said Eddie, gesturing to the armed figures standing guard up on the surrounding hills. 'Drink! Anything you want. Tequila, *mezcal, mota*. You having a good time? Don't worry. You go asleep? No problem. You sleep anywhere. On the ground. With the chickens. Anywhere. You safe. Policía right there. Nobody bother you.'

'Jesus, Eddie,' I said, 'you should be proud . . . I can't believe you did all this, put all this together.'

The goats' head soup was fabulous – one of the best things I'd had anywhere. Platters of roughly hacked roasted goat arrived, surprisingly tender and absolutely delicious. The stuffed stomach was revelatory – a wonderful spicy jumbo sausage of bloody, oniony goodness. I tried to eat everything, including the *ensalada de nopalitos*, salsas, grabbing for food with still-warm tortillas from the readily available stacks in napkin-covered baskets everywhere. I ate rice, more salads, enchiladas, tamales, an incredible quesadilla of fresh zucchini flowers and *queso fresco*. And is there any music on earth more sentimental, more romantic, more evocative of place than Mexican mariachi? (OK, maybe samba gets the edge.) But that evening, as the sun set over Eddie's hills, with the sounds of music and laughter and Mexican-inflected Spanish all around me, I had never heard anything so beautiful.

The vaquero performed lariat tricks. Another sang on horse-back, his horse dancing under him, rearing, lying down, kneeling at his lightest touch. Under rented floodlights and a string of Christmas bulbs, the sun long gone, the mounted vaquero dismounted, held his microphone with an officious gravity, and, in the tone reserved for announcers at sporting events, bellowed, rolling his 'r's' at maximum volume and gesturing toward me, '¡ Señor as y señores . . . el hombre, el chefe norteamericano, el chefe de Nueva York muy famosooo! Anthony . . . BouRDAIN!'

Uh-oh.

The crowd cheered. The music stopped, the mariachis looking at me expectantly. I knew what was required as I sauntered over to the horse waiting for me in the center of a ring of light. There was some hooting and HeeYaaaing coming from Eddie, the camera crew, and a few other smart-asses in the audience. I put one boot in a stirrup and hoisted myself smoothly into the saddle. (A few weeks at summer camp and two riding lessons at the Claremont stables served me surprisingly well.) I was drunk, unsteady, but it was a magical horse under me. Trained to dance, he responded to my every touch, breaking into a slow canter at the slightest movement of boot, turning on command. I made a reasonably competent turn around the yard, doffing my hat to all assembled, stopped at the appropriate spot, and swung down from the saddle like a rodeo dude, feeling both utterly foolish and thoroughly delighted at the same time.

Eddie's pal, whom he'd introduced as the head of the local Mafia, forcefully insisted the camera crew and I join him in a few rounds of what he called 'cucarachas.' It would be a friendly match – USA versus Mexico. One at a time, the two cameramen and I, followed by the Mafia guy and his two associates, were presented with a fifty-fifty mix of Kahlúa and tequila – ignited and still flaming. The idea, it was explained, was to stick a straw into the flaming elixir and drain it in one go, before the flames subsided. This was to continue until one team cried uncle or collapsed unconscious.

The USA team did well. To our credit, we acquitted ourselves with honor, each of us downing five of the devastating concoctions without igniting our hair or choking. The Mexicans, though, were right in there. Finally, through some thankful manifestation of international goodwill, it was wordlessly agreed that at the appearance of a sixth round, all the contestants – from both teams – would together stick in their straws and suck down a final round, saving face for everyone, as all of us, I think, were on wobbly knees by now.

Matthew made it out the gate of Eddie's ranch on two feet with the rest of us, but by the time we were in the car at the end of the dirt drive, he had his head out the window, begging for us to pull over. Now, Matt had, over the last few months and continents, been less than sensitive to my own moments of gastric distress. He had never hesitated to get me to choke down some cinematic but nauseating gleet – even when I was ill – if he'd thought it would make riveting television. He'd never had a problem shooting me sick in bed, crying for relief, crawling toward yet another cold tile floor. So when we pulled over so poor Matt could flop senselessly about in front of the headlights, then crawl into a drainage ditch on his belly, I had his camera in my hands. This was my moment. Payback. Video gold. All I had to do was aim, press the button, and then everyone back in the offices in New York – editors, producers, all of us – could play and replay the comeuppance of my longtime tormentor. The lighting was perfect. It couldn't have been more dramatic: a deserted country road, total black beyond the narrow circumference of the headlights, a dark canefield in the background. I raised the camera, pointed . . .

I just couldn't do it. I didn't have the heart.

We ended up hoisting the poor bastard back into the car, and carrying him to his room later. We took off his shoes. I left his camera and his exposed tape by his side.

When he woke, those would be the first things he'd be looking for.

He's a professional, after all.

CAN CHARLIE SURF?

I WAKE UP IN my room at the Bao Dai Villas, the onetime summer home of the last emperor of Vietnam. I hear reveille out the window, followed by patriotic music at a nearby school, and the sound of children assembling. Rain patters on leaves; roosters crow. Someone is chopping wood on the grounds and there's the familiar shush of a straw whisk broom sweeping tile. Out on the water, just around the point, a freighter's engines throb idly in the early-morning mist.

All my clothes are soggy and beset by mosquitoes. I remain under the netting over my bed until I can remember where I put the repellent. There's a knock on the door. It's Lydia, wondering if I have any Lomotil. I went alone to Nha Trang beach yesterday, ate whole sea bream with my fingers under a palm tree. Chris ate crab soup at the hotel. He's deathly ill with food poisoning. Of course I have Lomotil. The traveling chef's best friend. I give Lydia a few and wish Chris well. I know how he feels. It looks like I'm on my own this morning.

After locating the repellent, I spray down my clothes, find the driest ones I can, and get dressed. There's a scooter and motorbike rental by the desk, and I pick out the one with the most juice, hop on, then head into town for breakfast. Technically, foreigners aren't allowed to drive anything over a low-cc putt-putt, but the rental guy didn't give me any trouble, so in a few minutes, I've joined the thick stream of morning cyclists heading in on Nha Trang's main beachfront drag. It feels great. I'm surrounded on all sides by men and women in their conical hats, whipping by palm trees, a long stretch of white sand and gentle surf to my right, the beach mostly deserted. The Vietnamese are not really beachgoers. Pale skin is seen here – as it is in Cambodia and elsewhere in the East – as an indicator of high status and good family. A lot of money is spent on skin lighteners, acid peels, and various fraudulent and often-harmful procedures intended to make one whiter. Women in Saigon often cover themselves from head to toe to protect themselves from the sun's rays. So Charlie, it appears, does not surf. Not in Nha Trang anyway.

As I turn off the main road, away from the sea, the traffic intensifies. Cars, trucks, more and more cyclists – on motorcycles, bicycles, cyclos, and scooters – join the fast-moving pack. Crossing an intersection is a heart-stopping maneuver, frightening and thrilling at the same time, filled with the roar of engines all accelerating simultaneously as we swarm across a square, only a foot or two from people on both sides. I squeeze past a line of trucks on the bridge across the channel. In the water, the gaudily painted red-white-and-blue fishing boats are coming in toward shore.

Local legend has it that when Nha Trang was the base for US military activity in the area, the CIA and Special Forces used to kick prisoners out of helicopters over this channel – wire a few tire rims to their necks and out the door. Now, there's little evidence of what was once an enormous American presence. As elsewhere in Vietnam, there's plenty of infrastructure, which the Vietnamese have all too happily adapted to civilian use, but the obvious signs are gone. No more shantytowns built out of cans hammered flat and scraps of military detritus, housing whores and cleaning ladies and laundresses. Quonset huts, officers' clubs, barracks, and parade grounds are gone – or converted to more practical purposes. The large hotels and villas once used to house high-ranking military personnel are now the property of government officials or rented out to tourists. The only people on Nha Trang beach are a few French, Germans, and Australians, most staying in the modern foreign-built resort-type buildings clustered together at one end of the bay. Yesterday on the beach, a kid approached me with a box of used books in English. It was the ubiquitous Vietnam collection: pirated editions of Tim Page, Michael Herr, David Halberstam, Philip Caputo, Neil Sheehan, and Graham Greene – pretty much like the collection on my bookshelf at home. But among the crudely Xeroxed covers and the dog-eared copies of left-behind drugstore paperbacks, the kid extracted a novel by a Vietnamese author: Bao Ninh's *The Sorrow of War*.

'Not legal this book,' said the kid, looking theatrically in both directions.

Needing a good beach read, I bought the book. The author, a war hero, served with the NVA's Glorious Twenty-seventh Youth Brigade. Of five hundred officers and enlisted men who went into battle with him, only ten survived. It's a remarkable document. Change the names and it's an Oliver Stone movie. The members of the hero's platoon have nicknames, just as in every American war movie you've ever seen. The conflicts described are bloody, pointless, and horrific. The soldiers are frightened and superstitious. They get high on weed, on any psychoactive substance they can, whenever they can. Innocents are cruelly and foolishly killed. The 'good guys' are responsible for brutal rapes and atrocities. The hero returns to Hanoi cynical, embittered, and hopelessly screwed up, only to find his girlfriend has become a prostitute. He spends most of his time with other similarly screwed-up veterans – all of whom spend most of their time drinking and getting into fights, having lost faith in everything they once believed in. It's a remarkable book, mostly for its eerie parallels to similar American works. It's a Vietnam book – like so many Vietnam books – only told from the other side.

By a Cham temple on a hilltop, I turn right down a narrow dirt road, splashing through muddy puddles until I find the fish market. People are eating everywhere. Among the pallets of fish and fast-moving deliveries and the crowds of marketers, large groups of people – old, young, babies, and children – sit on low plastic stools and squat, leaning against walls, slurping noodles from bowls, drinking tea, nibbling rice cakes, and eating pâté between baguettes. There's food cooking everywhere. Anywhere there's room for a fire and a cooking pot, someone has food going. Little storefront *coms* sell *pho* and noodles and 'roll your own beef.' Street vendors sell spring rolls, shrimp on a stick, scary-looking pâté sandwiches, baguettes, fried fish, fruit, sweets, and steamed crabs. Others seem to have just settled down at random, fired up some soup or noodles, and dug in – along with a large group of friends and family. I'm taller, by at least a foot, than anyone for two miles. Walking through the fish market to the water's edge, I get a lot of stares. A woman smiles and holds up her baby, a healthy-looking kid in a bright knit cap and new clothes. The woman herself is nearly in rags. 'Hello!' she says, holding the baby's hand and showing him how to wave. 'Bye-bye!' She asks me, by pointing and gesturing, if she can use my camera to take a picture of her son with me. Sure. Why not? She hastily confers with a group of women from a nearby fish stall. Someone locates a stool and the kid is posed standing on top. I show the woman how to operate the shutter and she frames the photo, a large group of women gathering behind and around her, all trying to look through the view-finder, all beaming with pride that their best and brightest is having his picture taken next to the freakishly tall and strange-looking American.

Only women work here. The fishmongers, scaling and gutting at long wooden tables by the water's edge, are all women. The people mending nets, unloading their catch from the colorfully decorated boats (they look like Amish barns), and cooking food at the stalls are all women. Women in *thung chais*, perfectly round dinghies made of woven bamboo and pitch, paddle their wobbly vessels toward the docks – a difficult balancing act (as I'd soon find out). Where are the men?

I sit down at a table with a large group of fishwives and their kids. The cook smiles and carefully places some cooked fish, some rice noodles, a few fish cakes, chilis, sprouts, peppers, and cilantro in a bowl, then hands me some chopsticks, a dish of black pepper, a wedge of lime, some additional chilis, and *nuoc mam* and chili sauce. There's a pot of coffee brewing over coals, and she pours me a cup. As with almost everything I've tried in Vietnam, it's fresh-tasting, vibrant, and delicious. Women keep coming over to the table and introducing their children. What they want, I have no idea. They ask for nothing except to allow their babies and small children to touch my arm, shake my hand, wave, the kids gaping wide-eyed and confused as the women scream with laughter and obvious delight. All these women have been up since way before dawn, many of them out on the water for hours, hauling in fish, loading them into their little round basket boats, unloading on shore. Yet no one looks tired. No one looks beaten down or defeated by their work. New arrivals stand upright in their dangerously pitching basket boats, smiling broadly as they heave pound after pound of dripping fish onto the market floor. The cook asks me if I'd like more coffee and pours me another cup, making sure my can of condensed milk is not empty. Fish blood runs across the wet concrete floor; a basket of squid is dropped a few feet away, then another basket of fish. The channel is filled with incoming fishing vessels, the awkwardly bobbing *thung chais*. Clouds cling to the mountains surrounding Nha Trang like tufts of white hair. I love it here.

Offshore are the islands of Hon Tre, Hon Tam, and Hon Mieu. Beyond those, farther out to sea, are a few tall rocks, surrounded by rough, dangerous surf, constantly patrolled by gunboats. This is where the salanganes (a variety of swallow) build their nests, high on the perilous snake-infested cliffs. The nests, formed out of the hardened salivary secretions of the swallow, fetch up to four thousand dollars a kilo from Chinese 'medical' practitioners and are much sought after throughout the East for bird's nest soup. Chris and Lydia have already asked if I'd be willing to climb up a cliff, past poisonous snakes, and crawl hundreds of feet over jagged rocks and pounding surf so they can shoot a bird's nest soup scene. I pointed out that bird's nest soup is medicine – not really food – and that I have about as much interest in bird's nest soup as I do in the next Steven Seagal ecothriller. The gunboat thing finally dissuaded them from having me attempt rappelling from any cliffs, but I feared the issue was not yet dead. I did, however, want to see some islands.

Linh and his friend Dongh, our driver in Nha Trang, said they knew a place on Hon Mieu, a little fishing village called Ba Mieu, where the seafood is supposed to be spectacular. I put a lot of faith in Dongh's opinions on food. He is a foodie, and as soon as he'd met me, he'd announced that I was a lucky man, for I was in the best town in the country for food. When we'd eaten dinner the first night, he'd kept pointing out highlights of the meal, asking if I'd noticed the amount of roe practically bursting from the green crabs, the freshness and flavor of the local lobsters, the clear eyes and noble conformation of the whole fish. He'd already fed me really well at a fish joint by the beach, and when Chris had asked about the food at our hotel, he'd rolled his eyes at the ceiling and given a decidedly lukewarm response.

Chris, it appeared, would have been well advised to pay closer attention. I'm surprised Linh is willing to take me here, that he is allowing us to see this – and film it.

As our hired boat approaches the surf off the island of Hon Lon, Dongh calls out to two thin, shabbily dressed men on the beach. A long, narrow launch sets out from shore, straight into the breakers, and eventually pulls alongside. There's room for only two passengers at a time in the leaky, water-filled launch. Lydia and I clamber in and are ferried to shore, riding the waves the last few yards. Chris is still back at the Bao Dai, probably getting up close and personal with the plumbing. This is a Vietnam I haven't seen yet.

It's a hard-packed, finely grained white sand beach around a small cove, strewn with trash, flotsam and jetsam, an absolutely godforsaken strip. A small village lies back among the trees on the muddy banks of what looks like a drainage ditch. Huts, hooches, shacks – as soggy and fragile-looking as you could possibly imagine – sag into unhealthy-looking brown water. There is no sign of electrical power, telephone communication, television, or any modern development dating after the mid-seventeenth century. There are a few bundles of sticks, and a *thung chai* resting upside down on the sand. I see no signs of life.

Lydia and I are alone on the beach, and I'm thinking about a swim. The surf is high, with a nice shape, the waves breaking far enough out to get a good ride if I want to bodysurf. Suddenly, we're under attack. Women come running from their huts, holding baskets of cheap seashell jewelry (the same Macao-made stuff you see on every beach in the world). The women are screaming, desperate-sounding, waving babies in front of them, shrieking, 'Look! Look! Baby! Baby!' They surround us on all sides, pressing in close, aggressively shaking fistfuls of necklaces and bracelets in front of us. It's impossible to deter them. I shake my head, saying, 'No, no . . . thank you . . . no . . .' again and again, but it's no use. They're pushing in, tugging our clothes. I move away, but they follow wherever I go. Lydia looks nervously at the boat, Linh and Dongh still waiting for the launch to return. I make the mistake of buying two pieces, hoping that'll satisfy the women, but it only makes them more desperate and inflamed. They begin arguing with one another, screaming, shouting, waving their fists. A woman presents me with her baby, a beautiful child with a single gold earring with a tiny gold bell – probably more valuable than the entire village – and begs me to buy a flimsy string of shells. I give in, which causes the others to redouble their frenzied efforts.

'I have a plan,' I say to Lydia. I run down to the water's edge, peel off my clothes, and dive in, then swim as far out as I can. Lydia chooses to remain ashore.

Nice curl on the waves. No reason at all for Charlie not to surf. I'm sure he must – somewhere. Some American soldier must have left an old longboard behind. There must be a Vietnamese surfer somewhere. Next time, I'll check Da Nang. I stay in the water for a long time, finally coming back ashore, to find Linh, stripped to his undershorts, energetically jogging down the beach, doing calisthenics, looking as happy as I've seen him. He smiles at me and charges into the surf. The women have given up on us. Now they just sit and watch, without much interest.

Progress has certainly passed this village by. I can't imagine what must happen during the rainy season, when it can pour for weeks and weeks without pause. That ditch must become a torrent. The houses – already tilting on broken stilts and crumbling into the water – must flood. The roofs and walls, such as they are, can in no way keep out the rain. I see no animals, no crops or gardens. Other than the lone *thung chai*, there are no boats. I ask Linh later, 'Who are these people? How do they live?'

'Very poor people,' he says. 'Fishermen families.'

When we've finished up, it's back to the leaky launch. The trip to the boat is pretty dicey: straight into the surf, water up to our shins, waves crashing over the bow. There are open spaces between the planks, and I can't see how we're staying afloat. Aft, one man furiously yanks a single oar back and forth, propelling us into the waves.

Hon Mieu, only a few miles away, is a completely different story. I can see another village of low ramshackle structures on the shore, but the bay is filled with tourist boats and water taxis, fishing vessels and *thung chais*, women shuttling visitors to shore. As we draw closer and tie up alongside another large water taxi, I can make out a strip of waterfront restaurants. Crowds of Vietnamese tourists fill long tables on their raised decks.

'This way,' says Dongh. Linh, Lydia and I follow, climbing from boat to boat across the bay until we come to a series of large floating docks, a maze of pitching, rocking walkways built around square openings that have been sealed underneath with fishing net. A whole enterprise floating a mile out to sea. Boats are tied up, fishmongers argue over prices, and customers cluster around large underwater pens containing the most astonishing array of live seafood. I stand there in bare feet, trying to keep my balance with the rise and fall of the planks beneath me, looking at enormous squid and cuttlefish, a pen filled with thrashing tuna, grouperlike fish, sea bream, and fish I've never seen before. Giant prawns, huge blue-and-yellow spiny lobsters, and crabs scuttle about just below the surface, awaiting my selection. I kneel down, reach underwater, and pull out a three- or four-pound lobster. Linh picks out some squid and some tuna while Dongh makes arrangements for our transport to shore. Lydia and I walk out to the end of a swaying collection of planks and climb very carefully into a *thung chai*; the two women in charge show us just where to sit, indicating that we should balance on the narrow lip, to best distribute our weight. Linh and Dongh take another boat in.

It seems like the most poorly designed vessel ever dreamed of. Absolutely spherical, like big Ping-Pong balls sawed in half and thrown into water, the boats bob and pitch with every move inside or out, threatening to toss one into the sea at any moment. One woman paddles, leaning ahead over the side, while another, directly opposite her on the other side of the boat's circumference, paddles in the opposite direction. Back and forth, back and forth, in a zigzag pattern to shore. I take an immediate liking to my skippers, two ruddy-looking ladies in the standard conical hats, which are tied tightly by sashes under their chins. They chatter cheerfully all the way in. As we disembark, carefully, very carefully, standing up and stepping onto a slippery dock, everyone remaining in the boat has to move around quickly to compensate for the changing distribution of weight.

In one of those magic moments that makes you want to hug the whole world, when Dongh (landlubber from town) and Linh (Hanoi city boy in nice white shirt) try to leave their little round basket boat, Dongh loses his footing and pitches face-forward onto the dock, nearly capsizing the boat – and just escaping a good knock on the head. All the women burst out laughing. From other boats nearby, people hoot and tease, really enjoying Dongh's embarrassment. It goes on for a long time, all of us laughing hysterically. Every time any of us catch another's eye, it starts again. One of those rare crosscultural moments where one realizes we're not that different after all.

Right next to the dock, up a few slimy wooden steps, a cook from the Hai Dao restaurant gravely examines the sea creatures we've brought and then weighs them on a scale. One pays for one's dinner by weight. Seated at a large uncovered table, Dongh, Linh, and I are soon joined by the pilot of our water taxi. At Linh's urging, we order a bottle of Nep Moi, Hanoi vodka. A waiter approaches with my lobster, still kicking, holds it over a glass, and thrusts a short knife into its sexual organs. A transluscent, slightly milky white liquid pours out – and is quickly mixed with the vodka.

'*Ruou tiet tom hum* . . . lobster blood,' Linh volunteers. 'Makes you strong.'

The Hai Dao is packed with customers, every table filled with enthusiastic Vietnamese families chowing down, some visiting from America, some vacationing from Hanoi and Saigon. Everywhere, there is the sound of those plastic packages of cold towels popping, the floor littered with discarded lobster shells, cracked crab claws, fish bones, cigarette butts, rolling beer bottles.

Food starts to arrive at our tables: *tom hum nuong*, my lobster, grilled over a wood fire; *muc huap*, steamed squid with ginger and scallions; *ca thu xot ca chau*, tuna braised in tomato and cilantro; *banh da vung*, rice cakes studded with sesame seeds, in a bundt mold-shaped hot pot over a little gas burner at the center of the table; *mi canh ca*, a sweet-and-sour soup of fish, noodles, tomato, onion, cilantro, pineapple, and scallion, and a few humongous green crabs, overstuffed with roe. It is the perfect setting for a damn near perfect meal. I am now totally indoctrinated to the casual Vietnamese dining experience. I love the way you garnish and season your own food: the ground black pepper and lime wedges you mix together into a paste and dip your food into, the dipping sauces and fish sauce with chili paste, the little plates of tiny green and red peppers, the bottles of soy, the plates of chopped cilantro and scallions.

Dongh has made it his personal mission to make sure I fully enjoy every scrap of Nha Trang's bounty. He refuses to let me touch the lobster or the crab until he's tunneled through every claw and spindly leg and removed every micron of meat. When he lifts off the carapace of a jumbo-sized green crab, he beams at me as he points out the beautiful, fantastically plump roe, the crab backs swimming with delicious fat.

We eat with chopsticks. We eat with our hands. We smoke between courses. We smoke during courses. We drink vodka and beer, scattering our refuse all over the table, like everyone else. The food is wonderful. Nothing but happy faces as far as I can see, children and grandfathers avidly sucking the last bits of meat out of crab legs and lobsters, picking out the good stuff from between fish bones.

I am ecstatically happy. I love it here. I love this country. I consider, for the fifth or sixth time at least, defecting.

What else do I need? Great food. The South China Sea's beautiful beaches. An exotic locale. An element of adventure. People so proud, so nice, and so generous that I have to keep a cover story on tap, should a cabdriver or shopkeeper invite me to his home for dinner (bankrupting himself in the process). It's a wonderland of food and cooking. Everybody has an opinion. Linh, naturally, says the best food in Vietnam is in Hanoi. Dongh sneers dismissively and argues for Nha Trang. They have definite opinions in Can Tho. And Saigon speaks for itself. To the Saigonese, North Vietnam is a joke – unfriendly, uninteresting, filled with stuck-up idealogues who underseason their food. Anyplace where everybody feels so strongly about their particular community, their cuisine, and their cooks, you know you're going to eat well. I could live here. And it smells good. I've already come to like the odor of durian and fermenting fish sauce, promising, as they do, untold delights, constant reminders that yes, yes, I'm in Vietnam! I'm really in Vietnam!

But TV makes its own rules. When I get back to the Bao Dai Villas, still reeling from the feast, they're preparing something for me in the kitchen. Chris is still out of the game for a while. (In coming weeks, he became thin and pale, unable to eat, constantly feeling ill.) But Lydia has arranged for a meal of the dreaded bird's nest soup.

'You've been dreaming of bird's nest soup,' she begins.

'No, I haven't,' I say, interrupting her. 'I don't give a fuck about bird's nest soup. I thought this was settled . . . I'm absolutely stuffed. I'm feeling a little seasick from the trip back. Please don't ask me to choke down bird's nest soup. I just had one of the great meals of my life. Don't ruin it. Please.'

But Lydia's like a dog with a bone between its teeth when she gets a concept in mind. She's shot a lot of odd bits of film, close-ups, kaleidoscopic scenes on 'progressive scan,' which she's convinced, after some additional *Apocalypse Now*-type footage of me lying in bed, shot from behind a slowly revolving ceiling fan, will make hilarious viewing.

'You've been dreaming about bird's nest soup,' she begins again, undeterred. 'It's the dream sequence.'

Far be it from me to stand in the way of art. I like Lydia. At the end of the day, I always end up doing pretty much whatever she asks. Looks like I'm eating bird's nest soup. And not just any bird's nest soup. Bird's nest soup from the same kitchen that put Chris on his back for the last twenty-four hours.

What the hell is in bird's nest soup? Bird's nest, for one. After cooking, it has the flavor, consistency, and appearance of over-cooked angel-hair pasta or cellophane noodles, slightly trans-luscent and, overall, pretty inoffensive. The chunks are the problem. Bird's nest soup is made by hacking up a whole rock dove (pigeon), putting the meat, bones and all, into a drained coconut, and then cooking it with the soaked nest, an assortment of Chinese medicinal herbs, dates, scallions, ginger, and the swallow's eggs. The coconut milk is poured back in and the whole thing is steamed for four hours.

It's disgusting. The nest tastes fine. The broth has a sweet-and-sour taste that's not too bad. But I just am not ready for the chunks. Not after my enormous seafood lunch on the island. Not ever. I struggle with chopsticks to pick my way through all the hard-cooked eggs, slurp strands of nest dutifully, if unenthu-siastically, managing to gnaw the meat off a few stringy bits of thigh and breast. But when the pigeon's head, beak, eyes, and all, comes popping up between the eggs and dates and bones and the rubbery sheets of coconut meat peeling off the shell, I have had enough. Linh and Dongh are digging into theirs as if they, too, have not just wiped out a monster-sized seafood feast. I eat as much as I can and hurry back to my room to lie under the mosquito netting and groan and toss, feeling like I'm going to die.

Two hours ago, I was dancing on the moon. Now? The horror. The horror.

WEST COAST

SAN FRANCISCO, AS ITS residents like to remind you, is nothing like Los Angeles. Anytime a snide, wise-ass New Yorker like myself starts slagging California, someone points out that 'San Francisco is different.' It's pretty. There are hills. Unlike LA, you can, on occasion, actually hail a cab by sticking a hand out in the street. Other than New York, it's probably got more talented chefs, and a more vibrant culinary scene, than any other American city. A good argument could be made that the whole renaissance in American restaurant cooking emanated outward from San Francisco, starting with Alice Waters and Jeremiah Tower. It's got a shabby, bohemian appeal, a rich tradition of bad behavior, good local ingredients. 'You'll love it,' my friends always told me.

So how come I can't fucking smoke? Somewhere north of San Francisco, I was sitting at the bar of a ramshackle roadhouse that, from all appearances, was exactly the sort of place I like. The bartender, 'Lucky,' or something like that, is in her fifties. She has a hoarse, rasping voice, two missing teeth, and a tattoo of a winged phallus above her wrinkled left breast. Charlie Daniels plays on the jukebox for a small group of regulars drinking bourbon and rye with beer chasers at ten o'clock in the morning. A chopped Harley sits out front and probably belongs to the guy in the cut-down denim jacket to my left, who offered to sell me crack a few moments ago when we passed each other in the septic bathroom – and I get the general impression that if I were to slide over to the left or the right, buy a few rounds for my fellow citizens, I could probably acquire an illegal handgun or two. This was the sort of place where I could walk over to the jukebox and play a couple of Johnny Cash tunes and nobody would say boo. Hell, they might even like it. This was the sort of place that when Johnny, singing 'Folsom Prison Blues,' comes to the line, 'I shot a man in Reno . . . just to watch him die,' people will sing along, getting wistful over similar golden moments in their own pasts.

On my second pint, I was getting into the ambience: the familiar smell of decades of spilled beer, a hint of Lysol, chicken wings in the deep fryer. Somebody down at the other end was drunkenly insisting, 'I barely touched the bitch! It was a fuckin' accident! Why she's gotta go and get a goddamn restraining order!' – before bursting into tears. I took another sip of beer, reached automatically into my shirt pocket, and fired up a cigarette. Lucky the bartender looked at me as if I'd just taken my pants off and begun soaking myself down with gasoline.

'Dude!' she wheezed, nervous, her eyes darting in all directions at once. 'You can't do that here! You gotta take that outside!'

You can't smoke anywhere in California. Rob Reiner says so. Celebrity fuckheads who live in walled compounds and use words like *working class* – never having sat down at a bar for an early-afternoon shot and a beer with any such animal in their lives – say so. For them, the bar is a place where we stupid, lumpen, and oppressed blue-collar proles are victimized by evil tobacco companies that have tricked us with their clever advertising into killing ourselves and our neighbors. For me, the bar is the last line of defense. 'It's an employee safety and health issue,' explained Lucky. The state is protecting her fry cook (I could see him in the kitchen, picking at an abscessed track mark) from the pernicious effects of secondhand smoke. Now, I can understand why they don't want me smoking in restaurant dining rooms. If I'm enjoying a delicate pairing of seared foie gras and pear chutney, I probably don't want somebody puffing away on a jasmine cigarette at the next table. I'm considerate. I can find a way not to smoke in the dining rooms of decent restaurants. Though bitterly resentful that I can no longer enjoy a cigarette with my fucking coffee in most places, I've learned to live with it. But the bar? The *bar*! What these miserable screwheads are saying is that it's OK to kill yourself with bourbon or tequila at nine o'clock in the morning – just don't enjoy yourself when doing it. It's only a matter of time before some well-intentioned health Nazi busts into your bedroom and yanks that postintercourse cigarette right outta your hand.

San Francisco is said to be one of the most 'liberal' and 'tolerant' places to live in America. That's a good thing, right? I'm avidly supportive of 'alternative lifestyles.' I'm 'tolerant'. But something's gone wrong here. It's a wildly expensive city to live in – even where I'm staying in the Tenderloin – too expensive for most people to afford. Yet San Francisco's acceptance of hope-lessness, prostitution, and drug addiction as 'alternative life-styles' seems to have ensured that many of its neighborhoods are choked with hustlers, junkies, the desperate, and the insane. I haven't seen junkies in such great numbers since the bad old days of Alphabet City – and in such bad shape. They're everywhere – dirty, diabetic, their limbs swollen, chalky, covered with sup-purating tracks and infections. West Coast skells make my old crew from the methadone clinic look like the Osmond family. San Francisco's main employment sectors, at a cursory glance, are the countless whorehouses, massage parlors, clip joints, live sex shows, and crummy-looking strip joints you see everywhere downtown. A great number of women in San Francisco seem to be sex workers, and while perfectly OK as a 'lifestyle choice' in my book, there are so many of them, and so disproportionately Asian, it feels more like Cambodia then any American city. As rents are so high, there's nowhere to live – and the dotcoms ain't hiring like they used to.

With all their kind hearts and good intentions, San Francis-cans, living in postcard-pretty houses atop high hills, seem to be sending a message: 'It's OK to come here. If you are prepared to lap dance for us . . . and then sleep on our sidewalks.'

Just don't smoke. That would be wrong.

I don't want you to think I don't like San Francisco. I do. It's a relief from Los Angeles. And some of my favorite movies were filmed there: *The Asphalt Jungle*, *Bullitt*, *Dirty Harry*. When I was a kid, reading *Life* magazine on a beach in France, all I wanted to do with my life was run away to the Haight and live in a house with the Jefferson Airplane, drop acid and draw underground comix. I grew up on R. Crumb's incredible line drawings of San Francisco, dreamed feverishly of all that free love I'd be enjoying with hippie chicks – if I ever turned thirteen. When it became clear that living in a commune, or sharing a crash pad, meant arguing over whom the last yogurt belonged to, when I realized, finally, that I'd been right all along, that the Grateful Dead really did suck, regardless of what my brainy friends said, and that 'the revolution' would never, ever, ever happen – and that that was probably not a bad thing – that particular dream died. The putative leaders of that revolution probably wouldn't let me smoke now, either. And of course, by 1975, when I first saw the Ramones, all thoughts of ever living in a city other than New York evaporated.

My first few days in San Francisco were fine. I ate oysters and Dungeness crab at the Swan Oyster Depot – exactly the kind of eating establishment I dearly love. I had durian ice cream at Polly Anne's out by the beach. I had a superb meal at Gary Danko – a too-precious dining room but very, very fine food, and a very likable group of hooligans in the kitchen. I visited a few New York transplants now working in the area, most lured by the town's reputation for good food and innovative restaurants and its selection of readily available fresh ingredients. I had a gluey, cornstarchy, dinosaur Cantonese meal at Sam Wo's in Chinatown, a throwback to my childhood forays to upper Broadway or Mott Street in New York. A cranky waitress hauled each course up a hand-pulled dumbwaiter. I purposefully ordered chop suey, wonton soup, and chow mein, not even having heard those words since 1963 – and thoroughly enjoyed myself – a little nostalgia for the old folks. I hung out with cooks a lot, as there are plenty of cooks in San Francisco. And one thing about cooks: Whether you're talking about New York, Philadelphia,

Glasgow, Melbourne, London, or San Francisco, we're the same everywhere. (Though I don't fully understand the Fernet Branca shot and ginger ale chaser thing.)

I was staying in a rock and roll motel around the corner from the O'Farrell Theater. There was a bar/nightclub set off from the pool deck and music pounded all night long; bearded metalhead band members sat in deck chairs while their roadies brought them drinks. I whuffed down a few cigarettes and then wandered into the bar for a drink. 'Are you Anthony Bourdain?' asked a security guy by the door. Knowing of no outstanding warrants or unsettled grudges on this side of the country, I said yes.

'Listen, man, my friend's a chef, and he really loved your book. He'd love it if you dropped by his restaurant. It's right down the street.' I'd heard about the place. Let's call it Restaurant X, a fairly swanky new joint a few blocks away. I'm always more comfortable in the company of chefs and cooks, so I figured, What the hell, maybe a few free snackies.

When I swung by, much later, the chef joined me and two off-duty shooters at my table. He was eager to send out some *amuses-gueules* and some drinks. A fairly young guy, in only his second or third chef's job, he was amiable but clearly stressed out, getting crispy from the pressure of opening a new restaurant, dealing with an overwhelming initial rush of business, and the responsibilities of managing a large crew. Nothing new there. We all have that look, to one degree or another. When he invited me in to see his kitchen, I gladly agreed. I like taking the tour through restaurant kitchens. (I'd been away from mine a long time – and I missed it.) He showed me a hot line of new Jade ranges, gleaming counters, an ice-cream machine and pasta maker, then took me through the walk-in, where he'd conscientiously organized and segregated the meat, fish, dairy, and produce. He introduced me to his cooks, the usual posse of pierced and decorated scamps, most in the final stages of kitchen breakdown.

The chef opened the door to his office and beckoned me in, as if to show me around – the familiar cluttered desk piled with invoices, schedules, old copies of *Food Arts*, *Restaurant Hospi-*

tality, faxed résumés, equipment manuals, stashes of saffron and truffle oil – and asked if I'd sign a grease-stained, food-smeared copy of my book, which I was all too happy to do. The greasier the better. Somebody shoves a book to be signed in my direction, and it's covered with food? I know it's for the home team. But when I looked up after scrawling my signature, the chef had closed the office door. He was sitting behind his desk, head in his hands, teary-eyed. 'What do I do? . . . I don't know what to do . . .'

I sat there, stunned, while a total stranger (I didn't even know his last name) cried in front of me.

'What . . . what's the problem, man?' I asked.

'My sous-chef,' he said, blinking away tears. 'He's . . . my best friend. But . . . he's like . . . talking behind my back. He's leaning on the cooks real hard. Yesterday, I had two cooks walk out 'cause a this guy! That's why I'm working the line tonight. I was supposed to be off . . . But I'm working the fuckin' grill 'cause two of my staff walked out. No notice, nothing.'

I felt my blood starting to percolate, simmer, threaten to boil. 'You tell this prick to lighten up?' I asked.

'Yes! I told him,' said the chef, clearly pained by the situation. 'He's my friend. My best friend. We came up together. I told him . . . I told him . . . But he just ignores me. He knows better . . . He says that to the cooks! I say one thing? He says another. The cooks can't take it anymore. I'm gonna lose all of them if something doesn't change.'

'You should fire the cocksucker' was my suggestion. I didn't have to think too long about it, either.

'I know . . . I know. I should . . . But . . . I just can't,' he said, rubbing his face.

'Listen. Let me get this straight,' I said. 'Just so we both know what we're talkin' about here . . . You're the chef, right?'

'Yes.'

'And your sous-chef, your underboss, is talking treason behind your back . . . disobeying your orders, causing discontent, disgruntlement, desertion . . . possible mutiny among the troops?'

'Well . . . yeah . . . I guess so. I mean, maybe he doesn't mean to. He's just trying to – '

'This guy's a fuckin' lone wolf! He's a loose cannon! He's gotta go!' I snarled, surprising myself with how viscerally involved I suddenly was in the chef's problem. 'I don't care if he's your bestest, dearest, closest buddy since you were babies. This mutt has gotta go. The sous-chef's number-one job is what? To make the chef look good. At all times. He's not there so that every time you come back from a day off there's some kinda problem you gotta deal with. Is he making you look good with this shit he's pullin'?'

'No,' admitted the chef. 'It's not good. Things are all fucked up.'

'That alone is enough . . . And he's talking trash about you when you're not around? Forget it! You gotta cut this cancer out before it kills you.'

'I know.' He sniffled. 'I know.'

'Look,' I said, softening. 'I know what you're going through. I fired my own best friend and sous-chef at least . . . what . . . three times. We're still friends. He's still my best friend. He's just not my sous-chef anymore. And you know what? After you kick this guy out, this kid'll go on and get his own chef's job. He'll be calling you up and apologizing for all the stuff he pulled when he was here. He'll know. He'll find out what a chef needs and expects in a sous. It's business. That's all. But it's serious business. That's what you forgot to tell him. Kiss this guy on the mouth and say, "Fredo, you broke my heart." Then whack him. But don't wait.'

'You're right . . . you're right . . .'

'Next time you're hiring a sous, do like I do. Take him out to a nice bar. Buy him a drink before you close the deal. Then give him the Talk. Let him know right up front. I say, "I'm the nicest, sweetest guy in the world. You call me at four o'clock in the morning needing bail money? I'm there for you. I'm not going to be riding your ass like some other chefs will. I won't humiliate you in front of your crew or anybody else. You don't have to address me as 'Chef' all the time. I've got a sense of humor – and in my off hours I'm a depraved, degenerate animal – just like you. You will like working with me. We'll have fun . . . But if you ever fuck me, talk shit about me behind my back, drop the ball, show up late, or show disloyalty in any way, I don't care if you're my dearest friend, I don't care if you saved my fucking *life*, I *will* fire your sorry ass like I'm blowing my fucking nose. Do we understand each other? Is that clear? And do you want me to write it down?" That's what's called "fair warning". You've drawn the lines. He crosses them and it's bye-bye. You let him know up front what a vicious, cold-blooded motherfucker you can be. That way, there're no surprises.'

The chef seemed considerably cheered by my inspiring little lecture. 'Thanks, man,' he said. 'I'm sorry for dropping all this on you. I knew what I had to do and all . . . It's just . . . I guess I needed to hear somebody else say it.' Then he reached into the pocket of his chef coat and offered me a bump from a big bag of white powder.

Maybe his sous-chef wasn't his only problem.

Reasons Why You Don't Want to Be on Television: Number Five in a Series

'C'mon, Tony! You've been to Cambodia, for Chrissakes! How bad can it be?' said the television producer. 'We can't do a whole show on one restaurant! This will be funny! They're looking forward to cooking for you!' What he'd arranged, what he had in mind, was for me to venture into the real heart of darkness, deep, deep into enemy territory, to Berkeley, and a vegan potluck dinner.

I've said some pretty hateful things about vegetarians, I know. In spite of this, many of them have been very nice to me over the past year. Though I think I have at various times referred to them as 'Hezbollah-like' and as 'the enemy of everything good and decent in the human spirit,' they come to my readings, write me nice letters. My publicist in England, whom I adore, is a veg (though I've forced her at gunpoint to eat fish a few times), as are a couple of the shooters I've worked with. They've shown remarkable good humor, considering how I feel about their predilections. There have been lots of vegheads who've been very kind and generous these last few months, in spite of the fact that they know that at the first opportunity, when they're drunk or vulnerable, I'm getting a bacon cheeseburger down their throats. That doesn't mean I wanted to sit in some hilltop A-frame eating lentils out of a pot with a bunch of Nader supporters and hairy-legged earth mothers in caftans. I certainly didn't want to visit 'them' on their home turf. If nothing else, I was reasonably certain that smoking would be a problem.

I'm going to try – really try – to be nice here.

I went along with the producer's scheme. Fair is fair. The opposition should be given every chance to prove the right-eousness of their cause – or at least the merits of their case. The people coming to the dinner, the folks who'd be cooking for me, were all serious vegans. Cookbook authors. Vegan cookery teachers. People who spent lots of time going to seminars, classes, corresponding with others of their ilk – on-line, in chat rooms, and at conventions and informal gatherings. Maybe, just maybe, they had something to show me. Maybe it was possible to make something good without meat, or stock, or butter, or cheese, or dairy products of any kind. Who was I to sneer? The world, I had recently found out, was a big, strange, and won-derful place. I'd eaten tree grubs and worms and sheep's testicles. How bad could it be?

Bad.

The vegans I visited did not live in a converted ashram on a hilltop, tending to their crops in bare feet or Birkenstocks. No one was named Rainbow or Sunflower. Only one person wore a sari. My hosts lived in a kempt modern luxury home in an exclusive area of the suburbs, surrounded by green lawns and shiny new BMWs and SUVs. They were, all of them, affluent-looking professionals and executives. Ranging in age from late thirties to early fifties, they were well dressed, unfailingly nice, eager to show me the other side of the argument.

And not one of them could cook a fucking vegetable.

Fergus Henderson, the grand master of blood and guts cookery, shows more respect for the simple side of sautéed baby spinach on some of his plates than any of these deluded vegans showed me in ten elaborate courses. Green salads were dressed hours before being served, ensuring that they had wilted into nutrition-free sludge. The knife work – even from the cooking teachers present – was clumsy and inept, resembling the lesser efforts of younger members of the Barney Rubble clan. The vegetables – every time – were uniformly overcooked, under-seasoned, nearly colorless, and abused, any flavor, texture, and lingering vitamin content leeched out. Painstaking re-creations of 'cheese', 'yogurt' and 'cream' made from various unearthly soy products tasted, invariably, like caulking compound, and my hosts, though good-humored and friendly to the hostile stranger in their midst, seemed terrified, even angry, about something nebulous in their pasts. Every time I asked one of them how and when exactly they had decided to forgo all animal products, the answer always seemed to involve a personal tragedy or disappointment unrelated to food.

'I got a divorce,' began one. 'I lost my job,' said another. 'Heart attack,' offered another. 'I broke up with my . . .' 'When I decided to move out of LA, I started thinking about things . . .'

In every case, it appeared to me (in my jaundiced way of thinking anyway) that something had soured them on the world they'd once embraced – and that they now sought new rules to live by, another orthodoxy, something else to believe in. 'Did you read about the PCBs in striped bass?' one whispered urgently, as if comforted by the news. 'I saw on-line where they're pumping steroids into cattle,' said another breathlessly, every snippet of bad news from the health front a victory for their cause. They seemed to spend an awful lot of time confirming their fears and suspicions of the world outside their own, combing the Internet for stories of radioactive dairy products, genetically altered beets, polluted fish, carcinogenic sausages, spongiform-riddled meat, the hideous Grand Guignol chamber of horror abattoirs and slaughterhouses.

They also seemed curiously oblivious to the fact that much of the world goes to bed hungry every night, that our basic design features as humans, from the beginning of our evolution, developed around the very real need to hunt down slower, stupider animals, kill them, and eat them. 'Don't you ever wake up in the middle of the night craving bacon?' I asked.

'No. Never,' replied every single one of them. 'I've never felt so healthy in my life.'

It was difficult for me to be polite (though I was outnumbered). I'd recently returned from Cambodia, where a chicken can be the difference between life and death. These people in their comfortable suburban digs were carping about cruelty to animals but suggesting that everyone in the world, from suburban Yuppie to starving Cambodian cyclo driver, start buying organic vegetables and expensive soy substitutes. To look down on entire cultures that've based everything on the gathering of fish and rice seemed arrogant in the extreme. (I've heard of vegans feeding their dogs vegetarian meals. Now that's cruelty to animals.) And the hypocrisy of it all pissed me off. Just being able to talk about this issue in reasonably grammatical language is a privilege, subsidized in a yin/yang sort of way, somewhere, by somebody taking it in the neck. Being able to read these words, no matter how stupid, offensive, or wrongheaded, is a privilege, your reading skills the end product of a level of education most of the world will never enjoy. Our whole lives – our homes, the shoes we wear, the cars we drive, the food we eat – are all built on a mountain of skulls. Meat, say the PETA folks, is 'murder.' And yes, the wide world of meat eating can seem like a panorama of cruelty at times. But is meat 'murder'? Fuck no.

Murder, as one of my Khmer pals might tell you, is what his next-door neighbor did to his whole family back in the seventies. Murder is what happens in Cambodia, in parts of Africa, Central and South America, and in former Soviet republics when the police chief's idiot son decides he wants to turn your daughter into a whore and you don't like the idea. Murder is what Hutus do to Tutsis, Serbs to Croats, Russians to Uzbeks, Crips to Bloods. And vice versa. It's black Chevy Suburbans (which, more than likely, US taxpayers paid for) pulling up outside your house at three in the morning and dragging away your suspiciously unpatriotic and overopinionated son. Murder is what that man sitting across from you in Phnom Penh does for a living – so he can afford a satellite dish for his roof, so he can watch our *Airwolf* reruns, MTV Asia, and Pam Anderson running in slow motion down a Southern California beach.

Hide in your fine homes and eat vegetables, I was thinking. Put a Greenpeace or NAACP bumper sticker on your Beemer if it makes you feel better (so you can drive your kids to their all-white schools). Save the rainforest – by all means – so maybe you can visit it someday, on an ecotour, wearing comfortable shoes made by twelve-year-olds in forced labor. Save a whale while millions are still sold into slavery, starved, fucked to death, shot, tortured, forgotten. When you see cute little kids crying in rubble next to Sally Struthers somewhere, be sure to send a few dollars.

Damn! I was going to try and be nice.

But then, I wasn't in San Francisco to be nice. I wasn't there to investigate, experience, or explain the full sweep of NoCal culture and cuisine, to bring enlightenment or illumination or a new perspective to a complex and interesting subject. I was in the region for one reason and one reason alone: to eat at the French Laundry.

I was worried about this part of the jaunt. Even getting a reservation at the Laundry can be a lengthy and difficult process, and the prospect of chef/owner Thomas Keller allowing me, Mr Obnoxious Don't Eat Fish on Monday, to eat in his dining room at short notice – while a camera crew shot the kitchen and dining room during service – seemed doubtful. Keller, very likely America's greatest homegrown chef, had, as I pointed out in an E-mail to him, absolutely nothing to gain by allowing my spiteful presence through his doors. A journeyman knucklehead like me was hardly going to dazzle or impress. Instead, I threw myself cravenly at his mercy, pleaded for any consideration I could get: Professional courtesy? Curiosity? Pity? I'd take it, I told him, anyway I could get it.

Being the shrewd, conspiratorial, paranoid second-guesser that I am, I made damn sure, while Keller considered my request, to pad my guest list for the proposed meal with the heaviest-hitting, friend-in-common, high-octane bunch I could find. Even if Keller thought me an utter swine and an opportunistic hustler, my dinner companions would be sure to get his attention.

I put my end of dinner at the French Laundry together like a bank job. Enticed through threats, promises, and guarantees of an all-expenses-paid trip to what was sure to be a memorable meal, they came one by one. They knew who Thomas Keller was, just as he surely knew them.

From Palm Beach, dragged away from Easter dinner with his family, came Michael Ruhlman, the coauthor (with Keller) of *The French Laundry Cookbook*. We'd met only recently, at an evening of senseless debauchery and overindulgence at the Siberia Bar in New York. He'd written two other books, *The Making of a Chef* and *The Soul of a Chef*, which I'd really enjoyed; I'd found from his prose that Michael, like no other nonchef writers I know, understands the glories of veal stock, the grim realities of kitchen grease, the hard kernel of truth about what really makes people want to cook professionally – and why. He generously agreed to join me in my bold but weird venture.

Scott Bryan flew in from New York. He's an old crony by now. I'd met him through his food. I'm a regular customer at his three-star restaurant, Veritas, and we've become friends over the years. If you ever read in the papers about some ugly incident at a midtown bar involving me, a blunt object, and a vegetarian, chances are Scott will have been in the room when they clapped on the manacles. I'd written gushingly (and sincerely) about him in my earlier book, and I assured him that even though there would be TV cameras floating around like airborne pests, there was no script, no plan, and that all he had to do was show up in San Francisco, pile into a car, and eat what would very likely be a fantastic meal.

Eric Ripert, the chef of the four-star Manhattan restaurant Le Bernardin, flew in from Los Angeles. Here's a guy who is everything I am not: He has four stars, a résumé of nothing but world-class kitchens, incredible natural talent, top-drawer skills, and movie-star good looks. He's not even American; he hails from Andorra, a minicountry in the Pyrenees. That he entered my life after reading my book, I always secretly attributed to his all-too-well-remembered apprenticeship days, when he must have experienced something in common with the desperate, debauched hustlers, strivers, and journeymen discussed in its pages. (Though I have a very hard time ever picturing Eric knocking out eggs Benedict like I did for so many years.) He has, by the way, what is perhaps the best independent intelligence network running in New York – and maybe the whole country. The NSA has nothing on this guy. If it happens in a kitchen anywhere, Eric knows about it ten minutes later. He's also the most bullshit-free 'French' chef I've ever met.

They arrived, one by one, at my motel – all of us, it turned out, dressed for dinner in nearly identical black suits, dark ties, and dark sunglasses. Whatever collective coolness I may have thought we had evaporated immediately when I got a look at the car the TV folks had rented to take us out to dinner. It was a half-mile-long gleaming white stretch limo, a hideous rubemobile that practically begged for us to change into powder-blue ruffled shirts and pastel orange tuxes. I was mortified. Already extremely nervous about our reception and this much-anticipated meal, here we were, planning to arrive in the rural Napa Valley community of Yountville in a car more suitable to some lottery-winning yokel on his way to the county fair to sell off his prize hogs.

When you talk to most really talented 'star' chefs, the words *I* and *me* and *my* tend to come up a lot. Nothing wrong with that – it takes a big ego to do what chefs do, to keep them going in the face of absurd odds, uncertain outcomes, long hours in hot spaces.

'My cuisine . . .' 'My cooking . . .' 'My kitchen . . .' 'My cooks . . .' 'My approach to food . . .'

You've heard that before. I do it all the time. So it's striking to talk with Thomas Keller, to listen to this quiet, surprisingly modest man describe his restaurant as an institution – not as a personal enterprise or as the spawn of his own personal genius. Here's the guy whose cookbook is widely seen as the ultimate in food porn. Upon the mention of the chef's name, other chefs – no matter how great – become strangely silent, uncomfortable-looking, even frightened. In a subculture where most of us are all too happy to slag anybody at any time, you never hear anyone – even the French – talk trash about Keller. (One Frenchman, I believe, even called him the 'greatest French chef in the world.')

What's missing from all the wild praise of Keller, his cooks, his restaurant, and his cookbook is how different he is. You can't honestly use terms like *the best* or *better* or even *perfect* when you're talking about Thomas Keller, because he's not really competing with anybody. He's playing a game whose rules are known only to him. He's doing things most chefs would never attempt – in ways unthinkable to most. Everything about him and the French Laundry experience is different from most fine dining experiences; and Keller himself is a thing apart, a man hunting much bigger game, with very different ambitions than most of his peers.

Talking with the man as he walked through a small farm that grows him vegetables, watching his chef de cuisine pull baby leeks and garlic right out of the ground for that night's dinner – and later, as he showed us around the grounds of the French Laundry after dinner, when he sat with us in the dark garden, sipping an after-work glass of wine – it was evident how unusual his priorities are and to what lengths he is willing to go to attain them. The building itself looks like an unassuming country home, rustic-looking wood and stone, surrounded by green fields, farmlands, and vineyards in the small community of Yountville in the Napa Valley. There are two stories, an upstairs deck with a plain wooden balustrade, and a pretty garden. The decor, like the service, is unassuming, comfortably casual, with everything – the room, the wait staff, the view of the hills outside the windows and through the French doors – conspiring to put the diner at ease. The service, though relentlessly sharp and efficient, is not stiff or intimidating. The waiters are neither too friendly nor too distant.

'It looks like France,' said Eric, gazing out the window. For

Keller, the French Laundry is a cause. It is the culmination of a philosophy shared by the people who work with him. Every detail is inseparable from the whole, whether it's new steps to the porch or a new dish on the menu. He brought up the famous Taillevent in Paris as an example of the kind of place he aspires to leave behind someday. 'You don't know the chef's name at Taillevent, do you? No. It's the restaurant you remember – the institution. The tradition.' Though he's a legendary perfectionist, lives next door to his kitchen, and takes a hands-on approach to every tiny detail, what he has created in Yountville is a place inseparable from its community and suppliers, where the absolute best ingredients are treated with the highest degree of respect.

Think I'm exaggerating? Maybe I've gone over to the dark side – flacking for a chef I hope will someday throw me a freebie, maybe blurb my next book? No, you haven't seen how he handles fish, gently laying it down on the board and caressing it, approaching it warily, respectfully, as if communicating with an old friend.

Maybe you've heard some of the stories. That he used to make his cooks climb up into the range hoods each day to scrub out the grease personally. How he stores his fish belly-down, in the swimming position. That every fava bean in his kitchen is peeled raw (never soaked). How his *mise-en-place*, his station prep, is always at an absolute minimum – everything made fresh. Maybe you've heard about his unbelievably beautiful, elaborate *fifteen*-course tasting menus, seen pictures of food so perilously balanced, so perfectly posed, that you don't know how it ever gets to the table. They feed about eighty-five people a night at the French Laundry. They employ, all told, about eighty-five people. An army of similarly dedicated purveyors comb lonely stretches of the Pacific Northwest at night, some armed only with flashlights, looking for the telltale phosphorescence of a particular wild mushroom. People grow things to his specifications. The simplest-looking garlic chip garnish at the French Laundry can require the skills of a microsurgeon. Maybe you've heard all that.

There was a break between courses – a sort of seventh-inning stretch – and there we were: four grown men – three chefs and an author – standing outside Keller's kitchen in the dark, our noses pressed up against the window screen, spying on the man, whispering.

'SSssshh! . . . He'll hear us!' somebody said.

'Look,' said Michael. 'See how happy he looks!'

'My God! He's got no *mise* at all!' said someone else. Standing there in the shadows in the French Laundry's garden, it felt like we were kids on Halloween night.

'That's a happy man,' agreed Eric.

'How many chefs get to do this?' Keller had said earlier. 'We're just really lucky. And I don't forget that.'

A twenty-course tasting menu, under the most favorable circumstances, is a challenge to any chef. A twenty-course (including *amuse-gueules*) tasting menu for a party of fellow chefs is, for most of us, reasonable rationale for a nervous breakdown. But imagine – try to imagine – turning out four distinct and different twenty-course tasting menus for that one table of chefs, only two or three courses in common, over sixty different plates of food hitting one party of four – and doing it at the same time as serving a full dining room of regulars, many of whom are also having elaborate multicoursed tasting menus – and you get the idea when I say that Thomas Keller is different.

The meal took six and a half hours, with very little, if any, waiting between courses. Four different little oyster dishes would arrive, and we would all first look at our own plate, then glance longingly at the others'. For a while, we'd taste a little, sawing off a tiny bite of oyster, for instance, then pass our plates counterclockwise so the others could try. After many bottles of wine, and many courses, some of us just stopped passing. How do you cut a single oyster into four portions? It's hard. Some get more than others. In the highly charged atmosphere where everybody wants to try everything, this can lead to disputes – maybe violence. By the time the meat and fowl began hitting the table, I just hunched over my plate and said, 'Don't even think about it. You can try this one next time.'

There was a lot of head shaking and sighing going on. Who

among us in the whole wide world of chefs would attempt this? It was, far and away, the most impressive restaurant meal I'd ever had. Let me give you a closer look. Listed below is the menu for that evening, what I was served. Keep in mind that Scott, Eric and Michael were simultaneously enjoying equally elaborate and yet different dishes.

The meal began with the French Laundry's signature *amuse* – tiny little coronets of salmon tartare, served in a cone rack like at Baskin-Robbins (the inspiration for the dish). We all knew they were coming. We'd seen them in the cookbook – in my guests' case, they'd had them before. In addition to being delicious, it's psychological manipulation at its most skillful. You can't help but be charmed. The cute little cones, wrapped in tiny paper napkins, press long disused buttons in the sense-memory section of the brain. You feel like a kid again, your appetite jump-starts, and a breathless sense of anticipation comes over you. You want – you need – to know: What's next? Here's what I had next: puree of Robinson Ranch shallot soup with glazed shallots, English cucumber sorbet with pickled cucumber and a dill-weed *tuile*, Yukon Gold potato *blini* with shiitake mushrooms and chive butter, cauliflower *panna cotta* with Malpeque oyster glaze and osetra caviar, *côte de saumon*, an Atlantic salmon chop with russet potato *gnocchi* and Périgord truffles. Salmon chop? you're thinking. Salmon ain't got no chops! Yes, they do. Up by the head, there's an oft-neglected triangle of delicious flesh. It's a tricky little piece, usually discarded when chefs cut salmon for uniform portions of filet, because it's an awkward shape and riddled with annoying little bones. At the Laundry, a liability has been turned into an asset. There it was on my plate, a perfect little *côte de saumon*, looking just like a baby lamb chop, one bone extending from a tiny medallion of fish. Sounds cute? It is. A lot of Keller's dishes reveal an abiding sense of whimsy.

Whimsy and its unlovely cousin, irony, make appearances on a lot of menus these days, more often than not, unsuccessfully. You'll see a menu item with a 'cute' transposition of terms – for instance, 'tournedos of monkfish,' which means nothing more than that the chef is bored with the word *medallions* or feels insecure about titling his creation 'little pieces of monkfish.' Rarely does the finished product bear any resemblance to the term in its original usage. Now, if you were to serve that little disk of monkfish, larded with bacon, topped with a slab of foie gras, and drizzled with truffled *demiglace*, you might be able to get away with calling it 'tournedos of monkfish Rossini' – a direct reference to the old beef classic. But why? It's a dangerous game playing with your food like that. The line between cute and cloying (or worse – pretentious) is a very fine one.

But Keller, typically, is playing at something else here. He's not looking to elevate a less than worthy dish by associating it with a beloved classic. More often than not, he's taking something refined and giving it an ordinary – even clichéd – name (the best examples being his famous 'coffee and doughnuts' dessert, his 'Caesar salad,' and his 'grilled cheese sandwich.' 'The one compliment,' explains Keller, 'that I enjoy the most is someone saying, "This reminds me of" – and they'll tell you of this wonderful experience they had somewhere else. And I hope that when they go someplace else, they'll say, "This reminds me of the French Laundry." ' Memory – that's a powerful tool in any chef's kit. Used skillfully, it can be devastatingly effective. I don't know of any other chef who can pull it off so successfully. When you're eating a four-star meal in one of the world's best restaurants, and tiny, almost subliminal suggestions keep drawing you back to the grilled cheese sandwiches mom used to make you on rainy days, your first trip to Baskin-Robbins, or the first brasserie meal you had in France, you can't help – even the most cynical among us – but be charmed and lulled into a state of blissful submission. It's good enough when a dish somehow reminds you of a cherished moment, a fondly remembered taste from years past. When those expectations and preconceptions are then routinely exceeded, you find yourself happily surprised. Keller had a surprise for me.

He'd done his homework, I guess, gleaning from my book that I'm an absolutely degenerate smoker. There is no smoking at the French Laundry – maybe the only place on earth I don't mind refraining. But, to be honest, by course number five I was feeling a slight need. To my embarrassment and delight, they had anticipated this in the kitchen. When the next courses arrived, mine was called 'coffee and a cigarette': Marlboro-infused coffee custard (with foie gras). My dinner companions hooted. I blushed down to my socks, thinking this a cruel but very funny joke at my expense. I certainly didn't expect the thing to taste good. Goddamn the man, it was good. (He'd actually used the tobacco from a very decent cigar, he told me later.) Best of all, after I'd polished off my plate, I felt a very welcome, much-needed nicotine buzz.

Next?

Une salade fraîche au truffe noire with celery branch and celery root vinaigrette. Hand-cut tagliatelle with Périgord truffles and grated Parmigiano-Reggiano cheese. (The truffles were shaved tableside from a magnificent fist-sized monster.) Herb-roasted Chatham Bay cod 'shank' with a 'fricassee' of new-crop potatoes and applewood-smoked bacon emulsion. (Again, a liability turned into an asset, as the small, usually unservable tail section of fish had been cut across the bone and served like a lamb shank.) 'Lobster Navarin,' sweet butter-poached Maine lobster with glazed pearl onions, spring vegetables, and sauce 'Navarin' (another crosscultural reference – 'Navarin' is usually associated with a heavy, old-school French country classic of braised lamb shoulder). Brioche-crusted 'confit' of North American moulard duck 'foie gras' with braised fennel, fennel salad, and Tellicherry pepper. '*Gastrique*' milk-poached four-story Hills Farm '*poularde au lait*' with 'crème fraîche' dumplings and '*bouquetière*' of spring vegetables. Roasted Bellwether Farms spring lamb with a 'cassoulet' of spring pole beans and thyme-infused extra virgin olive oil. (These were the most fetching, tender little lamb chops I'd ever encountered.) 'Roquefort' ricotta cheese 'gnocchi' with a Darjeeling tea-walnut oil emulsion, shaved walnuts, and grated Roquefort cheese. Hayden mango soup '*et son brunoise*' (I love the '*et son brunoise*' thing – very funny). Haas avocado salad with Persian lime sorbet (of all the plates that made their way round our table that night, this was the only one that landed with a thud. Scott's comment was,

'This is waaay over my head. But then, I'm not that smart.')
'Coffee and doughnuts' – cinnamon-sugared doughnuts with
cappuccino semi-*freddo* (looking exactly like a coffee shop
doughnut sitting next to a Chock Full O'Nuts cup filled with
cappuccino, but marvelous). '*Mille-feuille à la crème de vanille et
son confit d'ananas mignardise.*'

It was an absolutely awe-inspiring meal, accompanied, I
should point out, by a procession of sensational wines. Unfortunately, I'm the wrong guy to be talking about wine. All I can tell
you is that Scott, who knows about these things, used the word
wow a lot. I remember a big brawny red in a cistern-sized glass,
which nearly made me weep with pleasure. Cooking had crossed
the line into magic.

Keller himself is quiet, with a bone-dry, gently sardonic sense
of humor and the wary, observant gaze of a totally centered chef
who knows what he wants to do – and is doing it – every day.

He seemed annoyed when asked about the roots of his drive
for perfection. 'Perfect is something you never actually attain,' he
said. 'It's something you search for. Once you reach it, it's not
perfect. You've lost it. It's gone.'

Gush too much about 'creativity' and you'll get: 'There's very
little creativity – in anything.'

But instead of *I*, *me*, and *my*, he uses words like *respect*, *hope*,
institution, *future*. Big words and big concepts in a trade where
most of us look no further down the road than the next star, the
next book deal, the next investor, the next busy Saturday night.

I was going to go on. I was going to blather on about the
seamless integration of restaurant and locale. I planned to
ruminate on the marvelousness of a chef finding, after years
of wandering and false starts, a home. I was in love with the idea
that a chef of Keller's unique abilities and ambition could
actually be content in a small town in wine country, marrying
place, purveyors, personnel, and personal vision into an idyllic
rural retreat, far from the carnivorous environs of the big city.
The whole concept had great appeal to me. An ideal accomplished, if not by me, then at least by someone I liked and
admired.

Then I opened up the *New York Times* and saw that Keller is planning a French Laundry in New York, that he's moving in across the street from Jean-Georges, down a ways from Ducasse, and realized I'd learned nothing at all.

'Unfinished business in New York,' said my chef buddies as we sat around a table at a Lower East Side joint.

'Rakel didn't make it,' said one friend, regarding Keller's failed venture in Manhattan many years ago. 'It was great – but the people weren't ready for it.'

'Jesus,' I sputtered, 'Keller coming to New York . . . That's an act of aggression! That's like Wyatt Earp coming to town. Everybody's gonna be gunning for him. Who wants that kind of pressure? He's already got it all. New Yorkers go to him! Why come here and have to put up with all the nonsense?'

Needless to say, when the new place opens its doors, every chef, critic, food writer, serious eater, and casual foodie in the city will have been hyperventilating for weeks. To say the restaurant will be 'eagerly anticipated' would be an egregious understatement. I cannot even imagine what will happen. I'm afraid. I'm afraid he'll fail (if that should happen, it would be for reasons having nothing to do with food, of course). But more, I'm afraid he'll succeed. I like the idea of having to travel to experience a French Laundry meal. The journey is part of the experience – or was for me – an expression of the seriousness of one's intent, and the otherness of everything Keller. I liked looking out the window and seeing hills and countryside. I don't know if I want to be able just to pick up the phone, make a reservation, and, sooner or later, simply hop in a cab and zip down to Columbus Circle. One doesn't take the A train to Mecca. That experience, like the French Laundry, should be a pilgrimage. Not that that will slow me down in the slightest when the new place opens its doors. See you there.

HAGGIS RULES

'WE'RE NUMBER TWO—BEHIND TONGA,' said Simon, talking about Scotland's position on the scoreboard recording the incidence of heart disease worldwide. 'We've got to get that sorted out. Where is Tonga anyway? I've got to go there!'

The Scottish, Simon tells me, will deep-fry anything. To prove his point, he was taking me to a chip shop for some 'suppers.' We were decidedly not in Edinburgh. 'Too European . . . too . . . English,' sneered Simon. They put brown sauce on their fish and chips there, Simon revealed, an outraged look on his face just from remembering the brown home-brewed Kitchen Bouquet or GravyMaster concoction.

'Brown sauce on fish and chips? No, no, no, no, no,' said Simon. It's malt vinegar all the way, and plenty of salt for Simon, a proud Glaswegian with a typically sardonic sense of humor. He'd been feeding me Guinness all day and showing me around Glasgow, and now it was time, he said, to visit a proper 'chippie.' We ate the traditional fish and chips first, a batter-dipped and deep-fried filet of cod – or more and more frequently, now that the cod population is in decline, haddock – usually served in either a paper cone or a plastic to-go container. 'You got to get a good bit of salt on it,' said Simon, following a very healthy sprinkling with a long squirt of malt vinegar. 'I could eat bloody Elvis – if you put enough vinegar on him . . . S' magic.' The fish was great, the chips, as everywhere in the UK, were needlessly substandard, limp and soggy. Few chip shop owners bother to blanch their fries in low-temperature oil before frying, so they are never, ever crisp.

The appropriate beverage for this kind of on-the-run Glaswegian repast, said Simon gravely, is Irn-Bru, the popular caffeine-jacked orange-tinted soft drink.

We were not really here to do the fish and chip thing. The real wonders, the full potential of the Scottish chip shop, lay somewhere deeper: deep-fried haggis with curry sauce. The crispy cigar-shaped tube of sheep guts and oatmeal (more on that later) was wonderful – the perfect late-night munchie food after a long session drinking Red Bull and vodka, pints of heavy, or Buckfast (a cheap screw-top wine: the Ripple of Scotland). The 'king rib' – whatever that might be – was delicious, though its actual relationship to ribs seemed in doubt. Prefried orders of haggis, meat pies, sausages, and fish filets were crowded next to one another under bulb-lighted glass, ready to be snapped up by hungry drinkers.

Everything, everything at the chip shop, went into the same hot oil. Carlo, the counterman, unwrapped a Mars bar, dunked it in the universal batter, and dropped it into the oil. When it floated, golden brown, on the surface, he removed it, sprinkled a little powdered sugar on it, and handed it over.

'Careful,' said Simon. 'Inside, it's bloody napalm.'

Mmmm. I like grease. I like chocolate. And I like sugar. After addressing any concerns about potential mandibular or maxillary facial damage by allowing the thing to cool down a bit, Simon sawed off a half and presented it to me. It was still tongue-searingly hot – and not bad at all. Simon flashed me an evil smile and enjoyed telling me what was next. 'Deep-fried pizza?' I said, 'Oh . . . I don't know . . . That's maybe . . . I don't know, it seems somehow . . . unnatural.' I had a hard time believing that anyone would even consider such an atrocity. Sure enough, Carlo took a cold slice of premade frozen pizza, dipped it cheese side down into the batter, and dropped it into the all-purpose trough of grease.

'Not bad,' I said.

'Wait a minute,' said Simon as I made to leave. 'There's this one thingy we have to try.' He told a skeptical-looking Carlo to drop a pickled egg into the batter. We were breaking new culinary ground.

'I don't know,' I said. 'I don't . . . know about this.'

'This is where my granny would go "Holy Mary, mother of God,"' said Simon, taking a bite and handing me the rest. It was edible. I think one's enjoyment of the chip shop's more esoteric delights has a direct relationship to the amount of alcohol consumed prior to eating. Hot, salty, crunchy, and portable, the previously awful-sounding collection of greasy delights can become a Garden of Eden of heart-clogging goodness when you're in a drunken stupor, hungering for fried snacks. At that precise moment, nothing could taste better.

Glasgow has a working-class vibe and the familiar feel of parts of Brooklyn or the Bronx. In many ways, it's the antidote to everywhere else in the world, a city filled with gruff, no-bullshit, often very funny citizens with impenetrable but beautiful accents. On my way into town on the train, I fell asleep near a large group of Glaswegian football fans. When I woke, for a few disconcerting minutes, I thought, listening to the people talking and shouting around me, that I'd somehow stayed on the train too long, maybe slipped across the sea to Lithuania or Latvia or Finland. Only the repeated exclamations of 'Fook!' and 'Shite' brought me back to the correct time and place. (Note to travelers: Your choice of football team is an important one in Glasgow. Generally speaking, it's a Catholic versus Protestant thing, I think. Aligning yourself with one team over the other is a 'once in, never out' lifelong commitment. They take their footie seriously around these parts. It's a good idea to sound out one's friends carefully before saying what might well be the wrong thing.)

Edinburgh is, in my opinion, one of the most strikingly beautiful cities in the world. There's a castle sitting on top of a big rock promontory right in the middle of town. The place drips with history, a crowded tangle of cobblestone streets, ancient buildings, beautiful monuments, none of which weigh the town down. It's got good pubs, and bright, shrewd, very sophisticated, and often lavishly educated folks. I love it there (though I feel more at home in Glasgow).

This is mean of me, because I'm not going to give you its name

– and I'm certainly not gonna tell you where it is – or next time I go, there'll be a bunch of 'bloody Yanks' at the bar – but a friend of mine took me to his local awhile back, on a narrow cobble-stone street in Edinburgh. My friend writes very fine novels set in the city, and his fictional hero, a mildly alcoholic civil servant, hangs out at this very real pub – in between murders. If there is a perfect place in the world to drink beer, this is it. It's a modest, unassuming corner pub with a small sign and smoked windows. One can't see the interior from the street. Just inside the door are an ancient small bar, weathered wood floors, hand-pumped beers and ales, a few middle-aged geezers drinking pints and chatting with the bartender. In a back room, there are a few tables and an electric fire in the hearth, some fading football posters on the walls. It is a place of perfect stillness and calm, the first sip of ale inspiring feelings of near-transcendental serenity. This was it, the perfect refuge from the modern world, and all its worries. Within moments of hanging my coat on a well-worn hook and sitting down, I turned to my friend and said, 'I'm never leaving.' I know it's terribly unfair of me to be so coy about the place. But don't worry, Scotland is loaded with great pubs – and I'm sure I'm overromanticizing. I do that a lot.

For Simon, it's love/hate with Edinburgh. He was not happy that I'd be having my first real haggis experience there. But he'd found us a very decent place on Edinburgh's High Street, just down from the castle, and he assured me that even though we were in (to his mind) the second-best city, the chef here knew what he was doing.

What is haggis, anyway? For one thing, it's the punch line to a thousand jokes in America. The Thing Never to Be Eaten Under Any Circumstances . . . What Groundskeeper Willie eats . . . It does sound terrifying to the uninitiated: a hot gooey mix of sheep's 'pluck' (the whole esophagus, lungs, liver, and heart, yanked out in one go, then finely ground), oatmeal, onions, and black pepper. This filling is cooked inside a sheep's stomach (which you don't eat) and then steamed slowly, covered in the oven, then served with 'neeps and tatties' – mashed turnip and potato. As with so many dishes, it originated with the leftovers of the rich landowners – turned into a proud classic by an enterprising and desperate peasantry.

A kilted bagpiper's performance preceded the arrival of dinner. (With his graying handlebar mustache, he looked suspiciously like the original 'Leather Guy' in the Village People.) Another few seconds of screeching pipes and I'd be reaching into my pocket for a hundred-pound note – just to make him go away. I may love Scotland, but the sound of bagpipes is as alluring as a dentist's drill hitting nerve. Fortunately, our haggis soon arrived, a big plump flesh-colored steaming balloon, tied at both ends and rupturing slightly in the middle, ground meat and oat mixture spilling out like a slowly erupting volcano. As I quietly struggled for words to describe its somehow violent-looking appearance, the fully costumed piper did me one better, yanking a sharp, menacing-looking dirk out of his scabbard, approaching the near-to-bursting membrane, and swinging right in to Robert Burns's 'Address to the Haggis.' I couldn't follow too many of the words, though I did catch the phrases 'gushing entrails' and 'a wondrous, glorious sack,' and then the piper slit the stomach fully open with his blade and retreated, leaving us to enjoy our guts.

After one mouthful, I couldn't disagree with Scotland's greatest poet. It was glorious. Haggis rules! Peppery, hot, meaty – it didn't taste of anything you might expect in a dish cooked in stomach. Not really tasting organlike at all, no bitter livery taste, no chewy mysterious bits, no wet-dog taste of tripe. It was in no way offensive to even the most pedestrian American tastes, but subtle and rich in a *boudin noir* sort of a way. If you can handle *boudin noir* or black pudding, or even sautéed calf's liver, you will love haggis. The mashed tatties and neeps provided a perfect counter to the hearty, peppery, oniony, oat flavor. The shepherd's pie in your old high school cafeteria was far more challenging to the palate. If haggis, right out of the oven, didn't look the way it did, we might all be eating it in America. They'd be serving it from street stands in New York, fried and battered with curry sauce. High-end restaurants would be making 'haggis sauce' and '*feuilleté* of baby bok choy, Yukon Gold potato, and haggis with a whiskey sauce,' and stuffing it into metal rings, decorating it with squeeze-bottle designs.

Scotland has far more to offer hungry pilgrims than grease and guts, however delightful they might be. The Scottish are going through the same foodie gold rush as elsewhere in the UK and Ireland (and Australia) – and, as elsewhere, they are rediscovering what was good all along about their country. The seafood is unbelievable. In Leith, the old waterfront on the firth outside Edinburgh, there are a number of modest-looking seafood joints serving absolutely smashingly good scallops, salmon, mussels, trout, oysters, and other fish from the North Sea, the Atlantic, and Scotland's many rivers, lochs, and streams. At the most ramshackle, touristy-looking seafood barn, where you'd expect, at best, to get a decent piece of deep-fried or plain broiled fish, they're piling tasty little stacks of fresh fish on piles of tasty indigenous vegetables – the technique as good as almost anywhere in New York or London, and the raw ingredients frequently better.

Scottish beef is justifiably famous. And Scottish game – venison, grouse, pheasant, wild hare, and rabbit – is perhaps the best in the world. I capped off my Scottish wanderings outside of Inverness, in the Highlands, on the 25,000-acre estate of the Cawdor family. For a guy like me, it's hard to fathom how the rich and the upper classes really live – especially when you're talking about the UK. For Americans, the aristocracy means any talented hustler who's got more than four cars and a beachfront pile in the Hamptons. In Scotland, I found out, it means something very, very different. The rich talk differently. They all seem to know one another. And in the case of the Cawdors, and Colin, the seventh earl of Cawdor, they tend to go back a ways. His family have been living on this particular Rhode Island-sized expanse of grouse moors, salmon streams, farmland, and forest since the late thirteenth century. There's a castle in the middle, a structure referred to significantly, if inaccurately, as the residence of 'Macbeth, the soon-to-be thane of Cawdor.' The Cawdors were kind enough to let me stay at their Drynachan Lodge, a hunting, shooting, and fishing retreat on their property, where I'd come to eat wild salmon and to try, halfheartedly at first, to kill a helpless little bunny rabbit or two.

Things really were different here. I don't know any rich people in America who count among their employees not just cooks and servers and housekeepers but also gamekeepers and foresters. I don't know any wealthy American families that can point to a magnificent forest of tall trees and deep gorges and rushing freshwater streams and say, 'My great-great-great-great grandfather planted that forest.' It was breathtakingly beautiful. From my big brass bed, I could see mile after mile of checkerboard-patterned grouse moor, the scrub and heather burned down in carefully controlled alternating square sections to provide optimum living conditions for the much-sought-after grouse. Pheasants wandered carefree just outside my door. Roe deer kept the underbrush to a minimum in the thick forest. Wild salmon literally leapt from crystal-clear streams. For mile after mile, an entire interlocking ecosystem was maintained – and had been maintained for hundreds of years – on the sprawling, seemingly never-ending grounds running all the way to the sea. Roddy, the gamekeeper, took me salmon fishing, and he showed me, as best he could, how to cast a line. I reeled it in across fewer than two feet of quick-moving water, hoping that a salmon would become enticed by the fly. The salmon were jumping out of the water, looking me right in the eye only a few feet away, but proved immune to temptation. Nothing like being proven – again and again – to be more stupid than a fish. But I didn't care. To stand at the edge of a Highland stream, casting across the water, reeling in, then moving slowly downstream on a brisk, clean, late-spring morning, had a hypnotic effect. I didn't mind if I caught anything or not. Fortunately, Ruth, the chef at the lodge, had a good supply of wild salmon on hand, so I wouldn't miss eating some.

I'd agreed – once again for purposes of television entertainment – to go rabbit shooting with Roddy. The plan was to bag a few rabbits, take them back to Ruth at the lodge, and have her make us a traditional poacher's stew of rabbit, venison, and cabbage, cooked in red wine and stock. Though by now I was reasonably comfortable firing automatic and semiautomatic rifles, handguns, and grenade launchers, given my Cambodian adventures, I had never in my life fired a shotgun. Nor had I ever fired a weapon at a living, breathing, fast-moving target. I am in no way supportive of hunting for trophies or sport – would never do it and don't like it that others do. But if you kill it, then eat it, it's fine. Still, I only agreed to take part in the senseless hunt because I was certain that I'd be hopelessly inept at shooting any rabbits, that I was sure to come up empty. I counted on Roddy, the seasoned professional, to provide enough bunny rabbits for the following day's lunch.

I don't know what happened. With my shotgun broken over my arm – so as not to shoot any of the TV crew or gamekeepers should I stumble into a pothole on the rough terrain – and the safety on, I spied a rabbit racing for cover about sixty to eighty feet in front of me. I quickly had to snap the gun closed, raise it, click off the safety, aim, and then fire – all this at a speedy, barely visible little critter that was running and leaping across his own turf. *Bam!* Very little kick. To my shock and no small amount of dismay, I'd blown the spine out of something that had once looked very much like Bugs.

'Well shot, sir,' said an assistant gamekeeper, retrieving the limp, still-warm corpse. Holding my prey, I couldn't resist the need to pet it, so cuddly and adorable; my voice actually cracked a little when I talked to the camera.

After each shot, I'd break my smoking weapon and an assistant would remove the shell and replace it. I saw a movement to my left, swung the barrel around, rapping Chris's camera in the process, and bagged another one tearing along a wall a long ways off. Jesus! I was a murder machine! Now I had two sweet-faced little bunny wabbits on my conscience . . . This was not right. But, God help me, I was having fun. Another few hours and I'd be signing up for grouse season.

Back at the lodge, Ruth prepared an amazing packed lunch of rabbit and venison stew, nettle soup, slices of air-dried beef, Scottish cheeses, and homemade breads. Then all of us, Chef Ruth, Gloria, the mad and wonderful Glaswegian housekeeper, an assistant gamekeeper, and the crew headed out over the moors to a fishing shack by the edge of a stream. Ruth set up a buffet on a picnic table inside and we helped ourselves, then sat down on the porch and devoured the fruits of the not-so-great white hunter's toil.

It was sensational. Sitting there watching cattle graze on a hillside across the water, listening to Gloria tell Glaswegian jokes, drinking red wine and watching the tall grass and heather move in the wind, I could hardly imagine a better setting for an afternoon meal. I did, however, begin to fear for my own safety. When this stuff hit the airwaves, when the PETA folks got a load of this, I could be looking at serious trouble. I don't want any vegan terrorists throwing blood on me – particularly not if I'm wearing an expensive jacket. Hopefully, my potential adversaries don't get enough animal protein to pose any real threat to my health or wardrobe. But I can't be sure, can I? Maybe I should buy a Taser.

VERY, VERY STRONG

IT'S BACK TO MY Saigon routine: Mornings at the market, 555 cigarettes and 333 beer. I'm holed up at the Continental (where I should have stayed all along), just across the street from Givral's pastry shop and the old Théâtre Municipal. Faded photographs of the hotel hang in frames on the walls surrounding the Orchid Garden bar in the courtyard. They date back to the 1880s, depicting straw-hatted French generals, white-suited colonists, satraps, and rickshaws. A much larger, later photograph, dated 1975, shows NVA soldiers resting out in front of the hotel. Across the square is the Caravelle, where journalists, spooks, and MACV brass once watched from the top-floor bar as B-52 strikes and airborne Gatling guns carved up the countryside beyond the city. Graham Greene stayed here. His character Fowler used to drink at the café downstairs, the Continental Shelf, where *le tout* Saigon used to gather each evening to drink and gossip.

I think I've gone bamboo, as they used to say about British military advisers who'd stayed too long in this part of the world. I've gone goofy on Vietnam, fallen hopelessly, helplessly in love with the place. I'm now accustomed to bowls of spicy *pho* for breakfast, strong cups of iced expresso over crushed ice with condensed milk at Trung Nguyen (sort of a Vietnamese version of Starbucks – only better), lunch at the *coms*, cheap eateries where I'd have bowls of rice with fish, chicken, or meat. I've come to rely on the smells of jasmine, frangipani, the durian and fish-sauce aromas at the markets, the constant buzzing and

261

rumbling from the motos. I have a hard time letting any of the *don gah* pass me by – women carrying portable kitchens on yokes across their shoulders, serving bowls of soup or noodles that are always fresh. Everything is beautiful. Everyone is nice. Everything tastes good.

Linh has changed since introducing me to Madame Ngoc. A few weeks ago, he was all nerves and suspicion. When I told him, before leaving for Nha Trang, that Philippe might be swinging through town, maybe joining us in Can Tho, he'd stiffened at the prospect of an unannounced and unanticipated new arrival. He'd have to talk to the People's Committee, he said. People were watching us, he insisted, independently reporting on our activity. This addition to our party was an unexpected and potentially difficult development. Who was this Philippe? What were his intentions? Was he also a journalist? Was he a French or American citizen? During drinks at the roof bar of the garish Rex, when I left to go to the bathroom, Linh followed me, making an elaborate show of washing his hands while watching in the mirror to make sure I wasn't emptying a dead drop or whispering into a satellite communicator.

But since Nha Trang, he's been relaxed, and since he introduced me to Madame Ngoc, he's become an absolute pussycat.

Madame Ngoc is a force of nature. The relationship between the matronly middle-aged restaurant owner, dripping in jade and jewelry, smelling of French perfume, always smartly dressed in well-tailored businesslike Western attire, and Linh, the young translator and Communist functionary, is a mysterious one. When he first took me to her restaurant, Com Nieu Saigon, I couldn't figure out why he was so solicitous of her. At first blush, they couldn't seem more different: the cold, efficient Hanoi boy and the warm but mercurial Saigonese woman. Yet Linh never lights a cigarette without first lighting one for her. He pulls out her chair for her. He hangs on her every word, anticipates her needs. When she narrows her eyes, looks around the room, clearly desirous of something, Linh goes on full alert. But then so does everybody else. She may be a tiny Vietnamese version of a yenta, but underneath her soft features and almost overbearingly generous nature it's pure steel. She teases him relentlessly. She scolds, pokes, dotes on him, calls him 'Little Brother'. It is, I finally figured out after a few visits, love.

'Next time! You bring cookies. Chocolate!' says Madame Ngoc, pleased by my gift of flowers but preferring other things. 'Chris! Lydia! You happy? I love you . . .' she says, giving them both a big hug and a kiss. 'You too thin!' she says to Chris, who has never fully recovered from his crab in Nha Trang. 'Too thin! I think you sick.' She snaps her fingers, and across the room an assistant manager and a waiter rush over to serve her. She barks at them in Vietnamese, and a few moments later, the manager returns with packages of vitamins, Maalox, and herb tea. 'Tony, Chris, Lydia,' she says, looking worried. 'You must be very careful.' We each receive an identical package and a stern admonition to eat more carefully when outside of Saigon. A few days ago, it was bags of Vietnamese coffee (she'd heard me raving about how good it was here). When Lydia commented earlier on the toy dogs with bobbing heads on the dashboard of Madame Ngoc's chauffeured car, she'd presented each of us with a set later in the evening. We all love Madame Ngoc, and we think she loves us, too.

'I give my heart. Make people happy,' she says warmly, before snapping her head to the right and fixing a waiter with a brief look of withering scorn. Beers arrive at our table. Ashtrays are emptied. At Madame Ngoc's restaurant, people are happy. The clean white room is packed with Vietnamese families. Tables of eight, ten, twelve, fifteen people tear into food all around us, with new guests arriving every minute. They drive right through the dining room, three and four to a motorbike, then into the backyard parking area. Napkins are popping everywhere from their packets. Every few minutes, a clay pot shatters loudly on the floor and a sizzling-hot rice cake goes flying through the air. The colors on the plates at every table are electric, psychedelic, positively radiating bright reds, greens, yellows, and browns; and it smells good: lemongrass, lobster, fish sauce, fresh basil and mint.

Com Nieu Saigon is the slickest, smartest, sharpest restaurant operation I've seen in a long, long time. Madame Ngoc, a tiny little middle-aged woman, divorced, living – as she is all too willing to tell you – all alone, runs it like a well-drilled battleship. Every table, every corner, every crevice of latticework in the open-air dining room is clean, tight, and squared away. Underneath the broken crockery, even the floor is spotless. The cooks, the waiters, and the managers move like a highly motivated – even terrorized – dance troupe. It does not do, I have long since gathered, to disappoint Madame Ngoc.

She's figured out how to run a successful restaurant in a Communist country. Com Nieu is a loud, casual, comfortable family place with a distinctive gimmick. Madame Ngoc, reading up on Vietnamese culinary history, found a traditional preparation for rice baked in clay pots. The drill at Com Nieu is that when you order a rice side, a waiter retrieves it from the kitchen, smashes the crockery with a mallet, the pieces falling to the floor, then hurls the sizzling-hot rice cake across the dining room, over the heads of the customers, to another waiter, who catches the cake on a plate, flips it, sends it up in the air a few more times like a juggler, then cuts it into portions tableside, dressing it with fish sauce, peppers, sesame, and chives. The room resounds with the noise of breaking and broken crockery. Every few minutes, searingly hot disks of rice go sailing by my ear. It's a tightly controlled riot of food, folks, and fun, kids standing on their chairs, their moms feeding them, granddad and sons tearing apart lobsters, crabs, and giant prawns, grandmas and dads smoking between courses, everyone chattering, eating, loudly and visibly enjoying themselves.

Who is Madame Ngoc? As she tells you, she's just a lone hardworking woman, unlucky in love, who loves cookies, chocolate, stuffed animals (which she collects) and continental buffets in large Western hotels. (She took us as her guest to one of the bigger, newer ones – absolutely giddy around all those chafing dishes of French and Italian food, the cake stands of Austrian pastries and French petits fours.) She is driven everywhere in a new luxury sedan. When it rains, someone is waiting curbside with an umbrella. When she decides – at 10:30 at night

– that she wants us all to have our picture taken together, she snaps her fingers, barks a few orders, and a frightened-looking photographer arrives in a full sweat only a few minutes later, an old Nikon and flash rig around his neck. Com Nieu is jammed full every night – as is her other restaurant, a Chinese-themed place down the street. And Madame Ngoc is at one or both, reigning over her devoted staff and adoring public for most of her waking hours.

'I so tired. Very hard work. Very tired. Sometime I don't want to come. I want to stay in bed. Sleep. But no can. Always watching . . .' She feigns a deeply suspicious inspection of her rushing staff. 'I go to fish market to surprise. Maybe somebody steal from me. I must find out. I say, "How much for crab today? How much yesterday? How many pounds you sell me yester-day?" I must look. Careful.' She points to her eye, signifying eternal vigilance. At the arrival of a large party by the front entrance, she jumps up out of her seat and approaches them, all smiles.

'I love everybody,' she says. 'You must give love. Give yourself to be success. You love people. They love you back.' Food arrives at our clean, newly varnished and polished table. *Canh ngheu*, a tofu and dill soup. Platters of *bong bi don thit*, crunchy, delicious golden zucchini blossoms that have been stuffed with ground pork and seasonings, then batter-dipped and fried. *Cha goi*, spring rolls, and *rau muong sao toi*, flash-sautéed spinach with garlic sauce – an otherworldly bright, bright green. *Thit kho tau*, a stew of pork and egg in coconut broth, the halved boiled eggs tinged pink around the outer rim of white. *Tom kho tau*, lobster stewed in coconut and chili, redder than red, the plump tail meat a phosphorescent saffron yellow. *Ca bong trung kho to*, a whole fish fried and dressed with chili sauce. *Dua gia muoi chau*, stir-fried baby bok choy. And, of course, lots of *com nieu*, the wedges of crispy rice cake from which the restaurant takes its name. Everything is as fresh as I've seen it anywhere in the world, fresher even. The flavors practically explode on my tongue; the colors shimmer. At the end of the meal, platters of ripe custard apple on ice arrive, accompanied by sliced mangoes, papayas, dragon fruit, and pineapple. I have been Madame Ngoc's guest three or four times by now, and there is no question in my mind that hers has been the best food I've had in the country (this in a country where everything is already fabulous).

Like any really good restaurant lifer, Madame Ngoc's nervous system is hard-wired to every movement in both kitchen and dining room. She has the ability to sense a full ashtray on the other side of the restaurant, even when far out of view. One moment she's cooing over Lydia, or teasing Linh for being late to the airport the last time she was in Hanoi, or insisting I try the crab, or worrying over Chris's stomach – the very next second, she's giving orders to a shaking but very competent waiter who has somehow managed to displease her, rebuking him in terrifying imperious tones.

Then it's back to 'I love you, Chris, Lydia . . . Tony, you happy?' She places her hand over mine and gives it a pat. When she smiles, it's a broad, full-body grin. And I want to hug her like a beloved aunt. She's a cross between a Jewish mother and the head of the Genovese crime family, driven, relentless, smotheringly affectionate, dangerous, warm, complicated and attentive. Though very concentrated on money – and things – she has rarely, if ever, allowed us to pay for anything.

She's strong. She can be hard. She can be cold. But on our way out the door after dinner, as we say goodbye for the last time to our new best friend in Saigon, her face collapses and she bursts into tears. As our car pulls away, she is sobbing, her hand brushing the glass in a combination wave and caress.

New Year's Eve in Saigon is a jumbo-sized version of the *song tu do*, the weekend ritual of cruising downtown Saigon, circling the fountain at the intersection of Le Loi and Nguyen Hue boulevards. It's the Vietnamese equivalent of low-riding or cruising down Sunset Strip; thousands – tonight, hundreds of thousands – of young Vietnamese, dressed in their best button-down shirts, freshly laundered slacks, dresses, and *ao dais*, drive in perpetual slow-moving circles through the downtown city streets. They are going nowhere in particular. They don't stop. There is no place to stop anyway. Every inch of Saigon seems filled, tire-to-tire, with motos and scooters. It takes twenty minutes to cross the street.

My plan was to celebrate the New Year at Apocalypse Now, a promisingly titled expat bar a few blocks from the Continental. What better place to be when the ball dropped, I thought, than some sinister expat bar in Saigon? I expected opium-addicted ex-mercenaries, aggressive whores in silver minis, long-AWOL 'white VC,' black market hustlers, Aussie backpackers, shriveled French rubber barons, their faces teeming with corruption and the effects of malaria; I expected international rabble, arms dealers, defectors, and hit men. I'd had such high hopes. But from the moment I step inside, I am instantly disappointed. Apocalypse Now is a fern bar! There's food! A crowd of well-dressed tourists from America, Canada, and Taiwan sit in a rear dining room among potted palms and Christmas lights, near a buffet of hot entrées, salads, and what looks like Black Forest cake. They sell T-shirts with the movie's logo. Soccer is shown on an overhead projection screen near a small stage. Sunburned blondes with Midwestern accents and Tammy Faye hairdos drink colorful cocktails at a clean Formica bar.

I hate the place on sight and retreat back into the streets, finding somewhere to stand by a large stage set up behind the Théâtre Municipal. I recognize my moto driver from a few days earlier – from his Yankees cap – and we wave hello to each other. Onstage, a group of children are taking part in some kind of dance and theater presentation: patriotic songs, storytelling. No one in the crowd is watching; everyone has their attention fixed somewhere else. The constant growl of the motos and scooters drowns out nearly everything. Once in a while, loud techno-music plays over loudspeakers as the traditionally garbed per-formers leave the stage for a break. Everyone seems to be waiting for something, going somewhere, but nothing happens. As the hour approaches, I see a few people check their watches. One minute to midnight, and traffic has not slowed. No ball appears poised to drop. There are no fireworks. Midnight passes – indistinguishable from five minutes before or after. No one cheers. No one kisses. Not a single raised fist, shout of 'Happy New Year,' or any acknowledgment that another year has passed in the Western world. It's true the Vietnamese celebrate the Chinese New Year (Tet), but for weeks there have been signs everywhere reading HAPPY NEW YEAR, and people have been calling it out whenever they spy an American or a Westerner. Everyone seems poised to party, the milling crowds huge, the traffic heavier than ever, but I see not the tiniest indication of any intention to do anything but drive or stand. They've all come out for the event, all these kids, as far as the eye can see, and beyond. They cluster around a laser-light display outside a nightclub, as if not knowing what to do next. Dance music blasts from inside, but nobody dances, sways, even taps a foot or drums a finger.

It reminded me of my first high school dance – boys on one side, girls on the other, both sides afraid to move. Or have I misunderstood? Are the hundreds of thousands of kids driving and driving in circles all dressed up with no place to go – as the song says – or are they truly indifferent to the infinite delights of three chords and a beat? Vietnam seems to have shrugged off the worst of our culture with barely a look back. Is 'living freely', *song tu do*, just driving? Or is it waiting? And for what?

It's *tim ran* time. This time, I'm going to eat something that will, I am assured, make me very, very strong. The strongest. Huong Rung (Flavors of the Forest) Restaurant is a bright beer-garden-like space, enclosed by trellis, its foyer crowded with fish tanks. I enter, sit down, and order a beer right away, steadying myself for what will probably be the most . . . unusual meal of my life so far.

A grinning waiter approaches, holding a wriggling burlap sack. He opens it, gingerly reaches inside, and extracts a vicious, hissing, furious-looking four-foot-long cobra. As I've ordered the specialty of the house, I assume the staff is inured to the sight, but when the cobra, laid on the floor and prodded with a hooked stick, raises its head and spreads its hood, the whole staff of waiters, busboys, and managers – everyone but my cobra handler – steps back a few feet, giggling nervously. My cobra handler, a nice young man in waiter's black slacks and a white button-down shirt, has a sizable bandage on the back of his right hand, a feature that does not fill me with confidence as he lifts the snake with the stick and holds him over the table, the snake training its beady little eyes on me and trying to strike. I knock back the rest of my beer and try to stay cool while the cobra is allowed to slide around the floor for a while, lunging every few moments at the stick. The cobra handler is joined by an assistant with a metal dish, a small white cup, a pitcher of rice wine, and a pair of gardening shears. The two men pick up the cobra, fully extending him; the cobra handler holds him behind the jaws, while the assistant keeps him stretched just ahead of the tail. With his free hand, the handler takes the scissors, inserts a blade into the cobra's chest, and snips out the heart, a rush of dark red blood spilling into the metal dish as he does so. Everyone is pleased. The waiters and busboys relax. The blood is poured into a glass and mixed with a little rice wine. And the heart, a Chiclet-sized oysterlike organ, still beating, is placed gently into the small white cup and offered to me.

It's still pumping, a tiny pink-and-white object, moving up and down up and down at a regular pace in a small pool of blood at the bottom of the cup. I bring it to my lips, tilt my head back, and swallow. It's like a little Olympia oyster – a hyperactive one. I give it one light chew, but the heart still beats . . . and beats . . . and beats. All the way down. The taste? Not much of one. My pulse is racing too much to notice. I take a long swig of *rou tiet ran*, the blood and wine mixture, enjoying it, not bad at all – like the juice from a rare roast beef – robust, but with just a slight hint of reptile. So far so good. I have eaten the live heart of a cobra. Linh is proud of me. Many, many sons. The floor staff grin, the girls giggle shyly. The handler and assistant are busily carving up the cobra. An enormous mass of snowy white snake tripes tumbles out of the cobra's body cavity onto a plate, followed by a dribble of dark green bile.

'This very good for you,' says Linh as a waiter mixes the bile with some wine and presents me with a glass of *ruou mat ran*. It's a violent green color now, looking about as appetizing as the contents of a bedpan. 'This will make you the strongest. Very special, very special.'

I have long ago come to dread those words. I take a long swig of the green liquid and swallow. It tastes bitter, sour, evil . . . just like you'd expect bile to taste.

Over the next hour or so, I eat every single part of the cobra. First, *ran bop goi*, a delicious shredded-snake salad, heavily dressed with citrus and lemongrass and served in a hot pot. *Ham xa*, braised cobra with citronella, is also quite good, though slightly chewy. *Long ran xao*, however, the snake's tripe sautéed with onion, is absolutely inedible. I chew and chew and chew, grinding helplessly away with every molar. My chewing has not the slightest effect. It's like chewing on a rubber dog toy – only less tender. The tripe, while innocuous-tasting, is impossible to break down. I finally give up, hold my breath, and swallow a mouthful whole and intact. *Xuong (ran) chien gion*, the deep-fried bones of the snake, is delightful – like spicy potato chips – only a lot sharper. You might enjoy these at a Yankees game, though very carefully. If one bone goes in at the wrong angle, it could easily pierce your esophagus, making the prospects of lasting through the ninth inning doubtful. *Ran cuon ca lop*, the cobra's meat, minced and rolled in mint leaves, is also delightful – a festive party snack for any occasion.

The manager comes over to present me with a plate containing a large tree grub, white with a black freckle-like mark on one end. It's alive, undulating, bigger than a thumb. Oh, Jesus, no . . . It squirms around, thrashing on the plate. No, I'm thinking. No. Not that . . . Fortunately, the tree grub is cooked before serving, sautéed in butter until crispy. When it arrives back at my table, perched on a little bed of greens, I warily take a nice-sized bite. It has the consistency of a deep-fried Twinkie: crunchy on the outside, creamy and gooey in the middle. It tastes fine. But I would have been much happier not having seen it alive.

Overall, though, not a bad meal. And I've eaten the still-beating heart of a fucking cobra! (I'll be dining out on this story for a while.) For the very first time after eating food that will 'make me strong,' I actually feel something. I don't know if it's just nervous energy and adrenaline, but when I walk out into the street, I feel a buzz, a jangly, happy, vibrating sense of well-being. I think, Yes, I believe I do feel . . . strong.

'Monsieur Fowlair. Monsieur Fow-lairr . . .' someone is whispering.

It's the police inspector in Greene's *The Quiet American*, talking in my dreams. I wake up expecting to see Phuong, the heroine of the novel, preparing an opium pipe for me, and Pyle, the youthful CIA agent, petting his dog in a chair. I'm in my room at the Continental, carved fleurs-de-lis in the woodwork, ornate chairs, yards of intricately carved shelving. I can hear the clack-clacking of shoes on the wide marble floor outside the door, the sound echoing through the halls. Saigon. Still only in Saigon. The French doors leading onto the balcony are open and, though early, the streets are already filling up with cyclos, bicycles, motorbikes, and scooters. Women crouch in doorways, eating bowls of *pho*. A man fixes a motorbike on the sidewalk. Buses cough and stall and start again. At Givral's, across the street, they're lining up for coffee and the short, plump, fragrant-smelling baguettes. Soon, the 'noodle knockers' will come, rapping their mallets to announce the imminent arrival of another yoke-borne kitchen, bowls and bowls of steaming fresh noodles. Linh has informed me of something called 'fox' coffee, *ca-phe-chon*, a brew made from the tenderest beans, fed to a fox (though I have since seen it referred to as a weasel), and the beans later recovered from the animal's stool, washed (presumably), roasted, and ground. Sounds good to me.

I'm leaving Vietnam soon, and yet I'm yearning for it already. I grab a stack of damp dong off my nightstand, get dressed, and head for the market. There's a lot I haven't tried.

I'm still here, I tell myself.

I'm still here.

PERFECT

THE WHOLE CONCEPT OF the 'perfect meal' is ludicrous.

'Perfect,' like 'happy,' tends to sneak up on you. Once you find it – like Thomas Keller says – it's gone. It's a fleeting thing, 'perfect,' and, if you're anything like me, it's often better in retrospect. When you're shivering under four blankets in a Moroccan hotel room, the perfect meal can be something no more exotic than breakfast at Barney Greengrass back in New York – the one you had four months ago. Your last Papaya King hot dog takes on golden, even mythic, proportions when re-membered from a distance.

I'm writing this, these words, from a beach chair somewhere in the French West Indies. My hand is actually scrawling in wet black ink across a yellow legal pad. I'm not here to eat. I'm here to write, and relax, untroubled by phone calls, shoes and socks, visitors, E-mails, or obligations of any kind. I'm here because I've been on the road for over a year and I want desperately to stay put, to dig in, to remain in one place and maybe reacquaint myself with my wife.

I've been coming to this beach for a long time. The first time I visited, back in the eighties, I was still kicking dope, and the blood-warm water felt cold on my skin. My wife and I honey-mooned here, blowing every cent of wedding loot on a two-week kamikaze vacation, which left us tanned, happy, totally in love with the island – and utterly broke. Down here, I like to think that I'm not the brutish, obsessive, blustering blowhard control freak, Chef Tony; nor the needy, neurotic, eager-to-please, talkin-sound-bites Writer Tony – but the relatively calm, blissed-out, sunstroked, amiable Husband Tony – the nicest version of me Nancy is likely to see for forty days at a clip.

After a few lazy hours bobbing around in the warm, gin-clear turquoise water, and dozing on the beach, Nancy was reading me the police blotter from the local paper.

A man, 'G,' from Saint Peters, was detained last night on the Pondfill Road. A gentleman from Domenica complained that 'G' had mistreated him with a pair of nail clippers after a dispute over a game of dominoes at the Dinghy Dock Bar. Dutch side police arrived at the scene and gave 'G' a stern warning and he was released. Two youths from Back Street, 'P' and 'D', were arrested after stealing a gold chain from Kun Shi Jewelers on the Old Street. The youths asked to see a chain in the store, then ran away without paying for it. They were arrested at the bus stop on the Bush Road as they tried to make their escape by bus.

'Jesus,' said Nancy. 'It's a crime wave.'

A while ago, I looked up from my pad, wiped the sweat out of my eyes, and, after consulting my watch, turned to Nancy and said, 'Hungry?' She said yes, as I knew she would. We're creatures of habit down here. We have a routine. That meant a short walk across the hot sand to a thatch-roofed hut with a smoking barbecue grill, a rudimentary bar with five or six kinds of liquor, and two coolers of iced Caribs, Red Stripes, and baby Heinekens. Gus, the proprietor, has known us since 1984, and he had a pretty good idea what we wanted. By the time we ducked under the palm fronds into the shade, he'd already cracked two Caribes.

I ordered the barbecued ribs. Nancy went for the cheeseburger. The service at Gus's is never quick. Our order took about half an hour – normal waiting time on this island. But, uncharacteristically, I wasn't impatient at all. I didn't fidget. I didn't look nervously around. I didn't listen for the telltale sounds of a spatula lifting Nancy's burger off the grill – or the bell signaling an order was ready. I knew Keesha, the woman working the grill, and was aware that she did things at her own pace. I didn't care how long it took. I was happy to wait, drinking the beer in the shade of Gus's makeshift frond-covered shelter, sand between my toes, hair still wet from the sea, Nancy looking brown and happy and a little bit drunk across from me.

My ribs were tender, slightly crispy on the outside and seasoned with the same adobo spice that Gus puts on everything. If the ribs were marinated in something before grilling, I knew not what. Nor did I care. Any critical sensibilities had long ago been put on hold. Nancy's cheeseburger was small, cooked completely through, and topped with a single Kraft cheese slice and a too-large bun, also seasoned with the ubiquitous adobo. She never finishes her food, so I knew that I'd get at least a bite. Both plates were white – plastic, garnished with soggy french fries – just as I'd expected them to be. Gus's new Shaggy CD played on the sound system for at least the fourth time that day. It will, of course, remain the music from this time on the island. From now on, that CD will always and forever bring me right back here to this time and place, the taste of crispy pork and adobo seasoning, Gus's Beach Bar, the look on Nancy's face as she sighed distractedly, yawned, stretched, and then tossed one of my rib bones to a stray dog that'd been lurking by our table. The dog knew the routine.

I've learned something on the road. It doesn't do to waste. Even here – I use everything.

– August 2001

ACKNOWLEDGMENTS

Thanks to: Karen Rinaldi, Joel Rose, Rosemarie Morse, Kim Witherspoon, Panio Gianopoulos, Lydia Tenaglia, Chris Collins, Matt Barbato, Alberto Orso, "Global" Alan Deutsch, Bree Fitzgerald, Michiko Zento, Shinji Nohara, Dinh Linh, Madame Ngoc, Khoum Mang Kry, the incredible Zamir Gotta, Scott Leadbetter, Simon McMillan, Lu Barron, Edilberto Perez and family, Martin Vallejo, Abdou Boutabi, Luis and Virginia Irizar, Chris Bourdain, Jose Meirelles and family, Philippe Lajaunie, Colin and Isabella Cawdor, Mark Stanton, Abdelfettah and Naomi, Jamie Byng, Fergus Henderson, Gordon Ramsay, Thomas Keller, Juan Mari Arzak, Dan Cohen, Kim Martin, Liane Thompson, Christian Gwinn, Dan Halpern, Anya Rosenberg, Sarah Burns, Scott Bryan, Eric Ripert, Michael Ruhlman, Mark Peel, Tracy Westmoreland, and all the people who helped me on the way.

A NOTE ON THE AUTHOR

Anthony Bourdain is the author of *Kitchen Confidential*, two satirical thrillers, *Bone in the Throat* and *Gone Bamboo*, and the urban historical *Typhoid Mary*. A twenty-eight-year veteran of professional kitchens, he is currently the 'Executive Chef' at Brasserie Les Halles in Manhattan – meaning he gets to swan around in a chef's jacket taking credit for others' toil. He lives – and always will live – in New York City.